O, Sweet Master

to Dear Anita
and Jack,
We are so blessed
to have your friendship!
Love, Marti Fuller

Proverbs 3:5-6

O, Sweet Master

MARTHA FULLER

CROSSBOOKS
PUBLISHING

CrossBooks™
A Division of LifeWay
1663 Liberty Drive
Bloomington, IN 47403
www.crossbooks.com
Phone: 1-866-879-0502

First published by CrossBooks 06/13/14

ISBN: 978-1-4627-3775-8 (sc)
ISBN: 978-1-4627-3774-1 (e)

Printed in the United States of America.

All Bible references are from the King James Version.

This book is printed on acid-free paper.

Any people depicted in stock imagery provided by Thinkstock are models,
and such images are being used for illustrative purposes only.
Certain stock imagery © Thinkstock.

I would like to dedicate this book
to those who have shared
their deepest hurts with me
and who are learning,
along with me,
to forgive.

It is not my right or wisdom
to see the how and why
of all things.
God will work it all out,
as He always has
and always will,
to His glory.

I have glimpsed His Kingdom
through lives touched
by His grace and mercy.
I am grateful
for each day He has given me.

Chapter 1

Mama told me this story when I was old enough to ken it. She said that I was to learn to see life through God's eyes, in order to become a man. "Seeing the world with human wisdom alone is not enough," she said. "You need to breathe with the Spirit of God in your lungs and know that it is the heart of God that beats in your chest. Then you can begin to see the world through His eyes and know a small measure of His wisdom."

Mama's name was Miryam. In Hebrew it means 'bitterness, and rebellion.' What a burden of a name to carry! And my Mama! She surely did grow up with a chip on her shoulder. She confessed to me that she always wanted things her way. While growing up she was usually seen as being a good girl, behaving well and having good manners and common sense, but she told me that as far back as she could remember, she had held grudges inside her that made it hard for her to be happy.

My Da, Rohan MacVoy, did the best he could to please her but what she needed was more than he could give.

This is her story, from very shortly before I was born. It tells of the long journey her life made - away from that bitterness - to the joy I have known through her love, and Da's. The joy of knowing the love of God. Life began for me on a Monday.

1867

It was wash day. Mama was out of sorts as she filled the bucket from the pump. She could be heard muttering regarding the general inconveniences of life – especially in caring for men, who seemed to contrive more and more ways to dirty up the clothes she scrubbed until her hands ached. The sky was the bluest it could possibly be, exactly the color of her husband's eyes, but she took no notice of it on that particular day, you see.

The wind had picked up and that meant misery for a Monday. Though the air was good and hot for drying her laundry, it was also so humid that the clothes hung for hours without actually accomplishing this. She hoped that the dense heat of the day would dry the scanty array of her family's clothing quicker than the dust would cover them, but as the freshly washed clothes were hung on the line, the wind chased the dust all around the yard. She sighed aloud and kept on with her task. She would have to beat the dust out of the clothes before bringing them inside the house.

"Oy, to be back east again, where life was easier!"

She plunged her hands into the water bucket - right up to the elbows where she had rolled the sleeves of her oldest sprigged muslin dress. The dress was of the lightest weight material that she owned, but in the heat and exertion it clung to her back and bodice like a mustard plaster. She could feel her pulse slow as the cold water seemed to seep right into her skin. Removing the bandana from her neck she soaked it with the delicious coolness, washed the perspiration from her face and neck, and pressed the cold cloth against the inside of each elbow. Then she wet it again, retied the sopping cloth around her neck, and let it drip down her bodice and back. She added the water to the rinse kettle and continued with her chore.

How she hated Mondays! To Miryam, they were a bottomless pit that any silly *nebbish* should try hard not to fall into. Maybe for those with someone else to do the laundry it was different, but regardless of one's station in life, Mondays tended to come around every week or so. She also suspected that most folks had a proclivity to put off until Monday any chore that was unappealing, only prolonging the inevitable distastefulness of the first day of every week.

Years earlier, Mama and Da had decided to move west when it seemed that they were not able to have children. Miryam's parents were vocal in their disappointment, as if being childless was a choice she had made to spite them. And to them it was definitely Da's fault, rather than hers. Of course they felt that everything was his fault. He was not Jewish, and that made him suspect in each and every situation. She pleaded with him to take her away from the tension. The west was open and people talked of adventure, so the decision was made to seek a new life out here.

Far west of the Missouri was a land that had been promised as not only pleasant but delightful. They had traveled as far as they could on land by relatively convenient means, then they had spent a long week on a flatboat. On the "wide river," as it was called, the journey became more arduous. There were some passengers to speak with during the day, but what few chairs that existed were occupied by the elderly and the women who held nursing or sleeping children. At night the crew crowded with them into the only cabin to sleep in bedrolls, cheek by jowl, on the filthy floor. After the Missouri River crossing, a prairie schooner was purchased and outfitted with the odd assortment of supplies with which to make do as they traveled west.

She and Rohan had left Kentucky with a very small herd of sturdy stock horses to sell and trade along the way. It was the only 'currency' they owned. At each stop along their journey they had made a trade for whatever was needed, ending up with no horses on the east side of the river but enough cash for passage and to start over with a new herd. They hoped to arrive in a place where their "horse sense" would be a needed commodity. Nebraska seemed to be the choice of the travelers they joined up with. It had seemed agreeable to make the trek in the safety of numbers with the Kansas Wagon Train Company Corps.

They were submitted to the dubious guidance of a man with ample knowledge about the route and the conditions, but who carried the reputation of imbibing considerable amounts of liquid fortification. Along the way, they learned a great deal more than they had ever wanted to know about how to prepare the victuals that the wagon train rangers brought in from riding the trail. While daily relying on the dry goods that were packed in their own barrels, they also partook of snakes and unidentifiable rodents, made barely palatable by the cook employed by the wagon train company.

Nebraska had just been admitted to the United States. The brochures said that it might just be the brightest, most beautiful place to settle. But the roads were difficult. When not slogged down in mud, they were rock hard with potholes big enough to break a wheel, or lose a small child or a goat in. All things considered though, Miryam and Rohan were glad to finally come into the possession of a place to call their own. According to the Homestead Act, they found a tract of pastureland with a deep stream running through it. It was rocky ground, unsuited for farming as was most of the area. But, as Roh had said, "Horses dinna hav' a care aboot plows, but they mun be fair pleased wi' the braes. Tis guid land eh?"

Miryam had to agree. Though farming was difficult, they were better off than most. The land did grow plenty of grass and clover for a small herd. They'd started small and over the years added worthy stock whenever they could afford it, branching out later to add the more practical sale of mules. They now carried on a fair trade, since all the other families needed strong work animals for their wagons, and their plowing, and a few wealthy folks even kept finer horses for their carriages and occasional races.

Rohan came from a family of hostlers and knew his way around a horse like he knew his own body. He could tell by the quiver of a muscle where a horse might be injured, or by the hesitancy in her eye which direction to move so the horse would not bolt. In the old country, Rohan's great, great, grandfather was believed, far and wide, to be a kindred spirit to all horseflesh. In those days in Scotland the old folks claimed that he must be, truly, part horse. A Highlander, he had been imprisoned after the battle of Culloden for supporting Bonny Prince Charles, and later shipped as an indentured servant to America, leaving behind a wife and young son.

Through what some may have viewed as coincidence, he was traded in service to a rich stable owner in Kentucky where, because of his skill with the animals, he became a trusted member of the establishment. After his indentured service was over, he was hired as the head groom. Making a name for himself, he was able finally to send for his grandson, Roh's grandfather to take his place in his old age. Grand Da left Scotland, not to make his fortune, but as a last effort to earn enough money to support his large poor family, though from a great distance. Rohan's father was the romantic result of the last embrace of his grandparents. They never saw each other again after the tearful farewell at the dock, but Rohan's father was born and the family line continued in Scotland.

It was in the Highlands that Da grew to know and love horses. His expertise with horseflesh, however, was no match for Ma's parents' prejudice against non-Jews. He'd been a gangling red headed youth with a slow smile when he came to America. But his eyes were what first caught Ma's attention, such a blue that she always said they startled her. And was he smart! Though he still never spoke much unless he was spoken to, she told me that when he did speak, it was something you'd remember. When his words came forth, plucked from the tree of his thoughts at the proper time, they were always ripe for the hearing. They were rare fruit though. Like the treats she used to wait for with such great anticipation at Hanukkah, his words were always gone too fast, leaving her whetted for more, all the while knowing it would be a long time to wait.

Out here, in the middle of nowhere, the opportunity for everyday chats with other women at home in the east was what she missed most. If she worked very hard at it lately, though, she could coax a short conversation from Rohan, but most of the time she felt it was really not worth the effort. Now her heart yearned for all the things that could be, and lately for all the things that could not be. How she had loved Rohan! How she had lived just to look at his face! He was tall and almost gaunt, but so handsome that she was always taken up with his every movement.

As Miryam scrubbed his shirt against the washboard she smiled in her mind, recalling his first words to her. "Miss, ye - ye seem t' be standin' on my cap." She had been crossing the street in Mayfield, the city near where she'd grown up. As a horse and rider came galloping around the corner, she'd backed up quickly so as not to be trampled. Rohan had been walking right behind her. He'd told her, years later, that he'd actually forgotten what errand he was on, so intent was he upon her gait. He'd confessed that his thoughts were totally involved in watching for her small feet to emerge momentarily from beneath her skirt, moving in tiny steps along the cobbles. "Dainty as a wee cat," he'd told himself.

When the swiftly moving rider had come upon Miryam, Rohan had been too startled to prevent a collision. She'd backed up and he'd walked right into her. His cap had flown off his head and her parcels lay scattered on the ground. He'd gathered them up for her wordlessly, and helped her arrange them in her arms so that she could carry them. All the while he had said nothing. Miryam had apologized for the mishap and, captivated by his beautiful eyes, waited for some kind of reply. Rohan had been tongue-tied by her sweet face. After an awkward moment, though, he had stammered that Miryam was, in fact, withholding his cap. It was to be a way of life for them.

When the day had come that he asked her to be his wife, Rohan had taken pains to say, "I hope ye dinna mind my quiet nature." It had taken some long moments for him to continue, "Ye mayna ha' noticed it." he'd said. "But I hope ye ne'er tae it t' mean that I'm nae happy wi' ye. Tis just my wa' nae t' spend much time talkin'." Of course she'd seen it from the start - getting a conversation from him was going to be like trying to eat soup with a fork. If there was going to be communication between them, it would begin and end with her.

He had a strong presence, though, that drew her to seek his company. He also used to have a way of looking at her that had made her heart race. His was her first kiss, and when they'd kissed, the tickle and prickle of his mustache and whiskers made an everlastingly divine impression on her inexperienced mind. Though their kisses were not so romantic now as they once were, she loved the excitement of their intimacy and lately regretted the busy muddle of the passing of the days and weeks that seemed to take precedence over quiet time spent together. It had been quite a few weeks since they had lain in each other's arms. She glanced at the rise where the road met the horizon. He should be home soon - should have been home before this!

So they were married. But theirs was a difficult courtship, fraught with tension. Mama was Jewish and Da was Scottish. Jews did not marry gentiles – "goyim." Mama told me how it nearly did not happen, but that Da looked at her with such open longing to hold her, to woo her, to say to her, "Tha gaol agam ort. (I Love You!)" She said he was bold, with his love written on his face for all to see - and her parents did not enjoy seeing it.

How Miryam's mama had taken on with tears! She had insisted that her only child be wed under the *chuppah*. The marriage canopy would be the symbol for the shelter and safety they would find in their lives, living together in the traditions of Judaism. Papa reacted to their courtship with dire threats of eternal damnation.

"To be a Jew is an honor, and you forsake it by marrying outside. You know the law! You marry your own kind. We shall find a nice Jewish *boychick* for you! Enough of this!"

But she loved Rohan and they sought out a judge to perform the marriage ceremony. Rohan was not happy either, saying, "A man an' a woman should be marrit in a kirk, nae in an office!" What a day that had been! When they heard the news, Miryam's mama wept and her papa exploded. Jewish tradition ran deep in her family and a Scotsman was not quite what they'd had in mind for a son-in-law. Eventually they respected him for his common sense, and they liked that he didn't always have to toot his own horn. But the rift remained and widened. When she remained barren, it was Rohan's fault of course. Over time, his quiet nature was seen as respectful, but religion was a topic they would never talk about with Miryam again. It was better all around not to stir the pot of controversy. What was done was done.

When the opportunity arose to venture into the west, the appeal of a new start in life was what led to Miryam's consent. It would be a simpler life, she reasoned. Though moving away from her family was a difficult decision, she also needed the distance from them. She hoped that after some time had passed there would be visits and homecomings every so often.

Miryam's papa felt the separation keenly, having some small amount of remorse about his part in giving her reason for leaving. He was a deeply religious man in that he respected the traditions of his fathers, but did not have much more faith than an expectation that his dedication to these matters would be rewarded by God. In this regard, he asked that they gather for a last meal together and read from the Torah as was his daily habit.

"Hear, O Israel: The Lord our God is one Lord: And thou shalt love the Lord thy God with all thine heart, and with all thy soul, and with all thy might. And these words, which I command thee this day, shall be in thine heart: And thou shalt teach them diligently unto thy children, and shalt talk of them when thou sittest in thine house, and when thou walkest by the way, and when thou liest down, and when thou risest up."1

He had looked for a long stern moment at Mama after speaking. Then they continued with their farewell dinner.

Her mama had sulked as the arrangements for the trip were made, but on the day of their departure she had held Miryam tenderly as they said goodbye. She presented the couple with a quilt she had made in Miryam's youth, to be ready for her wedding day. Having not given it on that chaotic occasion, she presented it as they left for the unknown. She had never been much for sentiment and this was as close as she could come. Miryam looked back as they left, but her parents were already walking away. There was to be no waving goodbye.

As Miryam rinsed and wrung out her best dress she noted that it was still in fair condition since she wore it only on Sundays, and special occasions. It was her last remaining store bought item of clothing. The buttons alone were a treasure to her - made of mother of pearl. She made a mental note to fashion a pattern of it for the next dress she would make. It was quite becoming on her. She still had a length of fine linen fabric to work up whenever she might find the time. She missed the frills and style of buying new dresses. What she wore for everyday was serviceable, not much more.

Learning to sew was a skill Miryam had struggled long with. But she soon realized, once out on her own, that if she didn't learn to make their own clothes, they would soon be dressed in *shmatte,* rags! Her mother had sent her patterns, but they tore so easily and were hard to read. So, as an item of clothing wore out, she would take it apart carefully and cut new pieces of cloth to match each part. Then she'd put the new parts together to look like the old garment. There were quite a few failed attempts, and with each effort there was the inevitable gaffe where she had to tear apart a whole seam, having sewn the wrong side of the cloth to the right side.

But as the years went by she finally conquered the art of making clothing. It was something she must keep up with, or have the clothes split and fall away at an inopportune moment. She could just imagine Roh, bending over to pick up a heavy keg of nails at the mercantile in town, having his breeches split their seam right there in front of all the folks who regularly gathered in front of the store to chat and pass the time. She smiled a mischievous smile. What a sight that would be!

Rohan was particularly hard on his clothes as was evidenced by the thinning cloth at the knees, elbows and seat, though mended again and again. Many was the time she wished that she could make his garments out of leather to make them last longer. She had seen a few Indians dressed in buckskin over the years and had admired the soft, durable garments. But she had no time for all that curing and heavy sewing. Some of the women she knew had sewn work pants for their husbands out of the canvas left from their covered wagons. The material lasted a good long time, and when dyed black, looked fairly presentable. She wondered if she should ask Rohan to order some from the mercantile. All of her husband's and son's garments were either hand-me-downs or home made, but she was of a mind to keep them looking decent. They wore them out so quickly.

Chapter 2

Miryam and her son had driven their buggy the long four miles to the village yesterday in the relentless heat. They'd arrived at the church exhausted, with rivulets of sweat running down their backs, and the cleavage of her camisole was so soaked that she wondered if it would show through the bodice of her dress.

One of the men at the church had told her a story of another hot and humid summer when the building was new and the decorating committee had decided that the pews in the sanctuary needed to be varnished. The stripping was done and the preservative applied, but it never fully dried. The first Sunday after the work was done proved to be a disaster. The folks rose from their seats wearing as much stickiness as if they'd sat in pinesap. After that day they put their bulletins on the seats before they sat down. They stuck fast, and folks then had to lean down to read the number of the next hymn to be sung. When the cold weather of autumn finally came, the pews were scraped, sanded and left that way.

Miryam didn't much mind going to church as opposed to going to synagogue. At least, in the Christian kirk as Rohan called it, she could sit with her husband instead of having to sit separately as in the synagogue, the men with the men and the women together on the other side of a curtained partition. Her parents would scorn her if they knew! The kirk also provided her with a sense of community and the intensely necessary companionship of other women. She wanted to have a desire to know the god they spoke of, but it had been drummed into her since childhood that the god of the *goyim* was false. She just sat and let the words said in the service pass her by without so much as a whispered remnant remaining in her head, or so she thought.

She would daydream though, without realizing it. Her thoughts ran rampant – "Either this *goy* god is *Adonai*, or He's not. Either He's in charge, or He's not. Either He knows what He's doing, or He doesn't. What is the evidence for Him, and against Him? Can I know enough to make a decision? Am I in a position to judge Him? Either He made the world, or it materialized by itself, order from chaos? If He made everything, then He made me. If He made me, then He has a plan for me. Is there sense to this the world? Is the One who created the complexity of the world evil or good? Why would He allow imperfection to exist? Would compassion for others exist if everyone was perfect? How imperfect am I?"

Then there was the Christian Scripture, oddly enough in a book called Hebrews, which rang true to her memory. It said, "Without the shedding of blood there is no remission."[2] That was certainly something she had learned as a child in *shul*. Were there more similarities to her Jewish life in this *goy* kirk?

There was the man called Job who pondered the distance between God, who was beyond his understanding, and man. He wondered if there could be a mediator who could bring them together. These gentiles claimed that it had in fact already happened. A young Jew named Timothy had written it: "There is one God and one mediator between God and men, the man Christ Jesus."[3]

Today's reading startled her out of her reverie. Even more boldly than on other Sundays, the Reverend MacClure was telling about how Jesus had stood in a synagogue and applied the words in a Jewish scroll to himself! She listened intently as the reader spoke authoritatively.

"A reading from Isaiah, chapter 61:

*'The Spirit of the Lord G*OD *is upon me; because the L*ORD *hath anointed me to preach good tidings unto the meek; he hath sent me to bind up the brokenhearted, to proclaim liberty to the captives, and the opening of the prison to them that are bound; to proclaim the acceptable year of the L*ORD, *and the day of vengeance of our God; to comfort all that mourn; to appoint unto them that mourn in Zion, to give unto them beauty for ashes, the oil of joy for mourning, the garment of praise for the spirit of heaviness; that they*

might be called trees of righteousness, the planting of the LORD, *that he might be glorified.'"*[4]

As the reader continued, Miryam sat in utter confusion. "How?" she thought, "How could this Jesus even begin to say that he was appointed by *Adonai*?" It made her angry as she had not been before in this kirk. These teachings were just too close to blasphemy!

Again she was returned to the present by the high, small voice of a child who had been called upon to read what they called the gospel. She read from a book in their Bible written by a man named John, who proclaimed that Jesus said, *"I am the way, the truth, and the life: no man cometh unto the Father, but by me."*[5]

This was not the truth! How could it be if it excluded everyone she had known as a child, all the Jews she had grown up with and loved? But perhaps this 'truth' was defined differently for gentiles than for Jews. She wondered what truth would be universally accepted. What things could be relied upon no matter what your belief or religion? "It may be unexplainable," she pondered, "yet, in as much as I am alone as a Jew here, I do yearn for knowing things of *Adonai*. I know that I am small and He is great, as I was taught my whole life, but surely, there is truth that I know that does not include this man Jesus. Surely there is more... I must try." She began a mental list.

"What is truth like? What do I know that is true?

"Truth is like remembering a once forgotten melody – it moves your hands to clapping and your feet to dancing, it creates a humming on your lips, or a glad rendition of the words if you know them.

"Truth is like a child who runs into the open arms of someone whom he loves very much.

"Truth is like a tear, running down my cheek, shed in joy that cannot be contained.

"Truth like sudden laughter, coming up from the belly, ringing into the air.

"It's like a smile that doesn't fade for long time, and which recurs at random as wondrous memories replay in my mind.

"Truth is like the hand which holds mine tenderly, to share a sorrow I cannot speak of.

"It's like the hope of reconciliation, deep in my heart, calling out to one who has chosen not to listen, saying, someday… someday.

"Truth is like the sudden flight of a bird from its perch.

"Truth is like the comfort and rest I find in quiet.

"Truth is like the scent of a baby, fresh from heaven, like the whisper of his breathing on my neck, and the tickling of his eyelashes against my cheek.

"Truth is like the reassurance that, as the days grow warmer, there will be budding, growing things greening all around me.

"Truth is like an array of flowers, in all their intricacies, bright witnesses to a vast plan that causes each to bloom in its turn.

"Truth is like a campfire we watch late into the night, adding logs because we don't want the embers to die out."

But these thoughts left Miryam wanting. There was a place inside her that called out for solidity and strength. These ponderings of 'truth' left her with a deep sense of nostalgia and wistfulness which did not fill the need she had just now discovered in her life.

As Mama grew to know the truth better, she explained it to me, saying, "We all have a certain place within us, call it what you will - a soul, a heart, a spirit. This place is where we carry a vacancy that we hope we can fill with perfection, where our ideals will be reality, where the best fairy-tale ending becomes part of our lives, where we BELONG! We all want to be loved! But this place remains empty until we fill it with truth. The truth is that we just can't love each other as we need to be loved. We are incapable of fully meeting one another's deep longing with a love that is perfect. The truth is that we need a Savior."

This summer was the worst season since they'd come here. The ground was parched, and the people as well. Every trip into town brought Miyam and Rohan and Jon into contact with forlorn faces and tales of folks who had given up hope and moved back east. Every crop was sown with back-breaking work to till the land that was as hard as rock.

Scratching out a crop from the dry soil was sapping the strength of many of the plains families. The women were alone too much, the men always needed each other's help just to keep their farms running, and the children grew up too quickly with little time for frolicking and youthful dawdling. There was never enough water and the threat of fire ever present. Neighbors arranged signals in case of calamity, this fact alone portending disaster. But thus far there had only been a few brush fires, quickly quelled.

Miryam's natural bent was to grumble a bit, and though outwardly nurturing her family, she'd inwardly spent years rehearsing her druthers. She'd been raised not to *kvetch*, though. She knew it was wrong to grumble. In her parents' home murmuring was outwardly forbidden but practiced daily. So in her prairie home she did her chores and understood the necessity of doing them, but the endlessness of keeping the house running and coaxing the vegetables to survive in the kailgarden was not her idea of the good life. She felt that she needed a change from the drudgery, the same dull chores repeated by rote seemed to be sucking the life out of her.

She once had a hope of making a difference in this world, maybe as a school teacher or a nurse. But the opportunity never came. At last she became resigned to this life. It was fair sometimes, sometimes it was wretched. When she took the time to turn to the looking glass which hung above her basin and ewer next to the door, she chuckled to herself. She felt as if she could easily be described as "one who wasted no time with outward adornment," though once in a while she caught a glimpse of herself in a better mood and was pleasantly surprised to see a woman who was, indeed, still quite pretty.

The dreams in her heart had always included family, but that ideal had vanished when they ventured so far west. Her family should have been close knit, her *mispochah* always nearby. Parents and grandparents, aunts and uncles, cousins and nieces and nephews by the score should have been gathered for each of the high feast days. Her home should have been big and comfortable. She'd wanted to bring about these things. She'd wanted to be regarded as a fine and noteworthy lady, a *berryer*, respected and well loved by others. But her neatly ordered dreams hadn't materialized as she'd planned them, and her resentment grew up around her like the weeds she battled every day in her vegetable garden. *"Oy vey! What a stubborn bunch! If only the vegetables were so hardy!"* she had often complained. There were so many days when she felt utterly alone.

In her dreams her marriage would have been a refuge of intimacy, with plenty of lively conversation. Her children would be plentiful and a continual source of delight. Somehow the years had passed, but Miryam was still struggling with her desire to own a peaceful heart. She saw her family as a mixed blessing of *alivay,* "if onlys" - and the solid dependability of her husband and son. There was contentment and longing in her heart, forever battling.

If only Rohan would smile and laugh more often. How she longed for some silliness and hearty laughter - but then he always knew how to fix anything that needed it, and he did care for Miryam and their son, Jonathan, dutifully and well.

Jon had finally been born long after their dreams of parenthood had faded away. He was the light of their lives, but now a stubborn adolescent. If only Jon, just turning fourteen, would realize that he was not the center of the universe - but then he was always there for helping Roh with the heavy work and he could make her smile with his boyish pranks.

If only there were other Jews to celebrate the feasts days with – but she was glad to be away from her parents' strict interpretation of the Mosaic Law.

If only she hadn't ventured into this desolate plain, away from her family - but still, she had a husband and a son, and that was more than many women had. She seemed to live in a perpetual state of dismay, imbedded with acceptance.

The home they'd made in the emptiness of the open prairie was sturdy and sufficient. Rohan had built the house well. Their one large room held their lives in order. Some of the furniture was brought from the Missouri border in their covered wagon, some had been purchased in the west, and some was made by Rohan. The kitchen was to the right as one came in. The washstand with its basin and ewer stood just beside the door with a looking glass on the wall above. A clean flour sacking towel hung from a peg near it. Then one's eye went to the huge gleaming copper kettle on the woodstove. When filled she could just carry it from the stove to the table. The stove, laid on a pallet of brick, burned continually throughout the year. It had taken four men to bring it into the house before the final installation of the door. Her pots and skillets and long utensils were hung from pegs on the wall over the stove.

To the left of the stove was the large galvanized sink with two buckets underneath, one for the clean water and the other holding the used water, which drained when the sink's stopper was pulled. Miryam used all the dirty dishwater for her flowers and her vegetable garden. Above the sink was the house's first window, where Miryam could watch the world as she washed the dishes. There was a big shelf on the adjacent wall to the left of the sink which held all her dishes, her big mixing bowl, and the wooden box which held the flatware and smaller cooking utensils.

The enormous fireplace took up most of the wall on the right side of the house. What a chore it had been to build. Finding the fieldstone was the easy part, but fitting them and chinking them to construct a working fireplace and a sturdy chimney was harder than she'd thought it would be. Rohan consulted the older and wiser men in town and, upon their advice, he worked slowly and with an eye to perfection. When it was finished, Miryam could say with no reservation that it was a work of art. A hook to hold her kettle and a spit for game made the ever-burning fire the heart of the household. The far right corner was stacked with wood and a large box of kindling.

By the fireside, Rohan had made a bench with a back and provided it with straw stuffed cushions made of feed sacks. Miryam had covered this with a fine wool blanket and Rohan had declared, "There noo, ye've made a puir settle look right canty."

There was a rocking chair by the hearth that Rohan had bought when Miryam was expecting Jon. It was used then daily at naptimes and bedtimes to snuggle the child and soothe him to sleep. It was a miracle, they thought, that a baby finally arrived. And as the letter announcing his arrival had gone out to Miryam's parents, she felt a hint of secret smugness that they were not there to see him. They had never cared for Rohan. They didn't think he was good enough for Miryam. Now, she had reasoned to herself, she had borne a son with him and they would have to acknowledge his role as a father to their grandson. He was surely a more than satisfactory father, too.

They had just a few prized possessions, the latest of which was Mark Twain's book, <u>The Celebrated Jumping Frog of Calaveras County,</u> which had been a gift from Miryam's parents on her last birthday. Rohan had bought the clock on the mantle with the first wages he'd earned when he arrived in America from Scotland. When he stepped off the ship he knew what it was that he missed about home the most, the ticking of the clock on the mantle. His own precious clock had been transported with the utmost care all the way from North Carolina to Kentucky, and then to the west. Her parents had given them the looking glass as a wedding gift, but Miryam had always felt it was a way of saying to her, "Look at who you are! You are Jewish and don't forget it!" The quilt on their bedstead was the one her mama had made for her dowry.

In the center of the room was the long strong table that Rohan had built. It was always covered with a clean white cloth and always bore a jug of flowers, or a bowl of fruit or vegetables in season. With the four chairs they had bought from a craftsman in the west, it made dinner seem more than ordinary.

Jon's bed was in the back across from the door. To the left of the door was the home's second window and the big bed for Miryam and Rohan, which could be enclosed by a heavy curtain of blue dyed burlap, to brighten up the room.

The far left corner was for storage of everything imaginable, from blankets to boots, and from lard to liniment. These supplies were laid in months in advance of need so there were times when the small house seemed to burst its seams. The stores lay in wooden crates under the cover of a length of cloth. This then served as a shelf against the wall to hold a small collection of books and projects with which to fill the evening hours before retiring to sleep.

But now it had been seventeen years since they left Kentucky. Rohan's family was all in Scotland, and her own parents had never even laid eyes on Jon. They had missed all of his infancy and boyhood years. He had grown up without once seeing his grandparents. Letters came faithfully but could not make up for the presence of an extended family, and for the way of life that was so central to Miryam's own childhood - the Jewish feast days with all of her family, all their traditions, and the recitals of the old stories from the scriptures. She especially missed having family around for the Passover. Jon would have been the youngest child at the feast, and would have been the one to ask the special question at the Seder meal: "Why is this night different from all other nights?" With no one nearby to share the feast days, she wondered sometimes why she should bother.

She thought of the richness of the language she had heard every day of her life until moving west. The Hebrew words used in the readings in the synagogue portrayed a zeal for the worship of God which was inspiring, but in reality, unknown to her in day to day life. Why bother with so many expressions for praise? Why such elaboration? There was *hallal* to denote worship by celebrating, dancing, or acting robust; *shabach* meaning to shout praise with a loud voice; *yadeh* meant to show honor to God with hand movements; *zamar* was for worship using a musical instrument; *tehillah* was the word for giving worship from the heart; and *barak,* an act of humility shown by kneel or bowing.

Miryam recalled the words her father recited every night as they began their evening meal at the supper table. *Nachamu ami.* "Comfort ye My people." *Adonai Yimloch l'olam vaed.* "The Lord God's reign will never end." *V'lo ya'azvecha.* "He won't forsake you." The familiar phrases gave her solace, knowing that there was a God who cared enough to comfort her.

Chapter 3

Miryam loved Rohan. She knew that Rohan was a good man who loved her in his own plodding, steadfast way. He was sweet and comfortable, but he was not very much fun anymore. She supposed that she herself probably wasn't much fun either. They both worked too hard every day. Their lives centered on their chores and on the necessities of keeping the ranch running. She knew inside that she could be more alive than she was today. She could relax and laugh more, but there seemed to be no time for it.

She supposed she could seek out ways to make Rohan happy, but she didn't do it. She felt that their love was a thing of the past. She just didn't feel like putting the daily effort into it anymore. Maybe someday he'd let his sensibilities rest, take her into his arms and kiss her again right out in broad daylight! Maybe the spark would reignite. But she wasn't going to hold her breath waiting on that. That had been so long ago, they were now both long past the budding passion of their courting. There were sometimes days when, looking back, she wondered if it had ever fully blossomed?

Though there was that one night in particular… She closed her eyes a moment to remember a time when their courtship was quite new. He had taken her to a square dance. Thinking back, she could hear the fiddle's sweet, moving music in her memory - and see Rohan, coaxing the old Scottish ballads from the strings with his bow. He'd looked down at her from the band platform, and she'd watched him in return, wondering what it would be like if he kissed her. Then the musicians started a jig and he'd jumped down, taken her in his arms and swung her around to the music. Oh, how they had danced! Their feet flew with the notes, high, quick and wonderful.

Then there was the moment that was forever etched in her heart. Rohan had pulled her close, looked down into her face, all flushed from the lively dancing, and kissed her. Squarely and hotly.

She had resisted at first, mostly out of surprise, but he was gently insistent, until she surrendered and enjoyed the moment as much as she dared. Even with people watching, she had thoroughly enjoyed that kiss. The corners of her mouth curved upward even now.

But, Roh hardly ever touched the lovely instrument anymore. She could not remember when the music had stopped. He was just too busy. The days flew by with hardly even a fond look from him. At night, the curtain which was to be drawn around their bed to provide privacy was not needed often enough.

When Jon was born, Miryam had imagined that the world had suddenly become a much bigger place. Her love for her *bubbala,* and his need of her, filled her days. He had been a delightful little boy, the treasure of life for both she and Rohan. Every milestone of life was celebrated joyfully. The doorjamb was notched and dated as they marked his growth from time to time. Rohan gathered him up onto his lap for reading favorite stories, and when it was time to start school, Jon sat behind his Da's saddle and rode into town until he was skilled enough to ride to school by himself. He was still an obedient boy, though as an adolescent, he needed to grow out of his complaints. Miryam and Rohan were patient with him. They fully remembered what it was like to be young, to be a know-it-all, and want to run things. They knew that someday he'd realize that the running of things was a bigger job than he could handle. Watching him grow was bittersweet, though. All the precious milestones passed far too quickly, and no more children came to fill the empty place on her lap where Jon used to snuggle in the evenings before she tucked him into his bed.

Miryam knew now that she was not the force to order her world. She hoped, even almost believed that *Adonai* was real. She did have a measure of faith, but it was faith in her faith, which faltered with each change of the weather. She was a Jew, and had been taught that she must follow a strictly prescribed life. The rules and regulations were of utmost importance! And so she must be resigned to letting the Lord bear full responsibility for all things, though she thought life might be much easier if He followed her advice on occasion.

She kept the *shabbat,* and all the feasts as best she could. But there were no other Jews within a hundred miles as far as she knew, and keeping kosher was hard without the encouragement of her people. It seemed meaningless to perform the rituals when Rohan did not share her heritage. But she tried to do so because it was prescribed. She had been taught that it was essential to follow the law, but she often wondered "Why?"

She was well thought of in her community even if they thought some of her ways were odd, yet she no longer cared much about their admiration. The foremost thing on her mind each day was to just keep up with her workload. Today the dust got in her eyes as she struggled to get the washing done. It seemed to her that every piece of clothing was soiled almost as soon as she could fold it and place it in their trunks. Her arms ached from all the carrying, all the hanging out. Her sensitive hands were raw from the strong soap and from the hot water in the huge kettle slung over the fire in the yard. If Roh were here he would have carried the buckets from dawn 'til dusk and still had strength to spare. His calloused hands wouldn't even feel the scalding water. Too bad he was away on business.

She'd learned how to live with this taciturn man, but yearned to talk with him at the dinner table or over a cup of tea late at night. She wanted him to tell her all the thoughts and dreams in his heart, and for hmi to listen while she told him of her own dreams. He used to talk a bit more, not much, but surely more than lately! Each night she slept in his arms waiting for the day she'd have all that she needed, the camaraderie, the shared secret looks between them as lovers, the smiles of contentment, the laughter and brightness she'd witnessed in other couples, young and old alike. But at least each night there was a strong hand holding hers under the bedclothes. She could have done worse!

Miryam had truly and utterly fallen in love with Rohan. His life was the life she had chosen to follow. Though her love for Rohan was no longer a flutter or a feeling, it was a comfortable place for Miryam to abide. She missed his presence today. She kept looking to the horizon for a glimpse of his horse with its tall rider and the familiar tilt of his hat.

After his Scottish cap had finally been worn threadbare, Roh could not find another that reminded him of his homeland, so he began to wear the tall, wide-brimmed hat of the ranchers. He found it suited him here in the Midwest, where the sun beat down unmercifully in summer on his fiery red head and fair skin. He became ruddy and still burned if he was not careful to stay covered up on the hottest days. He always wore his hat at a distinctive tilt that reminded her of his much younger days.

Miryam pondered when she could expect him. It had been a full two weeks since he'd gone out to sell some stock. It was the longest they'd ever been apart. Glancing to her son, Jon, she saw that, though he was not yet as tall, or as strong as his father, in appearance he was very much like him. Like Rohan, his curly, reddish gold hair just touched the shirt collar at the back of his neck. Whenever she cut their hair, she took the loose tendrils outside and scattered them around her flowers. The deer didn't like the human scent, but the small creatures took the soft fluff into their nests and burrows. It was fun to watch the birds pluck up the tufts and fly off with them. It pleased her to imagine tiny birds or mice sleeping softly on the red curls.

Jon was finishing up his chores near home today so as to be close at hand if he was needed for wash day. The heavy kettle always needed to be emptied and refilled several times, and Miryam was only halfway through with the rinsing. He was keeping busy though. Making a harness repair, oiling a squeaky wheel, chopping a load of wood - all these could be done within hearing of the house. And it seemed that there was always a loose picket in the fence Miryam had insisted they put up around the yard.

Out here, in the middle of nothing, a fence made it seem like they belonged. She'd planted her rose bushes even before she'd fully unpacked the wagon. They'd been transported carefully all the way from Kentucky, and then the fence was built for the roses to climb along. She'd made sure that, even when their drinking water was precariously low, there was water for her precious plants. The hardy wild roses held on for dear life and once planted at their homestead they produced a profusion of dark pink blossoms every July. Their scent filled her with memories of home. Since then, she had been able to acquire tulip bulbs which bloomed without fail each spring.

This Monday's chore for Jon was to clear out the debris and redirect the flow of the creek that ran past the side of the house, on behind the barn, and then on to the pasture. Once in a while during a heavy rain it tended to give way in one certain spot, flowing over its banks and widening so that in a dry spell it petered out before it got to the stock. Today he'd shored up the low sides with stones and deepened the shallow places of the stream bed just enough to get it running smoothly again.

"He's grown into a man for sure," she thought, as she watched him carry his tools so easily back to the barn, his shirt open and untucked, the tails flapping in the wind. When he was little he had worked hard to keep up with Rohan, saying, "I do it myself, Da." Today he was no longer a child. He was doing a man's work and doing it well.

Shifting her sight toward a movement in the distance, her heart beat a little faster. The rider she was expecting was coming over the horizon. She'd best pull their noon meal forward to the warmest part of the wood stove to be ready for him. Who knows when was the last time he'd eaten a decent meal. After eating he could help with rinsing the last wash load and then empty the water onto the roses and her vegetable garden along the fence.

Mama had always said, "Don't waste your wash water, the growing things like it." Mama had lots of wash water. She washed everything she touched all day, as if someone had snuck into the house at night and soiled every doorknob and surface in the whole house. "I'm glad I'm not like her!" Miryam huffed.

Back inside the house it was only slightly cooler because of the shade tree, which grew next to the window. The house had been built on this exact spot because this lone tree would give shade in summer. In the house, at least, there was shelter from the dust. With his supper warming, Miryam removed her wet apron and the kerchief from her neck. She soaked the kerchief in the enameled basin, and again washed her face and neck, luxuriating in the water's coolness as it evaporated from her skin. She glanced into the mirror, removed the combs from her hair and ran them through the windswept mass quickly to reset them and hold in all the stray wisps that tumbled from her forehead. Her fine light brown hair was hard to tame, tending to curl up wildly in humid weather.

She set the table with a mug of milk she'd kept cool in the little cupboard set into the floor next to the wall. Just outside, where the creek ran past the house, Rohan had made a waterwheel that fed a trough, lined with metal sheeting, that he had built into the foundation of the house to catch the frigid water so Miryam could preserve a day's supply of milk, eggs and butter. The water ran through the trough and then back into the stream.

She laid out a plate, a fork, and blue and white gingham napkin from the shelf. She and Jon had eaten their big meal earlier in the day, but there was plenty left for Rohan. "I'm so glad you're home," she said aloud, as if he were already standing right there beside her. "I've missed you!" It was the times he came home from his trips when she realized most that he was a husband to be grateful for. He was a good man who had made a good life for them.

Her blue and white china always delighted her when she set it out for her family, recalling the day that Mama and Papa had sent it to her as a gift so long ago. Her flatware was much more practical, though, having been purchased from the same people who had outfitted them with the covered wagon. The heft of the knives, forks and spoons in her hand was testimony to the fact that, though not much to look at, the pieces would probably outlive her by centuries.

She cut some bread thickly, buttered it generously just as he liked it and then sat down to wait. It would only be a few moments more. She'd just let her eyes rest while he rode that last quarter mile. She woke to her son's voice straining uneasily.

"Ma... Ma!" Still in the half-life between sleeping and waking, she rose and stepped through the doorway onto the porch. There stood her son, hands behind his back, held in the rough grasp of a stranger. Jon had hoped beyond hope that she would bring the gun from over the mantle, but he saw that this was not so.

This man's intentions toward mother and son clearly were not honorable. Raw fear pierced them both like the vicious barberry thorn bushes out near the barn. She was afraid to move lest she be impaled even more deeply.

Miryam's mind fled and time stood still. She couldn't think about the danger standing before her. Her thoughts went to a place from long ago and rested there; a place where time stopped and where there was no fear. It was a sweet memory of something that had happened in her youth and had which had always enchanted her. The memory surfaced, to keep at bay the terror that threatened to relieve her of her sanity.

Mama had told me many times about the horses that came to her. A mare, and a yearling. It was when she was in her early teens. She was out by the trellis in their back garden gathering wildflowers for the dinner table. She heard a noise behind her and turned, startled.

The horse came right up to her, head hanging low – so low that Mama had to stoop to see the sad eyes.

"Such a gentle soul," Mama had thought. The mare heaved a great breath and brought her great head up to Mama's belly and rested it there, just rested. It was as if she had finally found her way home.

The Good Book says that when hope is deferred, one's heart gets sick. Yet Mama saw that this poor beast, even in its exhaustion and starvation, still carried some hope in its heart.

She was a deep chestnut with white fetlocks and a white blaze. Mama melted, overwhelmed with the utter trust of this dear, meek animal toward a total stranger. There was a lead around her neck but no saddle. She was bereft of any weight and had little strength, but was still so beautiful that Mama loved her instantly. Mama talked to her, softly and gently, offering courage and soothing hands as she looked her over.

There was evidence of past beatings. No new wounds were evident, but Mama could see that her feet were tender. Apparently the beautiful beast had been running hard and long at some point in days past. Now she was covered with dried sweat and trail dust.

Some minutes had passed when another horse appeared. It was a smallish yearling maybe, wearing only a lead as well. He was white and had just a single streak of black in his mane. He, too, was just as spent and lost, aimlessly following the mare. Though not as gentle, he offered no resistance she Mama

25

walked to him, speaking softly. He let her take his lead and bring him close to the mare for reassurance.

"Well, they certainly knew who to come to," she told me. "I loved horses then more than I loved my own life."

Mama had led them both to the creek at the barn and walked them right into it. They stood, cooling their feet, drinking until they could hold no more.

Mama had told me, "How I wished I could have spoken their language, to tell them that I'd take care of them, and," she had smiled, "of course, to hear about where-all they had been."

She named them right there, standing in the creek. The chestnut she called "Nut-brown Maiden" and the yearling she called "Salt."

She hoped that the name would help him see that he was 'worth his salt' as the old saying goes. He did prove his steadfast loyalty over the years and was still part of the family stable when Mama left home.

Miryam was brought back to the present by the scuffing of a dirty boot on her porch step.

Chapter 4

Rohan had driven until he thought he'd fall from the seat. His legs were numb and his eyes weary from the bright sun, but he was bringing home enough supplies to last until early fall. He tilted his hat further down his brow to shade his eyes, but the result was so soothing that when he blinked, he let his eyes close for a longer moment than he intended and woke with a jolt when the wagon hit a pothole.

On this trip he'd been successful in all of his dealings. He'd traveled most of the day yesterday and sold the last horse at a farm in the next county for a good profit. She was the filly of his best brood mare. He'd bargained well and come out on top.

Earlier this afternoon he'd stopped at a town along the way to get his wagon loaded with all the provisions he could think of. He'd found everything he'd hoped to have enough money for, even the new pump and the window for the outhouse that he'd promised for so long. The new pump would be noted and put to daily use, but Miryam would be immensely pleased to have a window in the privy! She wanted to be able to look out at the world - even while ensconced in that dreary, smelly place. Months ago, in great anticipation, she had already bought the material from the mercantile for yellow calico curtains which she would hang, gathered on a wire between two nails. Last year she had asked Rohan to make her a placard to affix to the door of the little facility, which she had then painted gaily and lettered to read, *"Gay Avek!"* It was in her language, saying, "Go Away!" To Miryam it meant, "This is the only time I have alone all day, so go away and let me sit for just a few minutes, for heaven's sake!"

Rohan had also bought material for shirts for himself and his son, and the ultimate luxury of a ready-made dress for Miryam. He knew that it would be as much a treat for him to watch her face as she pulled on the strings and opened up the brown paper wrappings, as it was for her to receive the gift. She always had plenty of work keeping the men folk of the family clothed. This time he was going to give her the luxury of not having to make her own dress as well. Food stores filled the wagon bed as well and he felt like a wealthy man. It was a almost an hour's ride home but he would easily make it well before supper.

The time away from home had made him *frachetty*. He was too quiet for his own benefit, and he knew it well. He deeply loved his wife and his son for the brightness they brought into his life. He rarely spoke, but, thanks to them, he smiled often. He knew that he needed their conversation just as he needed fresh air and sun. These past weeks, as he'd been alone, he realized that he didn't care over much for his own company. He'd had the solitary time in which to ponder his life and its motives, and he knew that although he was not a scoundrel, neither was he a godly man. He was always ready to help others, and always did his share. He attended the kirk regularly, but somehow he just couldn't understand what was said there. God was still a very much a mystery to him.

Mama always said that Da had the heart of a dreamer. She could see it the first time she met him. He knew that there was a rich place – heaven? – a fulfillment? - somewhere, somehow - but it was always just out of his reach. She could hear it come out of him, though, when he played his music. "Such a longing and a yearning!" she would tell me. "I could see it the first time I looked into his eyes. They were so blue, like the sky on an autumn day…" She would always say the same thing, "You know when the leaves are such rich hues of red and pumpkin and yellow and every shade in between? To see that intensely blue sky with those leafy colors together, it's so beautiful it makes me weep. And somehow I knew that there was a place inside him that wept, too. That's what color his eyes were when we met."

"Did they change color, Ma?" I'd always ask.

"As he got sadder, his eyes seemed to get darker. And he stopped playing his music. Do you remember the sad days?"

I always told her, "No."

And I didn't.

"That's the grace of God," she'd answer, every time. "If you ever have

doubts, remember how many times I have told you this. How much God loves you!" Mama was always emphatic when she said this!

She implored me, "This isn't a plea for you to believe as I do. It's a plea to believe as much as you can, and take the time and effort to search out the truth even where it might be hard slogging. There will always be questions in your mind and quite often questions in your heart. That will always be the case.

"It's the same with me and with everyone," she continued. "But I believe that there ARE answers. The answers can be elusive, but worth pursuing. And yes, there will be questions which will not be answered. But I think that there are enough answers to maintain the view that life is very good and worth living to the fullest."

Rohan knew that there was a flood of emotions in his heart, which grew as the years passed. His affection toward his wife and son were strong and lasting, and yet there was a depth missing in the past months which he could not explain. He'd given all he knew how to give, and still he knew that he was lacking somewhere. He had needs of his own, and they were met for the most part. But there was a place in him that asked, "Is there naught more t' this world?" He had this odd notion that, when he found the missing pieces to this *stramash* of life, he'd be whole and not have to wonder any more. Surely, somewhere, there must be answers to be discovered.

The wagon rattled under its heavy load, the miles swallowed up in the river of his thoughts. After daydreaming for a while, he brushed aside those things that seemed too deep to pursue. It was a fair day to travel, so he turned his mind to the delights of this day and the prospect of settling into the good honest work of tomorrow. After suffering with his own camp cooking the last few weeks he was looking forward to well rounded meals, and Miryam and Jon's company. After weeks of travel, he was in familiar territory now. The short distance from home made the idea of Miryam's cooking almost close enough to taste.

As he turned a bend, he shouted at the mare and pulled hard on the reins. *"Sheas!"*

By the looks of it, a traveler had also turned there recently, but only on two wheels. There was a rig rolled onto its side and the driver was desperately trying to release the horse from its traces. The man was frantic with haste to accomplish this task and continually implored the animal to hold still. But it was to no avail, for the poor beast was shaken to the teeth by the scare it had taken. As he drew closer he could see it was Doc Wilton, who looked up and called for help, shouting that there was a baby due at a homestead nearby, and he had to be there. He was the only doctor for many towns, and overworked due to the large area he had to cover to see his patients. This time, the distance and the need for expediency had taken their toll on the doctor's buggy. He was beside himself to get on with his journey. His patient's pregnancy had been a difficult one, and he suspected the birth would not be otherwise.

Together the two men worked. Rohan held the frightened horse, speaking in the old language, ever so softly, not lacking for any abundance of words when conversing with an animal. "Weesht w' ye, bonny lass. Dinna fash yourself. I ken it verra weel. Ye were verra braw, e'en though ye were so afright. But tis all o'er noo. Weesht. Ye mun weesht noo, bonny."

The doctor unhitched the becalmed horse, then using ropes and the farm wagon to pull, they soon had the buggy upright. But when it was straightened out, it was plain that two of the wheels had been badly mangled and were useless to the doctor now. They removed the two broken wheels and rigged up the other two so that the buggy could be towed by Rohan's wagon.

As he climbed bareback onto his horse the doctor begged Roh to deliver the buggy to a house, some ways ahead, knowing that if it were left aside the road it might be scavenged. "Weel," Roh thought, as the doctor galloped away at breakneck speed, "Tis on the wa', an' there's nae a choice aboot it anywa'." With his progress now slowed by the additional weight and the constant bucking and bumping of the raggedy wheeled buggy behind his wagon, he fell again into deep thought.

What was the missing link in his life? He had lately become aware of an ache in his deepest heart. Where was it coming from? He knew that he could easily work the days through and avoid these thoughts, but he also knew that this search for meaning had been in him often lately and it wasn't going to be resolved until he pursued it to its end. Was there an answer? As he spoke so tenderly to the doctor's frightened horse, his mind had said to him, "When ha' ye lately said such tender words as these t' your wife, or your boy?"

As a child, his family had attended the kirk regularly. He had a few family traditions to fall back on, but he didn't really get their meaning. Maybe the answer did not lie within him, maybe it was somewhere out there in the vastness of the world around him - waiting to be found, like the gold that was being discovered out in the frontier. He'd heard that it was found by sifting through rocks in stream-beds, and by digging deep into the hillsides. "Hoo far mun I dig? What mun I sift through," he wondered, "t' find wha' I'm lackin'.

How could he find the wholeness that eluded him? Surely it wasn't a tangible thing that he sought. Surely it was real, though. He knew that God had created everything - the sun and moon, crops and animals, rivers and winds and such. He knew that he believed that! It stood to reason that this God had created him as well. But the whole idea of actually knowing God was as far from his mind's grasp as the wide, wide ocean. It went on farther than the eye could see. It had taken him long two months to cross it by ship. Since then he had heard all sorts of stories about the world and its many far away, strange places. If all that he'd heard was true, how could he even hope to understand the nature of the God who had planned and created all of that?

He pondered the basis of faith in this God whom he did not know. The idea, as far as he could gather it from the words that the rector said on Sundays, was to give one's very life into His hands. How, pray tell, could one do that when He could not be seen nor touched? In return, this God would give one daily food, safety from one's enemies, and rest when one was weary. It seemed an unlikely exchange. In contrast, Miryam's God was all tied up in special prayers and special ways of doing things. It was a puzzle, to be sure, but it was too much to worry about now. He finally pushed the idea to the recesses of his mind again.

I have learned that so many people are unaware that God is ever present. He is with them at every moment of their existence, always speaking to their hearts. He knows who is ready to hear His Word of freedom and delight. I want to reach out to those who are eager to find what their hearts are searching for. I want to let them know that, in the kingdom of God, there is a song to be heard if we but listen. There is a dance to be danced in the presence of our Lord Jesus. To those who will not listen I would like to say that I carry an exquisite burden which weighs heavily upon me.

This burden can only be relieved by my passing it on to you. But do you want to hold it? Do you want to share the pain? Do you want to to see the gain? For, you see, this burden is one of joy, freedom and strength. Why, then, is it so difficult to carry?

Because I cannot convince you. Only God can do that and perhaps it is not time yet. You do not yearn with your whole heart yet to hear the song He sings. You are content with so much less than is freely offered to you. Your struggles seem to be far too precious to give up for a life of joy. So the burden of this joy cuts me to the quick, this agony of not being free to share this wonderful love with you.

The homestead to which the doctor had fled was in sight and an impatient father-to-be was pacing about in the yard, holding an unlit pipe. He was followed by a dog, who was very confused by the prospective father's actions. The poor animal just wanted to keep up with his master, yet the man changed his direction again and again. Where the man was going by his circuitous and zig-zagging route, the dog could not guess, but only hoped to learn by the faithful act of following its master's footsteps, haphazard as this seemed.

Rohan pulled into the yard through the split-rail fence and halted near the barn. He jumped down and walked to the distraught farmer extending his hand in greeting. The short, stocky man was a bit older than Rohan, with blond hair that stuck out in all directions. He was dressed in heavy clothes that looked as if they were from the old country, with leather suspenders on pants that stopped just below his knees, and thick woolen stockings tucked up under the pant legs. He continually ran his hands thru his disheveled hair, making him appear much like he'd been recently dragged thru a field by his feet. Rohan's gesture and his presence went unnoticed by the fellow, so he stood and waited at length until, abruptly, the tired man looked up.

"Och... sorry ... I did not dere see you."

"I brought the doctor's buggy. My name's Rohan MacVoy. I was told ye ha' a wee bairn comin'."

"Yessir, unt a long time it hass been we have been vaitink – unt her in dere veepink, unt I not knowink what iss for her I can do."

Rohan blinked several times in succession. This man's accent was thick as the proverbial molasses in January.

"Weel," he spoke out slowly, "either tis all fair an' ye can breathe oot the relief o' it..." he paused interminably, "or tis nae." His thoughts went home to Miryam in the vivid timelessness of a day he'd rather have forgotten. He pulled himself back to the present, realizing that he'd left this man with a statement that needed a promise of resolution. "Ye gang on as best ye can. I ha' seen it from both sides an' canna be tellin' ye more than tha'. We'll wait it oot t'gether."

"You a bebee have also lost?"

"Aye." It was their second child. Miryam's pregnancy and Jonathan's birth had been momentous and frightening for him, as a father, and as a mere bystander to the physical part of it. But it was all just truly natural in the grand scheme of things. The women had all commented on Miryam's strong health and the easy delivery. If that was easy, Rohan could not imagine what a hard labor would be like. Never had he seen such anguish as on Miryam's face right before the midwife firmly ushered him from the house. And the sounds that came from her! A wounded animal was sweet music to his ears in comparison. But in the end all was well.

The second child, however, was never easy for Miryam to carry. She didn't feel right and couldn't work like she usually did. There was no baking done, no preserved vegetables from the garden, the floor was not swept for weeks at a time, and then only when Miryam begged him to do it because she could not lay in bed and look at the dirt for even one more hour. He lost many a workday looking after her, fixing terrible tasting meals, and wearing dirty clothes, but she had made it through. The baby didn't.

The weary father sat down on the bottom step of the porch. "Ve a bebee last year lost, unt my vife de same hass not been. It seems everytink poorly since den hass gone. De corn by de bugs eaten iss. De cow her milk no more givink iss. De last supplies uff uss nearly gone iss. I am not knowink how vill I mannich! I no money haff - unt a bit only uff hope." He looked up at Rohan. "Again, I sorry am. I do not to vitt all uff diss burden you." He ran his shaking hands through his hair again and then covered his face. "Sorry."

Rohan turned away to ruffle the dog's neck and give the fellow a chance to compose himself. "A man's got t' ha' the tellin' o' somethin' sometimes t' ta'e the worry from his heart," he said at length.

Two hours later, after they had both borne, by proxy, each cry and moan from the laboring woman, they could hear a baby's cry in the house. The men grinned in relief at each other. Presently the doctor came out onto the porch, announcing the birth of a girl. The father ran in to his wife, taking all three of the porch steps in one leap. Rohan and the doctor shook hands and grinned.

"He and his daughter did a good job getting things ready while he was waiting for me," he said. "There was hot water and clean sheets right there."

As he and the doctor untied the buggy from his wagon and pushed it out of the way to the corner of the yard, Rohan thought again of heading for home and what a pleasure it would be to be under his own roof with his family around him. At this he felt such a sudden pang that it startled him. Here he was with such bounty in his wagon and these folks were near the bottom of the barrel in their supplies. At once it was plain that he could not leave his new acquaintance in such a sad state. His own wagon was overflowing with flour, molasses, salt, tea - enough of many staples to last them until harvest was over. Surely he could ease the cares of this fellow. If the circumstances were reversed he knew that he would regard it as an act of sheer kindness, and not just pity.

"I hope ye willna ha' trouble gettin' tha' buggy fixed," Rohan said as he reached out his hand in farewell.

"I reckon I'll have to get some new wheels made and bring them out here," replied the doctor. "I thank you kindly for giving me a hand back there,"

"Welcome."

After the doctor left, Rohan began to sort through the supplies, loading near the rear of the wagon what he knew was an extra bag or box, and near the front what they could not do without at home. At last he stood up, pleased with the results. It was near an even split. The bulk of the dry goods was enough to get them both by for two months or more. By then he hoped for the sale of another horse and he could make up the difference.

He smiled as he picked up a paper-wrapped parcel which held a length of heavy cotton for new towels as a surprise for Miryam. It would do for nappies for this wee new bairn. The beaming father came out of the house with the infant in his arms, wrapped in an apron, the ties hanging down like ribbons on a bonnet.

"Do come unt my new girl see!" he shouted. "My vife guut unt tired iss, but fine, unt diss one, mine little Rosie, at last hass come." They stood close, admiring the perfection of the tiny child.

"I don't know if any help vould I haff been myself for de bebee bringink, unt mine daughter too young iss for helpink. Vitt a cow, I do not about her feelinks vorry. I a hundred times haff done it. A voman? A different matter iss. I tenk you," the father spoke huskily, "helping for de doctor to come.

"Ye would ha' done the same for me," Rohan said softly as he took the infant's tiny fingers and wrapped them around his own. "I'll be leaving ye wi' some o' these provisions. Ye'll be needin' 'em t' keep your missus an' the wee lassie strong."

The man's eyes brimmed with tears as the emotions of the day came to their peak. "As much I can't tenk you," he mumbled into his chest, and the baby cradled there. "De kindness, if I am able effer, I vill repay."

"Ye're not t' be obliged. This time, I can help. Your time'll come one day."

"My name Gustav Himmel iss," said the new father. He adjusted the baby's position, extending a free hand. "I am pleased to your acqvaintance make."

The men exchanged neighborly words, with Gustav bearing the weight of the conversation. Rohan being not very wordy, but friendly. Gustav gently placed little Rose into the large crate which held the cloth for diapers, where she promptly fell asleep. As they unloaded the wagon they made plans to bring their families together when the mother and child were ready. And so it was that Rohan was coming home hours later than he expected. Depleted in worldly goods, he was far richer in spirit. He would not have voiced it in that way, he thought only of the happiness he felt. He was glad it had worked out that he could be of service, and that the gift was received in the same spirit as it was given.

Chapter 5

Miryam was unable to speak aloud but stood holding fast to the door jamb, her mouth dry, her heart racing. She tried to hear what he said, but could not focus.

"Yes ma'am, I been riding a long ways, an' yer a sight fer sore eyes. Yes, ya surely are."

Still she could not respond, but looked at him with unblinking eyes. "Let this be a dream," she cried inwardly. It was as if she was seeing it all from a distance, but not belonging to it. Yet she knew it was real.

He interrupted her thoughts, rudely playing at conversation by making it up in his head. "No ma'am, how kind of ya ta ask! I ain't et... and I ain't only hungry for food, now that I seen the likes of ya. I'd be obliged for some vittles though, and to have the pleasure of yer company."

As he set his foot on her stairs she thought, "How can this *fershtinkiner* be speaking of being obliged, and the pleasure of my company from the same mouth, with its wicked grin and the suggestive licking of his lips?"

He rose the next step, forcing the boy in front of him. He was not tall, like Rohan. Why had she thought it was him from a distance? He stared her down. She could not look away. She had to look him in the eyes while he let her know that there'd be no struggle, for to do so would be to die a slow, painful death. She'd seen no weapon, yet she knew that in the unlikely event he had none, she'd perish by his bare hands if she did not do as she was told.

She felt dead already as she saw the look in her son's eyes as he was pushed the last step onto the porch. This porch would no longer be for them a place to listen to the breeze at evening, to put one's feet up at the end of the day and relax. The sunsets would not be as beautiful to watch from her rocking chair on this porch, holding hands with Rohan as he sat next to her in his rocking chair, with Jon seated on the step with his harmonica.

Jon seemed like a small boy again to her as she looked at him. She looked with such regret into his blue, blue eyes. He was holding back his fear, but she could see it there as his eyes searched hers for some reassurance that what was happening would somehow be resolved. She saw the vast sprinkling of freckles and remembered their first appearance when he grew out of his toddling years. She looked at the set of his trembling chin. It was like the time he'd been thrown by his horse and was determined not to cry. She watched as the stranger led her son to the far end of the porch and there tied him to the junction of the post and rail, facing outward, overlooking the pasture. She could not move a muscle, as if her feet were nailed to the floor. How could she protect Jon?

Miryam looked at her son's hands, now in front of him, tied so tightly that they were already reddening. The stranger turned then, and strode, purposefully swaggering, toward her, looking deep into her soul and wringing from her every drop of strength and self confidence she'd ever possessed. She saw herself in her mind's eye, running away across the yard, her skirts slowing her, her breath not coming fast enough. But, in fact, she just could not move. He stunk of strong drink. He was in no way weakened though, as he lifted her almost off her feet in a vise-like grip just under her arm - and still she couldn't move. "So this is death," she thought.

"Let's git somethin' ta eat now, dearie," he spoke intimately into her ear as he pushed her through the door into the house. Once inside he shoved her roughly toward the stove. She moved by rote as she drew the lid off the pot, dished up the food onto her treasured china and placed it before him, staring at his dirty, weathered face. He grasped her wrist and held it way too tightly with one hand as he ate with the other. His vacant eyes watched her every move, giving her permission only to breathe, nothing more. He moved the food around on the plate as his eyes bored holes into her soul. She felt as if she was losing her mind.

Miryam lifted her other hand to brush away a hair from her face and in a flash, like lightning, he let the fork clatter onto the beautiful plate and a blade appeared from nowhere, slashing her arm. A thick line of blood welled up, stinging like a burn from her skillet.

"Don't move, Etta. I'll show ya what I think of ya and yer fancy man out there." He pointed to the porch where Jon was tied, and sneered, showing the half chewed food in his open mouth. He ate noisily and drank the sweet milk in great slobbering gulps. The only other sounds in the room were the ticking of Rohan's prized clock and the pounding of her crazy heartbeat. It was like a rabbit caught in a snare, trying everything - anything - to get loose. Papa had always said she had *chutzpah*, but where was her courage now?

Mama said that she would have screamed if she could have, but it would be even more frightening for Jon if she had done so. She would have bashed his head in with her skillet if she could have summoned any sense from her mind, or any strength from her body. But "I had neither," she told me. "I was consumed with fear."

The bread she'd made that morning was so fresh and smelled so good that it was not right for him to eat it. As she watched him gobble it up the tears welled up in her eyes. "Dirty *fresser*," she said to herself, "He eats like an animal." She hadn't sliced her bread for him, not for him. She hadn't buttered it so generously for the likes of this monster.

He released her arm and shoved her. "Stand over there where I can see all of ya," he said wickedly. She backed up, wide eyed, until she bumped into the wall.

Stuffing his mouth with the last of the meal, he leaned the chair back from the table lifting a dirt-encrusted boot onto her clean white tablecloth. He unbuttoned his shirt deliberately pausing between each button to take in every inch of Miryam from head to toe and back again. She felt like a horse on the auction block in the stock yard, but unlike the calm horses, she felt naked and helpless.

Slowly he pushed away from the table with a loud scrape of the chair on her polished floor.

Miryam surely could move now, nothing could stop her. She'd run until she died! She'd run so fast that he'd never be able to catch h…

He brought her arm up so sharply behind her that she was sure her shoulder would come out of the socket and her elbow would snap like a dry twig.

"Go!" His voice grated as he moved her toward her bed. Strange, the things that came to mind as Miryam stumbled those few steps. The quilt Mama had stitched for her had made the house a home for them in those early days, until she'd had time to make her own things... a pillow with cheery bright colors, potholders and a pure white tablecloth to match the curtains.

"No... no..." she cried aloud as he pushed her.

He was a small man, looking straight into her eyes. His clothes were coated with grit, his face and hair a mask of sweat and grime. He looked through her as if she wasn't there, and she wished she was anywhere else.

"Yer *my* wife, Etta. See to it ya remember that!" he growled. His breath was rancid. He turned her to face him, then shoved her forcefully backward onto the bed.

Miryam stared at the ceiling with unblinking eyes as a thought rose in her like bile. It was something she should have remembered. "Rohan hadn't ridden the saddle horse," she saw in her mind, "he took the wagon."

The knife glinted in the afternoon sun.

Mama's life would have been so different if the next few moments did not occur. But she now believes, as she has told me many times, that as hard as she struggled to survive it, physically and emotionally, there was a measure of eternity there. The pains we bear, when released fully into the hand of the One Who has allowed the agony, will produce that which is of untold value.

Thomas Edison said it well: "God has a purpose for every difficulty we encounter. Although this purpose is seldom obvious at the time, we must always remember that God does not want to destroy us through adversity. Rather, He wants to shape us for His glory and to conform us to the image of Christ. He does not send suffering to crush us; He wants us to triumph through suffering. God is our hope! And because of His faithfulness and power, we can face the adversities of life without fear, and with triumph!"[6]

The grazing horses in their pasture were unmindful of the fear gnawing in Jon's belly and the raw place in his mind. He tried to think of what to do to stop the spilling of this invaluable time - this time that was being wasted and lost in despair, pain, and futility. He knew that he could do nothing and that he would stand powerless and solitary until these violent moments roared past and were gone.

Jon heard his mother's cries through the open door, try as she did to suppress them. He stood, as rigid as the post he was tied to. He flinched with each muffled groan and whimper. He wept, thinking "Will she live through this day?" The tree rustled in the wind as the daylight waned and the cow lowed, ready for milking. He felt like a man stranded alone in the desert, no water, no hope, and the life draining out of him. Sweat poured from his hairline down his face as he stood watching the afternoon sun descend. He tried so hard not to hear what was impossible not to hear. He tried so hard not to acknowledge what he knew was happening. Then it was over. There was an off tune whistle of satisfaction inside the house and then a haughty chuckle.

"Etta," the stranger said to Jon's beloved mama, "yer a good woman in bed, so I'll let ya live!"

Miryam's soft weeping began. Jon heard rough scraping footsteps coming out the door, slowly toward him. He stared into the distance, bracing himself for whatever might happen next. He might die now and he knew it. The stranger was behind him, silent. The man picked up a piece of the firewood that Jon had stacked on the porch yesterday. He stood slapping it against his palm rhythmically, endlessly.

Then Jon felt the wood strike his skull and he fell with pain and sorrow. Another blow came, this time with a curse. "Ya thought ya could have her! Well see if ya want her now!" The footsteps receded slowly into the distance, then he heard the stranger gallop away. Jon blacked out.

Chapter 6

When he came to consciousness, his mother was there, speaking softly to him between her sobs. She took her butchering knife and carefully cut the rope that bound his hands, which were now purple. He gasped and reeled as the blood returned to his fingers. In his heart and body he knew he'd never felt such pain. The lumps on his head were still growing larger and he could not stand up. But these hurts were nothing compared to the torture of not being able to help his mother when she'd needed him.

He felt her tender touch and the cold cloth she pressed to his wounds. She sang to him a song from his childhood, so long ago, and they wept together. But they were alive, alive to hold each other close and know that they'd survived. He wept in Miryam's arms until he finally slept.

Miryam rose from the porch floor slowly, stiff from sitting so long, one foot asleep. Stepping carefully to get the feeling back into her foot, she barely kept her balance. She slowly staggered out to the barn in the dimness to milk poor Wilhelmina, who had not ceased bellowing her discomfort. She moved in a daze, finding the familiar path hard to follow. It was hard to walk at all, she hurt so. It was nearly full darkness. Time would not stop to let Miryam recover from the day's horror. She knew that she must go on, putting one foot in front of the other until the farm was settled in for the night. Accompanying all of her pain was the fear for Roh's welfare. Was he safe? Was he hurt somewhere along the road? He'd promised to be home today! Where could he be?

Jon slept in merciful oblivion. He did not know that his mother wept grievously as she laid her forehead against the warm side of the cow while the foamy milk rose in the pail. Wilhelmina seemed to her to be so stable, so pure, so normal... she didn't want to leave the stall. Life was flying by, though. Jon needed tending to. Rohan was still out there, somewhere. And she was here, utterly broken.

Miryam mustered her strength and poured the bucket of fresh milk into the can and capped it. She struggled awkwardly to roll it to the creek bed to keep it cool until morning. It was not one of her usual chores. All the heavy work was usually left to the men. But where was Rohan?

She stood near the creek, shaking uncontrollably. There was no help for it. She felt unbearably filthy. There was usually a quiet time set aside for her to bathe at the end of a washday, her hardest day of the week. It was her time to be alone in the house while the men folk stayed away until she was finished. Rohan would get the hipbath from the nail on the back of the house and bring it in next to the fireplace. He'd fill the big iron kettle in the yard with fresh clean water and then, when it was hot, he'd bring in bucket after bucket, just for her. Of course they all had baths on Wednesdays and Saturdays, but Monday was Miryam's special time.

When the bath was full, she would smile at him and then take off her apron. It was the time for Rohan and Jon to go. Roh sometimes lingered, undoing a few buttons, telling her how much he would enjoy kissing her soft fresh skin after her bath. As she closed the white linen curtains she would see the two of them in the lamplight, father and son, seated at the barn door. In cooler weather they went inside the barn where the smithy fire would be lit. They'd most likely sit in silence and enjoy the night sounds, or talk about their chores. They would amble back into the house whenever she pulled the curtains back to cast a square of yellow light into the yard.

On Mondays Miryam got out the fine lavender soap that her mother sent to her every year on her birthday. Each sculpted piece was wrapped in tissue and kept in her bridal trunk for this weekly ritual. Each year she used them lavishly at first and then, as her supply dwindled, more sparingly. It was something which she had noticed that Rohan liked, the smell of the lavender soap. He'd bury his face in her neck and she could feel his breathing on her skin as he took in the scent. Their nights often turned to passion on Mondays.

As she took the lye soap from the laundry tub she despaired, "I never finished the clothes." Undressing hesitantly in the privacy of the darkness at the side of the house, she started at each owl's hoot and each night noise. Making her way to the water's edge, she moaned out her heartache. This night was much different. No warm water or heady lavender scent, only frigid pain, as she waded in the stream up to her knees. She quickly bathed in the deepest water she could find, gasping at the temperature of the water and snuffling with muted sobs. As hot tears ran down her face and neck they mingled with the icy cold of the creek water as she splashed it on her bruised body. She gasped as she felt a sharp stinging on her breast. He'd cut the mark of an X into her skin there.

"Ta prove yer mine!" he'd said.

She set her jaw in determination not to allow this day to rule her life, but to go on, looking ahead and not back. But she knew that it would be impossible. It had been shamefully humiliating and so horribly painful! She fell to her knees, the gravel cutting into her skin. She choked on cries that would not cease. She winced as she scrubbed herself with the coldness and the harsh soap. If not for Jon's presence, she would scream long and loud.

Eventually she could breathe almost normally. She had to get out of the icy water. She felt completely demeaned and worthless. Her world was crumbling and there seemed to be nothing she could do to stop it. Why had this happened? Where was the Lord, *Adonai*? Surely He'd seen what had happened? Her grip on reason was loosening and she felt she would slip away forever.

Her mind returned to the lost horses who had found refuge with her in her youth. "If only," she thought, "if only there was a place for me to go – a place where I knew that I could take refuge and be cared for... Will I ever rest again?"

The house was dark as pitch when Miryam came in. She wondered again where Rohan could be, and lit the lantern in the window for him. She took a clean dress from her trunk and put it on. She wadded up the filthy dress, carried it to the wash kettle and pushed it down deep into the water, drowning the thoughts associated with the blood stains on it. She went to the porch and looked long at Jon. He slept soundly, as if a child again. Miryam knelt at his side and gently tried to rouse him. At least, she thought, she could make things seem normal if he was in his bed, where he belonged at this time of night. He groaned and held his head. She tried unsuccessfully to lift him, but finally he rose under his own power, grunting from the effort. Leaning heavily on Miryam's small frame, he walked to his bed and fell upon it. She carefully removed his boots and woolen stockings.

He was now fully awake but the effort of moving was too painful. Miryam labored to shift him, inch by inch, to get his long legs onto the bed. He was so overwrought, but he had to talk, he could not think this through alone.

"Ma?" He hesitated, how could he say it? "Did he...?" It was too awful to voice and his eyes pleaded with her to ease the burden for him.

Miryam could not look at his face. She felt so shamed and so dirty, as if she'd been a willing participant. "Jon, it wasn't your fault. You were so brave not to struggle too much and get yourself killed... I'm so sorry," she sobbed. "I should have kept the gun handy, I wasn't thinking..." Miryam stopped to find control of her voice. She held her emotions deeper inside than she'd ever had to before. The hidden pain was searing her heart just like a branding iron leaves a foal with its owner's mark. In fact, she had been branded by this man.

"We've just been through the hardest thing we may ever have to face, but we're through it now, it's over...." Her voice broke as she reached for his hand. "*Zeeskeit*, my sweetheart," she paused to gather her own courage, "if we let this put us under, then the day can't be redeemed... *Fershtay*? Do you understand? We have to let today become the past, let it fade and not relive it. Tomorrow will have its own cares to handle. Won't we heal? Won't we go on?" Miryam wished with all her heart that she could believe her own words, and that Jon would take solace in them. Were they true?

He lay back, still holding her hand. His world was weakened, emptied of meaning and yet promising a purpose somehow, because of her words. He took hold of them with everything he had left. He must keep the evil that had taken place at bay somehow. He had listened to the preacher say it many times, but he didn't know how to accomplish the command of Jesus.

"Mama, how can I tell? How can I know when to be angry and when to turn the cheek? How can I forget? I'll never be able to! He was evil and... and sickening!"

It was not until I was nearly grown that she told me these things. She never wanted to burden me with them. But she knew that it was something that would soon enough cross my mind and I'd need to be forewarned and prepared. By then, Mama had gained the advantage of perspective, and some insight of God's workings.

She told me, "You see, God has ways that He uses to bring people into His arms. They aren't what we'd choose, more often than not. But His ways work very well to help us to learn about ourselves and about Him, how to build a tiny connection into a working relationship. Since He made us, we can be sure that He knows us, what we can handle and what we can't.

"Bad times will come into every life, but then He offers His hand for us to take hold of. We aren't spared from our troubles, even while holding His hand, but we learn to trust Him because of how He brings us through them."

As the dark gathered in the valleys and the crickets chirped, Rohan rode along thinking of his lot in life. He was able to set aside his doubts, due mostly to his fatigue. Right now, life was good and didn't much need to be improved upon. He had what he wanted, a good wife and son, and what he needed to make a living and enjoy it. That he had neglected some area of his life occurred again to him briefly and fleetingly, and then was forgotten. After all, the day had been well spent.

He rounded the last curve and saw in the distance the lamp he knew would be burning in the window. Finally he pulled up in the yard and swung stiffly to the ground, yet he took the porch steps by twos, as was his habit. When he opened the door, he knew immediately that something was not right - the house smelled sour.

He found Miryam asleep next to Jon in the boy's bed. He sat down beside her, looking at her beautiful face, then he spoke her name quietly. She stirred uneasily but did not waken so he shook her lightly and spoke again only to see her cower and stare at him wide eyed in fear, pleading, "No! Don't hurt me anymore, I beg you!"

"Tis me. I wouldna hurt ye. Tis only me, Roh."

"Oh Rohan!" Miryam flew into his arms and wept. She grasped at his shirt as if to hold him forever. Rohan ran through in his mind what could have gone wrong in his absence, looking over Miryam's shoulder at Jon to see that he was all in one piece and breathing. Having satisfied his fear for Jon he took her by the shoulders and gently pushed her away so as to see her face.

"Wha' is 't?" he asked, looking into her tears.

"I... I... he was hurting Jon and I tried to run, but I couldn't, and I... he... had a knife and he cut me... and he... he..." Miryam collapsed into agonized moans, tearing Rohan's heart wide open. He held her tightly, rocking her and smoothing her hair. It seemed an hour passed before she was calm enough to rest back on the bed beside Jon. Rohan lifted the blanket from the foot of the bed and covered her, whispering that he'd be close by, then he stood to survey the room. What had happened here? Who was the man with the knife and what had happened to his family?

There was no overturned furniture, or significant mess to indicate a struggle, but there was a hidden violence that he could feel somehow, a darkness in the corners, a more sinister presence than he'd ever felt before.

There was only one setting of dishes on the table, unwashed. There was a large smear of dried mud on the corner of the tablecloth. Miryam usually kept the house spotless. It was odd, but did not lead Rohan to the problem. He left then, after checking to see that Miryam and Jon were fast asleep, to unload the wagon. He brought the supplies into the house, drove the wagon into the barn, lit a lamp, then checked on Jon and Miryam again. He returned to the barn, unhitched the horse, brushed him down, put out the lamp and went to the house, all the while looking for clues as to why Miryam was so undone.

The wash kettle was still full. That was to be expected if Jon had been too busy to empty it after his chores. But there were too few clothes on the line. There was usually an overabundance and some of the heavier items sometimes adorned the fence until they dried by Tuesday morning. What on earth? Come to think of it, Miryam was not wearing her Monday wash dress, but the second best dress she owned, the wool she'd made last winter. But why on such a hot day?

He climbed the steps to the porch, and gathered some firewood for the morning. Why was one piece not stacked with the others? What was this piece of rope around the post for? He could not add it up. Violence was foreign to Rohan so he did not think that ordinary things like firewood and rope were a part of it.

He entered the house, and that sour smell hit him in the face again. He suddenly he recognized it as the smell of dirty flesh and alcohol. Someone awful had been in his very own house!

Miryam startled awake as he came to where she lay, softly asking, "Are ye ready t' come t' bed now?"

"No! No!........" she wailed as she hid her face from him.

Rohan stared at her, the realization of the crime that had taken place dawning in his heart. He spun and ran to their bed, finding it disheveled, the precious quilt torn and covered with mud at the bottom. There was a dark stain in the middle of it. Rohan shook with rage, pulled the quilt from the bed causing the pillows to fall to the floor, and fled the house. Miryam heard his hoarse crying in the yard but could not bring herself to go to him. She wept again until she was spent. At last she slept.

Whenever Mama talked about Da crying, I wanted to cry, too. I knew I had been spared seeing him cry, but the thought of my big father weeping overwhelms me even now. People ask, "How can God exist and allow evil to prevail?" Yet how can we judge what is evil without a comparison to good? The ultimate good is God. But our evil has set in motion all the heartaches that have ever filled the world.

Chapter 7

His head was pounding. The crows caw-cawing above him in the pines made an awful racket. His mouth tasted wretchedly of alcohol and dust. Where had he been and where on God's green earth was he at now? As he looked around he began to recognize the place. Apparently, he was in the back field of his own property. "May as well be in hell," he thought to himself.

Dan had not drunk alcohol in twenty years, he knew what that could lead to. Blackouts had been a frequent occurrence in his younger days, and fights, and waking up broken, often in jail. He'd vowed it would never happen again. But here he was, living proof that he had gotten drunk and somehow landed himself up in the field. In the distant valley he could see his house, but no smoke coming from the chimney.

She wasn't there. Of course. He began to remember. That fancy man had come, was it yesterday? Last week? Last month? What day was today? She'd been seeing him on the sly in town when she said she was going to do the marketing. They'd made all the arrangements behind his back. Her trunk was packed with all but her oldest clothes. No wonder she'd looked so slovenly lately. They'd left him standing in the yard stammering in anger. He'd heard them laughing at him as they drove away into the hills.

He thought about it as he sat in his field with his hangover. "Well, there's no use in stayin' to home," he'd reasoned. So Dan had taken off cross lots, just riding wherever the horse took him. He'd dumped a pan of biscuits he'd just made into a flour sack, and some apples from the barrel, saddled up his horse with a bedroll and just rode. He'd slept where the road took him, drinking water from creeks, eating when he realized a meal was way too long overdue. He could hardly keep his pants up with his belt in the tightest notch. He remembered that eventually he had sat on a barstool where the barkeep was called 'Catamount' or some such nonsense. He'd been too tired to wonder if it made any difference anymore. He'd ordered a drink. Losing Etta had pushed him over the edge.

He didn't know how long he'd spent there at the bar or what had happened since. "I hope I didn' kill nobody," he grumbled as he stood and gathered the reins of his horse as it faithfully stood by grazing. "I reckon we best be about livin', horse, cause I ain't dead yet - this mornin' at least."

He found the house just as they'd left it, but with an empty space at the foot of the bed where Etta's trunk used to be. She'd left him the household wares anyway. Pots and pans and blankets and such would come in handy since there was no money to buy new. Was that why she left? They'd been through hard times before but she'd stayed and worked next to him 'til the crisis had passed. Why not now? He peered into the looking glass above the bowl and pitcher on the washstand. Oh! What a face! Never did he think he could be so dirty looking and still be standing on his own two feet. "Six feet under is what ya look like, buster," he muttered to himself.

His beard had grown two inches and was crusty and brown while it used to be the jet black of his hair. Just How long had he been gone? He took off his hat and surveyed his matted mane. There was a bloody lump on top where he supposed he'd been hit on the head with a bottle, or perhaps a broken chair leg. It looked like the lumps he'd brought home in the old days. "Musta been gone a while this time." Dan was used to having someone around to talk to. "Better take a bath in case they come to string me up. Don't die dirty, Ma always said."

He set about making the fire in the hearth, and set the cauldron over it filled with water. Though he'd been married, he'd had to do all the domestic chores as well as the rest of the farming. Etta was, what do they call it? A slug-a-bed. She could not cook and would not learn. Oh, she was beautiful though, but she knew it only too well. And he'd coddled her 'til she was of no use for anything but looking at.

When the washtub was filled and tested for temperature, he plunked the bar of laundry soap into the hot tub to melt down a bit. He needed all the soap he could get to soak this grime off. He decided to wash his clothes later so he heaped them next to him on the floor, then stepped into the hot water and sank down, letting a sigh of contentment go as he eased into the full depth of the tub.

Dan let the water calm his mind while he relaxed deeper into the suds. As he rested there, the smell of the soap eventually led his tired subconscious mind to a homestead where a woman was washing her clothes over a kettle in the yard. She was pretty like Etta. But he had not seen her as pretty, he had been so angry with her. He'd shown her not to run off with another man! But the man was gone, and there was a boy. Who was the boy? There was a quilt. No quilt here, Etta had no sense for any of that. What had he done?

It was a bright day with a pure blue sky, birds singing and clouds making their lazy way across the horizon. But Miryam woke up stiff and bruised in Jon's bed wondering why she was there. Roh wasn't home yet? Oh! ... Oh! She hurriedly stumbled from the bed to the chamber pot and retched. She straightened up then with great care because of all the places she hurt so badly. Her brain was numb, and she didn't fight it. "Don't think about it. Don't try to remember. Just get on with what you need to do," she thought. But the memory was there, lurking like a wild thing. And she was its prey.

She saw that the dishes were still on the table. Miryam picked them up one by one with a dishrag and put them into the fireplace on top of yesterday's ashes. She threw the rag in as well. Then the tablecloth. But that was too much for her. She sat down on the hearthstones and let the tears roll down her cheeks again. "Must I throw away everything he touched?" she thought, "There'll be nothing left, and nothing left of me! I can't give up everything that's always been dear to me, but what can I do to rid myself of him?"

So she pulled the tablecloth, the cup, the plate, the fork and knife, and the rag from the hearth and resolved to begin again. Surely there was a way to put this behind her. There was work to be done to put the house to rights again. There was life to be lived again. There was a family to love again. She swallowed all the agony and stood up.

Rohan came through the door, looked at her and then turned again to go, not knowing what to say or how to face Miryam. Their eyes met for a brief moment, yet an eternity passed between them. "Don't leave," she implored. He stood facing away from her, rigid as an oak.

"I need you... to... we need to... put things away and... and... I... Rohan, I... please..." Miryam was gasping for air between her words and her tears as she stood holding the precious dishes along with the things she so wanted to forget. Couldn't he turn and hold her again like he did last night?

But then Jon woke up moaning, holding his goose-egged head. Rohan went to him to examine his wounds. He had finally figured out this morning that the rope on the porch had bound his boy while his wife was being raped. The odd piece of firewood was stained with blood, blood he couldn't have seen the night before. Jonathan's wrists were chafed raw, but the abrasions were not deep and would heal. Rohan was worried though about the other injury. Jon's head was oozing fresh blood and the pillow was covered. He was pale and shaky.

"Can ye walk? Do ye need t' go t' the privy?"

"Yes, sir," Jon answered, but could not stand up. He fell back onto the bed, so Rohan brought the chamber pot, but soon realized someone had vomited in it.

"Uh!" He felt ill himself, but pulled himself together and left to empty the pot. When he returned he held it for Jon to use it, then left to dump it again.

As Rohan came in with the empty vessel, he decided to just stick to doing what was practical. "Best t' give him somethin t' eat. Build up his strength. I'm gettin the balm." With that Rohan strode out to the barn, leaving Miryam still trembling, still holding her burden. She straightened her shoulders, took the contaminated table setting, and the once clean white tablecloth outside and put them into the wash kettle in the yard. Rohan's eyes widened when he watched her as he passed on his way back to the house but said nothing. He cleaned Jon's wounds, applied the healing salve and a strip of cloth for a bandage, and left again. There were chores to do, and he was glad to be away from the house.

Miryam went through the motions of preparing breakfast,

mechanically stoking the fire in the stove, boiling water, adding the oatmeal, making coffee, slicing bread, frying eggs. But Jon heard the rattling of pots and dishes cease every so often, and then sniffling would begin. Then a low, keening cry. Then ragged sobbing. He lay, choked up in sympathy for his mother, but he didn't know if he should let her know that he heard her. After a time, Miryam gathered her strength and continued cooking their breakfast.

Rohan entered with the morning milk. "Your parritch is ready," said Miryam woodenly, using Rohan's Scottish word. Over the years their cultures had overlapped and melted together. She dished up eggs onto the toasty bread and some porridge for Rohan, poured his coffee, then mixed a thin gruel for John with plenty of milk and butter and sugar. She wanted to tempt him to eat so he'd regain his strength. It wouldn't do to have him turn up his nose if he was not very hungry. He rose on his pillows and obediently opened his mouth like a baby bird. Miryam dared not look into his eyes for fear he would show her his fear, or his pain. She knew she'd cry again and she couldn't afford to. It took too much energy, and there was little enough of her left.

He watched her face. She watched his mouth. She dabbed at the corners whenever her trembling hand missed the mark or carried too much on the spoon. Then he could bear it no longer. "The dish is not so full now, Ma, I can do it." He melted inside as she surrendered the dish to him. Too late he realized that now she'd have to find something else to do to occupy her mind, and Da was still there, and there were words that needed to be said. He wanted to be up and out of the way so they could talk, but he just could not summon the strength.

Miryam poured herself a cup of coffee, took time to stir in the sugar and cream, then sat down across the bare wood of the table from Rohan. She bowed her head, watching the swirling in her cup until it settled. When she looked up, he was staring at her, and past her, and through her, all at once. Their eyes met.

"I...forgot the..." she tried unsuccessfully to take a deep breath, "... gun... I'm sorry." She bit her lip, hard, waiting for the shame to stop ripping her apart.

Rohan didn't mean to appear so hard. He just couldn't speak about what was in his mind. There was so much fury, so much anger at the circumstances. But Miryam read his expression as a judgment of her, as if it was her fault this had happened. She reached for his hand. He had been clenching and unclenching his free hand unconsciously, while holding his coffee cup in a white knuckled grip. He never used the handle. His hands were toughened enough that he never felt it was too hot to wrap his whole big hand around the cup. His eyes fell to her hand, so soft and small on his, then his gaze went to the gash on her arm where the sleeve was rolled up. "He cut ye bad?"

"Not too bad. But it stings"

"When did it happen?"

"Late afternoon."

"I..." He couldn't hold it in. It was eating him up that he wasn't at home when he should have been. His eyes welled up, but he would not let the tears fall. "I was delayed."

"Oh, Rohan, I'm not holding you responsible!"

"Ye're nae t' blame either. Anybody might ha' forgotten the gun."

"What... do we do now?"

"I dinna ha' answers for ye."

"Rohan," how could she say it? "I'm hurting so bad." She whispered, head lowered, tears flowing yet again. "I think there's something wrong in me."

Rohan set his jaw and swallowed hard. This was draining every bit of strength he had just to sit here speaking of such things. But he knew he must be able to stay calm for Miryam and Jon.

"Twas surely a lot o' blood, *aleannan*. I burned the sheet, but your mither's quilt I put awa' in the barn," he said.

She was so thankful for his expression of endearment that could barely speak, "Thank you."

"I suppose ye could ha' washed it wi' the rest... but I..."

"No, I'm glad you did it. I would never have slept under it again... I only saved the other things because I realized, after I put them in the hearth to burn them, that I can't throw away everything he touched or we'd have nothing left... Including me..."

Rohan glanced up with a desperate look to Miryam's well being. Would she hurt herself? But she seemed in control of her emotions.

"I guess not..." he said at length. "I scrubbed the porch," he offered. "I'll finish the washin'. Can ye keep up in here wi' Jon?"

"I think so."

He turned to go, to be anywhere but in the house.

"Wait. Roh?" Silence ticked by. "I need you, Rohan."

"What?"

"I'm so *fermisht*, I feel like I'm about to fall over... Could you just... hold me for a while?"

"Aye," Rohan consented, but this inactivity while a criminal who had ravaged his family was on the loose was killing him. He sat down again, after pulling his chair out away from the table. "Come noo, an' sit doon here," he said as he drew his long knees together for her.

She sat in his lap, and he rocked her, stuffing all his hurt and anger way down in his ribs. He would not cry!

"I was so worried about you. What happened to you yesterday?" Miryam asked.

"A wee new babby has come, o'er at the old Armstrong stead. The new folks is called Himmel. His name is G... It's summat like t' a goose."

Miryam lifted her head from his shoulder, brows knitted in confusion. But Rohan raised his own red eyebrows with his own lack of understanding and went on with his story. "He canna speak his words strung together proper t' save his own soul. Anywa', I was on the road an' I come upon the doctor as he was on his wa' t' deliver the *wean*. But his buggy had o'erturnit when he was goin' 'roond tha' hairpin turn, so I helpit him set it aright, then I took it o'er there."

"So you met the new folks?"

"Aye, weel, only Goose. There's a daughter, and the wife, but the leddy was quite busy, ye see." He gave Miryam a little squeeze and tried to make her laugh at his joke.

"The baby?"

"A lassie."

"All's well? Was... he nice?" Miryam was stuttering and taking ragged breaths, but trying so hard to talk normally, as if she weren't huddled on Rohan's lap in the early morning when she should be about doing her work.

"Aye. He said his wife is doin' fair well. He dinna say her name. The wee lass is to be called Rose."

"That's lovely... Roh? Hold me closer, I'm shaking so."

Da told me, when I was old enough to hear it, how he'd felt. He had so much to overcome. His anger and frustration was such that he wanted to run, to summon all the strength that was in his entire body, and give it to the running. He did not know his destination though. It was futile, he realized, to spend all of his life in a race that he knew he could not win. It took all the power of his mind, which was already running that frantic race, to stay and hold Mama. He knew that he was not what she needed, and he could not imagine what might be able to bring her peace. He felt that he was utterly destitute and unfit to give any solace.

He was so angry! What galled him most was that he felt he should have been there to prevent it from happening. He should have at least sensed that something was wrong and hurried home. Now it was bed time again. He'd been able to persuade Miryam that sooner or later they'd either have to use the bed or he'd have to build a new one. He assured her that the mattress tick had been beaten until he was weary, and he had put on clean sheets and a blanket to replace her mama's quilt. They got into bed together, the air heavy with unspoken words.

He was near cursing and silently blaming himself when she cut him short. "Just be here, hold me and let me rest. Don't grieve anymore. Just be still." She eventually slept from sheer exhaustion.

Miryam woke in the dark stillness of night and could lie there no more. She rose quietly and went outside. It was cool and peaceful as she sat in the dark on the big rock beside the outhouse, crying mutely. She reached inside the bodice of her dress and felt the ragged edges of the "x" on her skin. Would it heal and not show anymore or was it permanent?

She made her way to the barn on the familiar path and was able to find the bag balm right where is always was on the shelf inside the door. She applied some of the soothing salve to the wound on her arm and to her breast where the "x" was so painful. Rohan would not handle it well if he knew about this last, visible indignity. Realizing that she was still physically drained, even though her mind would not calm down, she returned to bed.

She listened as Jon tossed and turned in his sleep. His head wounds had finally stopped seeping blood and his wrists had been treated and bandaged. He could sit up in bed for a quarter of an hour before getting woozy. He would probably be himself physically in another week. But what about their life as a family? How does one step from the past to the present with no looking back?

Rohan didn't have any answers either. If his thoughts had been fire, they would have blazed like a barn full of hay. He could not quiet them, but for Miryam's sake he lay there beside her, smoldering within so as not to disturb her since she had finally come back to bed. When she left the house earlier in the night he'd gone to watch her out the window. It was all he could do to stay inside and let her be. But he didn't know what to say or do to help her, so what was the use? She returned and at last she breathed slowly and evenly. He knew that she slept.

Yet sleep was still far beyond him. He eased himself off the bed and went to the porch. The night sky was pricked with stars like a tin-work lantern. How could something be so beautiful when he was in such a *moil?* Perhaps he could find solace in the company of his horses. He lit a lantern and trudged to the barn, glad to leave the bed, and the house, and the grief.

But in the barn he realized that this awful thing followed him wherever he went. He swore under his breath, then grabbed a horse blanket and shoved it against his face and screamed at full voice as the hurt rose again, a great lump in his throat. It felt better to let it out so he let loose again but with a little less volume, then began a fairly loud muttering in terms better not used in mixed company. Normally he didn't approve of expanding one's vocabulary by swearing, so in giving way to cursing he was ashamed, but felt better for having let out the awfulness.

The horses didn't seem to mind after the first startling outrage, but sought the handful of oats he usually brought them. The velvet noses and lips searched his palm in vain. Finding nothing, they whickered and allowed Rohan to lean against their solid steadfast bulk, as he visited each in turn. He buried his face in their manes, stifling the groans that escaped him involuntarily. He took in the smell of the clean straw under their feet. He wished he could feel protected from the harsh world by these gentle beasts. As he touched each one, speaking their names to them, he knew that he should be of more comfort to Miryam – as the horses were to him - but he could not let his feelings surface with her. He was far too close to a tumult of fireworks.

The night was almost gone but sleep still eluded him. Sitting in the feed box with his horses whickering to him, he put his head in his hands and the hot, angry tears came unheeded. Where was this great God of the kirk all this time? How could this have happened to the most loving, most gentle person he knew? Confusion and anger wrestled in his mind and he knew it was to be a long fight. Life had challenged him, he reasoned, but he must stand up to the test.

Decades later, when Da and I talked it over, we decided that God wrestles with men today in much the same way that He wrestled with Jacob. It's a relentless struggle on our part until finally He pins us, and we realize that we cannot live on our own. He made us for Himself. We were designed to belong to Him. He wants our companionship, our love, and our obedience.

But, like long ago in the garden, when the opportunity was given, man disobeyed. And we are still like Adam. He ate the apple, imbibed the knowledge of evil. He ingested poison. This changed the spiritual chemistry of every generation for the remainder of history. This poison dissolved the bond between God and man. Intimacy with Him was no longer possible.

Our own strength, and our own wisdom will never sustain us, for this world, and we ourselves, are of God's making and we are not created to be independent of Him. So He wrestles with us, like a father with his son, to establish His leadership and say to us, "See, I am the Creator and King. You are my child. Now live with Me, in My ways, in My kingdom - in My peace."

As daylight appeared again, Rohan watched Miryam making their breakfast. He marveled at her strength. This was as hard a thing as he'd ever come up against and he didn't know how to live the life that was now before him. His anger and his guilt were too much to bear and he wept inwardly, unable to speak of them to Miryam, or to anyone. He thought of his words to the new father just two days ago as Gustav had poured out his troubles. Rohan had said that sometimes a man must tell someone else his troubles to take the worry from his heart. But who could he share this anger with? Who would understand his profound shame?

He knew that Jonathan was watching them both, needing their reassurance and their maturity, yet Rohan could not give it. He felt like getting up a posse, as impossible as that seemed. But he knew that he could not subject Miryam to the scrutiny of the sheriff's men, the embarrassment of the townsfolk's knowing about the rape, and the terror of seeing the perpetrator again, should they actually catch up with him.

The next few days came and went in almost complete silence in the MacVoy home. Friday came. The Sabbath was to begin at sundown. Miryam had baked the *challah* bread and put out the wine for Rohan to open. It had been difficult to get wine every week without causing a stir in town. The saloon offered hard liquor and beer only. The general store, nothing. Finally, after doing without, Miryam had arranged for Papa to send a case. So, twelve bottles of *Shabbat* wine arrived with the mail every three months. Very few folks imbibed in any alcohol regularly. Though there was a saloon in town it was rarely filled. Few men had time for drink, except for those who made their own beer, and the medicinal use of whiskey. No one grew grapes anywhere. After many months, however, the eccentricities of the local 'Jewish wife' became old hat.

This night she tried to find a sense of normalcy she did not feel. The *Shabbat* meal was ready, and her chores were complete so she would have a day of rest until sundown on Saturday. Miryam lit the candles and began the prayer she always said.

"*Baruch atah Adonai Elohenu, Melekh ha-olam...*" Blessed are You, Lord, Our God, King of the universe. The familiarity of the ways of her childhood soothed her, giving new strength to let the horror go and move into the days, weeks and months to come.

Rohan felt as he always had on the Sabbath night. This Jewish woman was still a mystery to him. Try as he might, he could not give his full attention to her God or to her traditions. It seemed to mean so much to her that he had to comply, but he never understood the significance of it all. "A lot o' flapdoodle." That's all it was to him. After dinner he went to the barn, "t' care for the stock," he said, though there was really nothing left to do.

On Saturday he gave Jon some small chores he could do at the house for the day, since his head had healed enough to get up and about. Rohan stayed near the house, too, doing all the work he could possibly do and still be close by. But his mind couldn't to relate to his tasks. He dropped the hammer while mending a picket in the fence. He was seen to stop and stare into the distance, deep in thought. Miryam watched him hang his head low onto his chest more than once. He sighed audibly, not knowing he'd done so. He kicked a fence post savagely, chopped firewood that they didn't need with a vengeance, became sullen and cross when spoken to, and yielded no quarter to his favorite Percheron stallion as it struck up the usual stubborn routine they'd been playing at for years. It was a game of chance that the horse and Rohan both loved. Who would get bested today?

The horse would hang back in the stall and wait for it to be opened. Even when it was ajar he'd stay back, standing stock still until Rohan took hold of his halter. He'd move up to the gate and step forward, while not leaving enough room for a body to pass through as well. The objective was to crush Rohan against the jamb, in an affectionate way, of course. If Roh didn't move fast enough, the enormous beast posed a severe threat to him. Though not mean, he did not know that he could break Rohan's ribs, or shatter one of his feet, in an instant.

Rohan knew that this animal meant no ultimate harm since he himself had raised him from a foal and hand fed him since then. If he was able to get quickly past the huge horse out of the stall, it forfeited the game and moved obediently out into the paddock. If he was not quick enough, the stallion just stood in the gate, which forced Roh to wait in the stall until the beast eventually moved to permit him an exit. Today was no exception to the rule. They went on with the mysterious dance as usual, but when Rohan had had enough, the horse received such an elbow in the ribs that it fairly ran outside.

Miryam rested and wondered how to get through the Sunday services the next day. She loved Rohan, but like him, she did not comprehend the idea of those three gods they spoke of in his kirk. She knew what her parents had taught her in their most important prayer, "*Sh'ma Yisrael. Adonai Elohenu. Adonai Echad…*" She knew it meant: "Hear, Israel. The Lord is our God. The Lord is One…" Roh's religion seemed all wrong, but she also knew that since she had chosen to wed him, that meant to abide with him in all things as well.

I'm so glad that Mama and Da had chosen to marry in spite of their differences. It was a rich heritage that they brought me to. I realize that through them both, together, I was given the best of Jew and goy, and that God's plan is perfect. The tension of their two worlds brought a realization that the ways of man can never be sufficient for the discerning of His ways and purposes. But He provides direction continually to those who seek Him.

Chapter 8

Though initially Rohan was understanding of Miryam's pains, and helpful with work that she could not do, he soon became grouchy and quarrelsome. Miryam repeated to him in their private moments that she did not feel right inside, there was pain where she had never had pain before. This only made him feel more guilty and reticent. She gave up and did her usual chores, asking help only from Jon, and only when she was in too much pain to manage.

Rohan's manner and attitude worsened as the weeks went by, then settled into a more silent man than ever before. He was seldom able to exchange even the necessary information for the fulfillment of the day's tasks. He'd point to the wood when it needed chopping, or to the pump when he wanted Jon to haul water, or worse, let the chore go undone entirely. Miryam went from day to day carrying her burden alone as well. She hoped Jon would be resilient enough because of his youth to forget the awful day that she herself would ever remember. She decided that she would not speak of it to him.

There was little if any communication from Rohan on any level, no consolation, no feeling left between them at all. So she bore the weeks of waiting in solitude. The day came when she knew there should be the monthly change in her body, but it did not happen. She began to feel queasy in the mornings as she prepared breakfast, especially while making the coffee. The truth became too apparent. Her early morning trips to the privy became urgent runs with her hand over her mouth as she fought back the nausea.

Miryam came to Rohan one day and asked to talk together. He nodded, knowingly. They went to the shade of the barn and sat together on his whittling bench. Miryam took both his huge weathered hands in hers.

"Roh, you know I haven't been feeling right since... well... for some time now." He just stared at her hands, silently.

"I'm going to have a baby, I've been keeping track." His eyes went quickly to her face. This might be the change that they all needed to set the world right again. How he'd loved seeing Jon grow and change so quickly from infant to toddler, from lad to boy, and finally to a young man. The next words were a heavy blow.

"It's his." She went on, "I need to know how you'll be from now on. I can't shield an infant from your anger. Jon can mostly deal with it because he understands you. But a babe will not see that. You can't keep this up any longer."

He thought long and finally nodded assent. His denial ran strong, but deep inside, he knew that what she said was indeed true. He'd mentally noted the days as well as she had, and in his mind he knew that it was impossible for the wee babby to be his. He had been out of town several times right after Miryam had finished her last monthly cycle. There had been many nights when they were too tired to love, and there had certainly been no intimate moments since he'd come home. He also knew that he'd behaved badly lately. He'd tried to stop the overflow of his temper, but found instead that it controlled him, and tainted their whole relationship.

He had also realized that what had been missing from his life was a force that was greater than he was. Now anger was that force, though a deadly one. He was bound by it as surely as this babby was bound to his wife. His days revolved around the nursing of the wrongs done, and the impossibility of redeeming any of the situation for the good. Yet here was Miryam, waiting for him, needing him to speak.

He answered slowly, measuring each word. "I ken I ha' been wrong...I canna help myself... Tis deep inside me an' it strikes me, hard!" He had to stop to regain control of the tremor in his voice. "E'ry day it hits me. I fight it, but the hate, tis still there... I pledge t' ye tha' I shall do all I can. I swear it, but I ha' nae been doin' so well thus far. I dinna ken how t' get free o' this."

Miryam had been thinking on this for some time, knowing that it would be a mountain for her to climb as well. Could she love the child of the man who had raped her? Could she see a helpless infant and not think of that awful man?

But truly, her desire for another child had consumed years and years of her life. This was not what she'd have chosen, for sure, but now there was a baby in her womb! A baby! She'd had to cross over a line in her mind and it had taken a huge battle to do it, but Miryam had decided to love the child. It was an innocent child! Was she to leave it in the dust after having carried it to birth? Was she to give it away after having nourished it with her own body throughout nine long months? No, she was determined. She would love the baby. But to bring Rohan to that point was another matter.

"The only way to beat hate is with love, Rohan. You're going to have to love this baby. He's an innocent child."

"I dinna ha' love for him who did this t' us!" he spat out, pulling away from her.

She had tried in her own struggle to think of what her childhood *rebbe* might say to Rohan. The patient rabbi was the wisest person she had ever known, giving counsel to her youthful inquiries far batter than her parents had. Miryam laid her hand upon his and implored him to believe the truth of this by using the words she felt the *rebbe* would have said. She was certain he would have said, "It's not your love that's needed. It's only the love of *Adonai*.

So she spoke those words to her husband.

"It's only God that can forgive so great a wrong."

Seeing her hand on his own drew Rohan to the reality of the fact that this man had touched his wife in a way that no one ever should, ever! He rose from the bench abruptly.

"Who is God!!!" he shouted, daring her to answer him.

The question arises in our hearts all the time, doesn't it? Mama says that our sin is far worse than we want to admit, but through Jesus, we are loved more than we could ever hope for. She says that every single thing we go through prompts a belief about God, or a doubt. We must bring even that doubt to Him in our worship. To leave a question without an answer is to let it grow, unchecked, in the dark undercurrents of life. Have our struggles eroded our trust in God's kindness and sovereignty in our lives?

"Why do you doubt?" Mama once asked me. "Is there not enough evidence that God exists? Who else do you know that has ever made a bird, a rose, a mountain?"

Now, I can honestly say it. Yes, there is sufficient evidence in the world around us that nature was created by some force that is outside nature, supernatural. Who tells the geese to fly in a "v" and rotate the leader every so often so that no one goose tires out? Who instructs the bears to hibernate, and give birth to their young in the darkness of winter? Who brings a caterpillar to spin a cocoon and transforms it into a butterfly? Who created within man an emptiness that can only be filled by "belonging to" and "believing in" something, a "Someone" outside of himself?

In my own life I have prayed with my eyes closed to the reality of my own darkness, seeking peace without admitting the presence of sin in me. But in closing my eyes to the darkness inside me I also closed them to the brilliance of God's redeeming light, His love, and His promises. Now I know that I can bring my longings, fears and questions before His throne of grace and let the light of Jesus' presence shine into every dark and confusing place.

Chapter 9

The various greens of the trees and prairie grasses turned to browns, reds, yellows and oranges. The woodpile was growing daily as Rohan and Jon took the wagon into the woody places looking for felled trees to cut up. They dared not fell more or next winter they might be hard put to find enough to keep warm. Kindling was never a problem but the logs were always scarce. Rohan had been raised with the burning of peat, with its acrid, and pervading scent. He loved the memory of it, and did not worry about how to keep warm. There was always the old way to fall back on.

Miryam just might have to put up with burning sod or dung, much as she hated it. That had been all they'd burned the first few years of their adventure west. Their first home had been a soddy, saving the precious wood for building the house.

Every plank was used to the fullest. Not a scrap was wasted or burned. Rohan knew that furniture must come next and replacements for wheel spokes. But now that they were established in their home and their household furnishings they could burn wood as long as they were frugal. Now they used their old soddy for a smokehouse, as well as a reminder that life was better now than it had been at first.

I remember the unique smell of the soddy the most. A powerful scent, but in some way even sweet. The dungy smell was only a faint memory by the time I was a boy. For me, it was mostly the strong scent of wood smoke permeating every bit of the inside of the smoke house. We'd take the small cart filled with the butchered meat and wheel its overloaded bounty carefully right into the domed hovel, then hang it to let it cure in the smoke. Da and Jon would have already built the fire in the pit. The rest of the smokehouse was brimmed with wood, ready to be added as the fire burned until the meat was cured. All winter we ate like kings, Da always said. Though I had never met a king, I thought I knew how they ate when I felt the roundness of my belly after a meal of roast venison.

When fall came, Miryam stayed indoors much of the time, preparing for the arrival of her baby. She wondered about when the very first tiny fluttering movements might be felt in her womb, not having to fret yet about how cumbersome she would later be as she went about her chores. There were apples to dry, corn to grind into flour, jackets and blankets to mend, hats and mittens to knit, and baby clothes and nappies to sew. In the evenings she sat in the lamplight making tiny garments while Rohan sat by the fire with his feet on a stool, his head back on the cushion, and his eyes closed. He did not want to see the small clothes nor acknowledge that there would be an infant to wear them. He and Miryam never seemed to be able to discuss the upcoming event, though her condition would soon become obvious to everyone.

One unseasonably warm day, Gustav and his family pulled into the yard, greeting Rohan heartily as they came. Miryam, who had long been without a woman's company, except at the church services, hurried out to meet them. "Hello!" she cried out. "I'm so glad you could finally come to visit!"

Gustav shook Rohan's hand, and put his arm around his wife. "Ava, diss here Rohan MacVoy iss, de man who helped to our place de doctor to come ven born vass Rosie. Unt here Ana iss," Gustav beamed as he drew a shy girl of about twelve years forward, "our olter daughter."

Rohan nodded. "Pleased t' meet ye. Here's my wife, Miryam. Our boy, Jon, is yon wi' the horses," he said, motioning to the corral when Jon was training a horse to wear a saddle. "Miryam, this is Goose, the fellow I telt ye aboot."

The women faced each other grinning. Ava was tiny, flaxen haired, buxom and bright eyed, a red woolen shawl loose around her shoulders. Ana was her twin, minus the years. Miryam reached out and pulled them into the house. The grown women giggled like school girls as they went. Ana followed quietly. Rohan's usually stoic countenance relaxed into a half smile. "I believe they'll bide well," he remarked with a conspiratorial smile. "Come in. I think we may ha' a plate o' oatcakes goin' wantin'." Gustav carried little Rose's basket into the house along with another market basket of necessities and some provisions for a meal together.

"Tenk you, Gus," said Ava in her high voice as she took the baby from him. Then to the baby, "Come, my little Rosie Cheeks, to Miryam meet." Taking in Miryam's rounded belly, she added, "She vill soon into diss vorld a playmate for you brink." The women cooed and fussed over Rose while Rohan poured coffee for the men. "I am tinkink how cozy iss your home, Miryam. So many pretty colors are your pillows unt all. If you vould like I to you for de bebee some of Rosie's little clothes vill giff."

"I'll let you know if I still need anything, but I'm still enjoying sewing my own things. I have some nightgowns and booties done already. Some blankets, too. I need Rohan to bring the cradle down from the loft." She turned to him, "Could you get the cradle for me? I'd like to show Ava how beautifully you carved the vines on it." She turned to Ava, "Jon loved it when he was tiny."

Rohan knew he was going to have to get it sooner or later so he rose from his chair with a nod. Gustav volunteered his company. "I a hand for you vill give."

In the barn they climbed the ladder to the storage area. The cradle was covered with a tarp in a far corner. Next to it on the floor was a bundle wrapped in burlap. "Wha' ha' we here?" Rohan wondered aloud. Too late he realized the contents of the mysterious package.

"How beautiful de needlevork iss!" exclaimed Gustav. "But vy keep it de barn in?"

Rohan tried to wrap the quilt up again but only succeeded in letting it sprawl onto the floor where the telltale brownish bloodstain was exposed. Tis ruined, but my wife couldna bear t' throw it awa'. Her mama made it."

"A shame it iss!" Gustav thought for a moment. "Rohan, it iss great de debt I to you owe. You diss know, unt I diss know. My Ava diss qvilt can repair. She can! Let me to home take it, unt I to you back vill giff ven it finished iss. Do not 'no' tell me. It for you de least iss dat ve can do."

Rohan would rather have forgotten that the quilt even existed.

Probably Miryam would, too, but Gustav needed to do this thing and Rohan decided to let him. He needed the friendship of this man so badly. He knew that someday he would need to share his burden, but today was not the day to do so.

"Verra weel. But ye canna say aught t' Miryam aboot it," he warned.

Gustav agreed. He put the burlap wrapped bundle into the cradle and helped Rohan ease the heavy wooden bed down the ladder. Then he stuffed the quilt under the wagon seat before going into the house after Rohan.

Miryam dusted off the cradle, remembering when Jon was tiny.

"Och, it lovely iss, Rohan," beamed Ava. "Your vork like dat uff my own fadder iss. You very proud uff it shoot be."

"Would you put Rosie in it, Ava? To see if she likes it?" suggested Miryam. She was eager to see a baby enjoy the bed again. "I think she's still the right size for it. It will be months yet until my baby can use it."

Rose gurgled and smiled a lopsided smile, kicking her hands and feet, delighting in the rocking she accomplished. Rohan had to admit that a baby in the house was a precious thing, though whose baby it was made all the difference in the world to him.

Jon came in, his shirt still damp from washing up in the barn. He was usually eager to greet newcomers but stopped short on seeing Ana. He blushed from the neck up and was tongue tied enough as to be embarrassed. But upon noticing Rosie in the cradle, he found a welcome diversion to his awkwardness. With all of Miryam's sewing projects he had found himself eager to have a baby in the house and was thrilled to see the cradle wobble with Rose's movements as well.

"Could I hold her? I mean whenever she's ready to get out of the cradle?"

"Och, of course," crooned Ava, scooping Rosie right up and shuffling her into Jon's inexperienced arms. It took a minute of arranging but he got himself and the child situated comfortably and then grinned at his audience.

"It's not too hard, is it?" But Rose was out to prove that she was a worthy challenge and tried for a nosedive toward the oatcakes. However, Jon's reflexes met the moment admirably and he was applauded for his efforts.

With the combination of the Himmel's contribution, and what Miryam had gathered earlier from the kailyard for supper, the group feasted and patted full stomachs after the meal. The friends sat by the fire and shared stories about their youth, their courtships, their hardships and their joys. But not all was disclosed. Rohan and Miryam were not ready to open that door yet.

Chapter 10

Dan moved slowly up the street, struggling against the wind that blew through his thin coat as if he wasn't even wearing one at all. There was no snow yet but the temperature and the billowing gray clouds told that it would not be long. He did not look forward to the prospect of spending anymore nights outdoors. The days, like today, were deceptively bright with sun, but offered no respite from the penetrating cold. The nights were far, far worse. He had stabled his horse at the livery late last night, and slept in the stall burrowing deep in the straw.

He kept a watchful eye as he walked, hoping that no one would call after him saying, "Ain't you the scallawag that rode in here drunk and busted all my windows?" or "That's the man who stole my horse!" He didn't know what he'd done, exactly, or where he'd been, but he did know that a fair chunk of time was missing from his memory and God only knew what had happened then. He didn't know when the day would come that he might be recognized, maybe even hung on the spot! But he hoped that his appearance had changed enough that he was not going to be easy to pick out in a crowd as the same man he had been six months ago.

He'd taken pains to see that his besotted visage was in the past. He had shaven off his beard and mustache, cut his straight, fine hair quite close, and always tried to be neatly dressed and polite. If someone thought that they'd caught a glimpse of the mean creature he had once been, they'd have to think twice and strongly consider his demeanor. Dan had been raised a to behave like a gentleman, and believed in acting the part. He respected others, as a rule. The fact was that Dan really was a meek man, except when he drank. And then he was like a cornered wolverine. When Dan drank, there was no one meaner or more cruel.

He desperately needed supplies now. He'd held off as long as he could at home, living on oatmeal and tea and jerky for the last two weeks, with an occasional rabbit. But aside from that, a man needed someone to talk to, though his horse was better company than Etta had ever been. Since he could no longer make the farm pay, he'd been hiring out as a handyman. Having exhausted the work near his home he'd decided to leave it. He'd traveled, knocking on doors asking for any kind of work, sleeping in barns when he could and under the open sky when he had to. He finally had some cash money from all the odd jobs. If this town seemed friendly he was thinking of getting a room where he could sleep in a warm bed, get a meal at least once a day, and keep his tools safe from vandals.

So far it was easy. Folks smiled, or greeted him eagerly as a newcomer to the area. He felt comfortable. But it was as he left the general store that he almost came face to face with Miryam. She was walking toward him with her tall, lanky son. He could see their faces clearly in the cold sunshine, but they could not see his face as he stood under the shade of the porch. He knew her the moment he laid eyes on her. His lost memory suddenly became vivid. It hurt him to the farthest reaches of his being to think that he could have been so violent toward her and her son.

She had been so frightened, and had cried so much. He knew then that he had utterly defiled her. Dan turned his face away just as they stepped out of the sunshine. He drew the brim of his hat low, pulled his neckerchief up as if to keep out the cold, and kept his back to the windows when they entered the store.

He packed his supplies hurriedly into his saddlebags and in the burlap sacks slung over the horse's rump. "Let's git outta here," he muttered under his breath to the animal as he mounted. This was not the right town to take up residence in. When he was past the last building he pulled up on the reigns and stopped. He'd been so wrapped up in looking at their faces that his mind just now took in the rest of Miryam's appearance. She was pregnant.

She surely wasn't pregnant when he'd... No, she wasn't pregnant then... If she was, wouldn't she have told him so he'd spare her? Now what should he do? Was she married? Was she scorned by her friends and neighbors? He knew right from wrong, now that he was sobered up.

And the right thing was to take care of this woman if she needed help. That is, if he was responsible.

Dan needed to think some on this. He dismounted, tied the horse, found a somewhat secluded spot which offered shelter from the wind, and waited for the lady to leave the mercantile. He needed to see where she went and what her situation was. It was a while, but then Dan was used to Etta taking way too long in the stores. At last she came out with her purchases piled up in her son's arms. They went to a wagon, arranged their belongings and drove away. There was nothing left to do but to follow at a distance. He kept out of sight, just watching. But after half an hour had passed Dan reckoned it must be too long a way to worry about and went back to town. At least this town was safe enough for the night.

At the rooming house Dan paid for the night and ate supper in the parlor with the rest of the guests. They were amiable enough. The hostess was a widow woman who seemed to know everyone for miles around. As the conversation went around the table, folks shared bits and pieces about their families. When Dan's turn came, he had a thought toward finding out the name of the woman and boy he'd seen earlier. He went fishing for information.

"Well," he said slowly, "I ain't got much family left, but I got a niece who's goin' ta have a baby soon. I don't know about such things but she's gettin' pretty round!"

As he had hoped, the hostess piped in with the local news that one of her friends was also in the family way. "What a coincidence! In fact I was just talking to her today at the mercantile. Why isn't that funny? What a dear lady, Miryam's her name. What's your niece's name? Wouldn't it be wonderful if it were Miryam?" She did not wait here for Dan to reply, which was just as well, since he had invented the story about his niece and his mouth was full of succotash. "And it's so nice that she's going to have another chance since she and Rohan had that miscarriage five years ago."

The woman went on and on with hair raising stories of more and more women who had had the remarkable experience of motherhood, even though she, herself, had never been so blessed. Dan was amazed that anyone could talk so much and so fast without saying anything of any consequence. Though he enjoyed the relative anonymity of the place he did not want to be an innocent victim of her prattling any more than was necessary. He decided that this rooming house might not be the quietest place for him to settle into. But he'd found out what he wanted to know. Miryam was married to a fellow by the name of Rohan. So no one here in town knew anything about his connection to her. He retired to his room and slept soundly in the warmth of a real bed.

Miryam's pain upon doing everyday chores was increasing. She needed to talk to someone who would know about such things in order to quell her fears. But who? The questions were beyond what she might share with the local midwife. Mrs. Dole was a good woman who had assisted at the birth of nearly every child within twenty miles, but she also knew and repeated each family's details, in a properly discreet voice, within the confines of her visits with her clients. Everyone soon was well aware of the cleanliness of their neighbor's homes and the intimate moments shared by husbands and wives all across the county, entirely due to the wagging of Mrs. Dole's tongue. She would never be the one to whom Miryam could confide.

She must ask Ava her questions. Jon hitched the buggy for her and brought the cushion from her sewing chair. A bumpy ride was not at all appealing to her condition. She set out to inquire for her own peace of mind.

Ana's bright halo of blonde hair shone in the afternoon sun as she hung the clean laundry on the line. The sun was hot on her shoulders and the wind picked up enough to animate the pant legs and shirtsleeves of the hanging garments briefly. The nappies, strung in a long line, beat a flapping rhythm to the breezes. At Miryam's greeting she turned and waved across the yard toward the house.

In the kitchen, Ava was dusted with flour and up to her elbows in baking, but was very happily surprised to see her friend. She fussed a moment about her messiness, but took off her powdery apron and embraced Miryam with a strength that confirmed the rightness of the bond that was to be formed. After putting on the kettle for tea, and settling Miryam into a chair, Ava donned her apron again and resumed her work. Her hands moved almost mechanically to form generously rounded loaves, and rolls, then from a different batch of dough came a braided loaf with buttered raisins and cinnamon woven in. The deft movements kept Miryam's eyes busy and her mind calmed, letting her form her questions in a logical sequence. After the first cup of tea was empty, she spoke.

"Ava, have you ever done any midwifery?"

"Och, to be sure."

"I was wondering, then… could I ask you some questions?" Miryam's confidence wavered a bit.

Ava's hands hesitated for just a few seconds in her stirring, then resumed the mixing of oats, eggs and sugar for her cookies. "For you, I am most happy anytink to answer. How much I care for you, you surely know?"

Their eyes met over the table. Miryam replied, "And I for you."

She accepted a slice of the coarse warm bread and buttered it as she expressed her concerns. "I am so much older than I was when I had Jon. And I've had a miscarriage. Am I going to have trouble carrying this child and with the birthing?"

"Vell… you are asking becauss you now are trouble havink? Tinks are not vell goink?"

"I do have some pains, but not like labor. It is more like I feel something is stuck in my side like a knife, especially when I straighten up from bending. I don't want to complain, but I don't want to harm the baby, either."

Ava removed her apron again and pulled up a chair next to Miryam's. Taking her face into soft, floury hands, she implored her friend, "I know for you to do, diss will difficult be, but slow down you must. Everytink else today must stop, or de baby vill stop, too. Do you hear vat I am to you tellink?"

"That is what I thought, too. But I needed to hear from someone who knows these things… How will I live, just sitting in my chair, or in my bed, doing nothing?"

"You will nothing neglect, but vill everytink differently do. You vill not go outside, maybe to de porch on a sunny day. You vill from your bed, to your chair, to your bed move only. You vill use the chamber pot set upon a stool. Rohan can safe make it so you vill not fall. You vill nottink lift, nottink heavier dan a glass of vater.

"But from your chair de food can come. You can de batter mix, you can de apples peel, you can de clothes fold unt mend. You can tell the men how everytink to do."

Miryam's heart fell. It was hard enough to expect help from Rohan now, and she didn't want to burden Jon with extra chores.

"I know, I know," comforted Ava. "I vill come and de men folk show. Dey vill do for you because uff love. You vill see it happen."

Ana was swept in the door on a stiff breeze with the fragrance of fallen leaves, her arms heavy with the basket of freshly dried nappies. "The next load dry vill soon be, Mama, vitt de vind comink so up." Her face was fair and lovely, but even more so with the bright blush of fresh air and exertion. Miryam had noticed Jon's interest in Ana last week and could easily see them together. It pleased her to think it. She enjoyed her visit with her new friends.

Gustav had struggled to maintain the farm since the day they bought it. He had been told the buildings were in sound shape but it was not so. The roof on the barn leaked something pitiful, and the house wasn't much better. He and Ava chased buckets, pots, and even teacups around the house until there was not a container left empty of rainwater. He asked in town for someone to give him a hand to put his new roof on and was referred to Dan. Dan agreed to work in exchange for a place to sleep, and his meals. He had stayed more than long enough at the rooming house!

"I to dees parts also am new, so I tenk you for beink villink a hand to giff," Gustav began as they rode the buckboard home from town, Dan's horse tied to the rear. Gus had picked up the shingles and nails they needed. "Sometimes folks don't de velcome matt to outten, so I appreciate dat helpink me you are"

"I'm new here, too, an' you're helpin' me as well. So we're both in the same boat. I need ta eat an' sleep an' earn the trust of the folks here so's I can make a livin'. Yer givin' me a start on buildin' a sound reputation."

"Vell, my vife a guut cook iss, so you vill not a vorry about dat haff," he chuckled. "Unt de barn a nice dry room hass. So dere you vill sleep. I all the tools vill take out of it. Dere is a guut voot stove for de heatink, unt I vill a cot brink. You vill haff to shut de door if you vant de cats to outten keep, but for de vinter you chust might vant dem for company to stay, eh? Dey are to sleeping in dere accustom, especially ven de vedder too cold gets."

Dan was happy about the new arrangement. "I'm sure I'll be comfortable. Cats are good listeners."

Ava met Dan with great relief, sharing her thanks that Gus would not have to accomplish the daunting list of repairs to the farm by himself. She took an instant liking to him and gave a standing invitation to spend his free time with them in the evenings. He would like her cooking, she promised him. Dan was looking forward to the next home cooked meal already. As they talked and ate together the three became fast friends, and Ana and little Rose won Dan's heart. He had always wished that Etta had wanted children, but she was of no mind to lose her figure or let her dresses get spit up on or mussed while she took care of a child.

Dan told the Himmel's a somewhat revised version of his life and marriage, but kept the latest events under his hat. Conversation eventually revealed the MacVoy family's friendship with Gus and Ava. Dan wondered if he should stay with them, but decided to take precautions not to come into contact with them, and remain with the Himmels. Their acquaintance was what he needed at this time when there was no one else in the world he could consider his friends. His utter loneliness made the decision for him.

Chapter 11

"Ralph, come in here!" Bettina called in her warbling voice through the back door. She imagined that he was always out doing something to keep from having to help her with the store. "Well," she thought to herself, "at least when he goes on this errand for me, he'll have a good excuse for being away."

Ralph entered, alternately squinting and widening his eyes after the being in the sun. In the dimness of the cavernous mercantile stood row upon row of dry goods, cloth, tools, and most all that a body could ask for. But Ralph's major delight was in the books. There were only a few dozen, but since not many folks could read or even had the time to if they could, he considered the books to be quite nearly his own. With effort, he peered into the darkness to find his aged wife, Bettina, standing before him, hands on her ample hips. He shrugged awkwardly out of his heavy coat, then turned to hang it on the peg on the wall.

Ralph was a rugged, squarish man, once just taller than average, but now permanently bent forward from the middle of his back. His gray head could swivel neither left nor right but required the rotation of his shoulders to look sideways. He did so, still trying to adjust his eyes to the comparative dimness of the indoors.

"Stop making those faces at me," Bettina pestered in jest. "There was a letter that came with the stage this morning and you've got to deliver it."

"Have you got the coffee on?" asked Ralph, ignoring her and blowing on his cupped hands.

"Didn't you hear me? You need to get out to the MacVoy's right now!"

"You mean that the sooner I go, the sooner you'll be able to find out what's in the letter." teased Ralph. For all his wife's bluster and fussiness, he was quite fond of her. Yet his teasing was based on fact.

"Not at all!" she protested. Bettina wouldn't admit it but she thrived on news from any source. She was quick to say, "I don't abide with idle gossip, mind you. I just think it's our duty to deliver the mail speedily, you know that." Yet she knew, that he knew, that it was the news that she really wanted. The people in the outlying area had little but farm news, so receiving mail was a big event.

Bettina's lower lip pouted at the accusation. Her face was a map of wrinkles that was reminiscent of a dried leaf. Her lips surrounded by a network of lines like the sun's rays reaching out to the rest of her bright face. This was prompted by her habit of pouting, albeit attractively, for Ralph's benefit, whenever she wanted her own way. He loved her little habits, though, and wouldn't change them for the world.

"Any new newspapers?" asked Ralph, making to remove his boots and have a sit by the hearth.

"No, only the ones from last month. Now Ralph, you need to go!" Bettina stopped him from unwrapping his scarf from around his neck, holding his coat out for him. He obediently put it back on. She systematically handed him each glove he had just removed, and placed his black and red checked hat back upon his silvered head.

"I'll have a hot thick stew ready for you when you get back," she cajoled, laying her soft hand on his cheek in farewell. She held both his ear lobes while planting a kiss.

"And then you'll ask whether Miryam read the letter and if she told me what was in it, won't you?" Ralph kissed the puckered lips of his mate with a loud smack, adjusted his scarf closer around his neck, and turned back to smile heartily at Bettina.

"Stew you say? And fresh bread, maybe? Madam, I am at your beck and call." Ralph chuckled as he peered out from under his scarf.

"Yes, alright! Now hurry back, will you?"

What I remember most about Uncle Ralph and Auntie Bettina (that's what Da and Mama said I should call them) is that they always seemed to have an understanding between them. She pushed a bit, but he was ever so willing to do whatever she asked. He would have "hung the Big Dipper upside down for her," he always told me, "if she'd have even whispered it."

Uncle Ralph always had twinkly eyes. He was bent forward dramatically at the shoulders, as if he'd carried a heavy load on them all his life. He never complained, but kept a smile and a chuckle handy for any occasion when one might be needed to lighten a mood or cheer someone's day.

Uncle Ralph and Auntie Bettina like to play practical jokes on people, too. Since they were the ones who received and then distributed the U.S. Mail, and also sold the tickets for the stagecoach from their store, they pretty much knew all the comings and goings of the folks who came through the village.

They would write fanciful letters from imaginary people to their friends, saying, "We're having such a wonderful time, but we wish you were here with us!" Their friends would often receive the letters, from people they didn't know, postmarked from a faraway place, sent on behalf of Ralph and Bettina by any salesman or traveler who would go along with their practical joke.

Miryam was baking when she heard the trap come into the yard. She glanced out the window, but was up to her elbows in flour and didn't want to be disturbed. Rohan appeared in the barn door and invited Ralph in to join him. There was a warm fire out there so she felt that enough hospitality was offered on such a cold day and went back to her bread.

When the dough had been divided into loaves and left to rise on the back of the stove she dusted off her hands and apron to make them some coffee. Since Ralph was still here, that meant at least one cup and a cookie to send him on his way home. Sure enough, she could hear Rohan, Jon and old Ralph talking as they closed the barn up and strolled to the house.

"Ah, fair damsel!" Ralph recited as he doffed his winter duds. "Rohan here has given me the impression that you might have a morsel and a hot toddy for me before I brave the storm again. I smell cookies... molasses?"

Miryam tried not to laugh at him. Ralph tended to make each sentence a grand and glorious occasion. He was well read and thrilled to share any and all that he'd gleaned from the pages of his precious volumes. There had even been occasions when he would burst forth with excerpts from sonnets or old drinking songs in the course of a conversation.

"No hot toddies I'm afraid... will coffee suffice?" she made a mock curtsy.

"Don't mind if I do, thank ye kindly!" replied Ralph with a low bow.

Rohan just stood back watching these proceedings with raised eye-brows, and then poured himself half a cup from the coffee pot. Miryam poured milk for Jon, and then Ralph's coffee as they settled into their chairs. Ralph cleared his throat dramatically while removing a letter from his breast pocket. When Miryam laid the plate of cookies and the steaming mug before him, he handed it to her with a flourish.

She scooped it up with delight, "Who is it from? Mama! Oh! But what if it's bad news?"

Miryam's nose crinkled up in indecision. If it was good, she could not wait to open it - if not, she'd best be about it as well. But she had no desire to actually read bad news without warning. "Rohan, do read it and tell me whether it's good or bad."

Rohan shrugged and went to find his glasses. "A lot o' bother. Ye know ye're goin' t' read it agin' an' agin' nae matter wha'," he grumbled. Having perched his new spectacles at the proper distance down his nose, he held out the paper and adjusted his arm's length before reading. Tis some bad news, but nae too bad. Plenty o' food for thought. Here." He handed the letter to Miryam.

Her gaze questioned him a moment before she turned her attention to her letter, reading aloud. She, too, knew that Bettina would be waiting to hear what it said.

"Dear daughter,

We trust this finds you well, and Jonathan and Rohan, too. Father and I have been in fair general health except for a minor incident which is my purpose for writing. Your Father was working with a horse last week when it spooked and sent him aloft. Don't you know that it took me the better part of an hour to convince him to send for the doctor? He has a broken shoulder. Doctor Pedersen assures us that in a matter of several weeks it will be right again. But due to many circumstances, there are not enough hands right now to run the ranch properly. Isn't there always something?

I know this may be an inconvenience to you, please let me know truthfully. We deeply regret that we have yet to make the trip west to visit you, but we wondered if you might be able to send young Jonathan to us for a spell to help out here. It would be a learning experience for him, and an opportunity for us to get to know him. Please respond at your earliest convenience.

Regards, Mother"

Miryam looked sourly up at Rohan, "She still has a way with words, doesn't she? How I wish she could show some affection, just once! …What do you think, Rohan? Should we send Jon? It's only a few days until Hanukkah. And would you want him away for Christmas? And then the baby will be coming in spring."

"We'll manage… but, if ye want, wait 'til after the holidays."

Ralph dunked his cookie and drank his coffee. "What does young master Jon think of all this?" he wondered aloud, peering at Jon out of the corner of his eye. The boy had never entertained the notion of going back east. He'd never laid eyes on his grandparents, didn't know if he'd like to live with them, and had heard since childhood that they had not visited once in all the years his family had been west of the Mississippi. Still, it would be an adventure!

"I've never been on a stagecoach or a train… but I could help out, I guess. I know horses. What are they like, your parents?"

"They're no-nonsense people," Miryam began. "Friendly, but not young at heart. They're wise in some ways and in other ways they can't see the forest for the trees. Mama is a bit of a *yenta*. You won't have much privacy from her nosiness. Papa is *haymish*, he gets along with everyone. But say you got homesick, they might not notice at all. You'd have to tell them, and even then, would they understand? They don't hold with hugging, but they'll smile. Maybe you could teach them a thing or two, Jon. What do you think?"

"I'll ponder on it, Ma. Don't write back yet, I need to do some thinking." With that Jon seemed to fall into a reverie of his own as the adults visited on all sides of him.

"There's a dandy church social coming up next Saturday night. I'm told there'll be musicians and dancing! Are you folks going to be able to come?" inquired Ralph.

"Oh, how I love to dance," cried Miryam. "I don't think I'll do much this time though," she said thoughtfully, rubbing her hands across her rounding belly. "Rohan, could we manage a slow dance, do you think?"

"Maybe so." He did love seeing Miryam pregnant. Her shape was comforting and sweet to him, almost enough to make him forget that the child was not his.

"I hear tell that this new fellow, Himmel, can stir up his feet with the best of them. I always love to watch folks kick up their heels. I used to do it myself in my younger days!" Ralph clicked his heels together a few times under the table.

As the adults talked, Jon was deep in thought. He had been looking forward to the birthing of the child his mother carried. He was uncertain as to the father of the wee one, but it would not do to ask such a thing. He'd speculated, though, because of his father's foul moods. He didn't want to miss such an occasion, but maybe the sooner he went, the sooner he could come home. "Would they let me come home if I wanted to?" he interjected. "If I didn't like being there?"

"I think," replied Miryam, "that we'd have to make that clear. And we can't pay much for the train fare home. They'll have to cover that. But we'll say that you must feel free to come home if you decide that's best. After all, you're not a child any longer. You can make decisions like that yourself. Does that suit you?"

"I think so. If Da can spare me, I'll go."

Rohan nodded his consent.

"I'll write the letter then. Would you get me my box?" Miryam's writing box was a plain wooden one that Rohan had made when they made plans to head west. He'd known that her loneliness would be easier to bear if she could send letters back home. After completing the beautiful wooden box, he had purchased some fine writing paper, a pen and some nibs, and a bottle of ink to furnish all that she might need. There was a corner compartment to hold the ink bottle upright, a slot for two pens, and an ample supply of paper and envelopes, kept flat and smooth by a wooden panel inserted on top.

"Ralph, can you wait just a while longer and take this back with you?"

"Yes, Ma'am." He was thinking how pleased Bettina would be. He not only knew the contents of the incoming mail, but of the outgoing as well. He knew that the MacVoy's would not mind him telling her, and that they were well aware that in giving Bettina this bit of news that it would soon be public knowledge.

"Dear Mama and Papa," Miryam wrote,

"We're so sorry to hear of Papa's accident, but happy that he is on the mend. Jonathan will stay at home for just a few days, until after Hanukkah, and then we'll send him on to you. We'll need you to give him train fare for the trip home but we'll buy his train ticket to get him to you.

Because I am in the family way, I ask that you give Jon the freedom to come home to us whenever he sees fit. He has not been away before and we don't know how he will settle into a new place. He doesn't want to miss the baby's arrival this spring, so whenever he wants to come home he should do so. We remember you always, and wish you a lovely and blessed Hanukkah!

Sending greatest affection and best wishes to you both,

Your loving daughter, Miryam."

Miryam sealed the envelope, wrote the address on the front, rose to her feet and handed it to Ralph. "Whatever the postage is, add it to our account. We'll be in on Saturday for the social and we can settle up then."

"Well, then," Ralph said, rising and putting on his coat. "I'm off... like a dirty shirt!" he chuckled. Thank you kindly for the pleasure of your company, and for the coffee and crumpets. I'll keep warm now on the trip home for sure."

Miryam blanched at the words 'the pleasure of your company.'

Rohan saw her step back and grab the back of a chair for support. "Miryam! Are ye ill?" Jon and Ralph came to her aid as well. She looked so pale and fragile.

"I... I..." She shook her head, "No, not ill. I'll be fine... I'm just going to sit down for a minute." The men stood by, waiting, watching. But Miryam resolutely breathed deeply and evenly until the panic passed. At last she managed a weak smile. "I must be just a bit tired, that's all."

"Oh, my dear! You frightened me! I think I may need another cookie, now, for sustenance on the trip home," Ralph chortled, trying to make light of it. He took another one from the plate before he pulled on the last glove. "Take care of her, Rohan! Jonathan! Good day and fare thee well."

"Thank ye kindly, Ralph." Rohan bundled up and walked out to settle the older man into his rented buggy and see him on his way. Jon shut the door against the cold. She glanced at Jon to see if he'd remembered the awful stranger's use of that phrase, 'the pleasure of your company.' It was clear that he did, but he was wise enough not to say anything. He would let his father think that he was shaken because of Miryam's moment of weakness, but she could read his eyes. They shared the memory for an instant, then looked away. It would not be spoken of.

"Ye sure you're well?" Rohan asked of Miryam when he came back into the house.

"I'm fine," answered Miryam with a determined smile, though it was hard to look Rohan in the eye.

Chapter 12

The social at the church was bright with decorations and buzzing with greetings, frills and fanfares. Everyone had brought out their finery for the occasion. Best dresses and starched collars were worn with delight by the women and discomfort by the men, respectively. Children who had been bathed and primped in their best duds looked delightfully clean when they arrived, but played on the floor and got as dusty as ever.

The musicians warmed up while folks renewed acquaintances, sampling wassail and baked goods as they waited for the dancing to begin. There was a clarinet player, a pianist, a drummer and a fiddler. When they began the first song, young and old alike took to the floor. Laughter, the tapping of the ladies' shoes and the clomping of men's boots almost drowned out the music, so the volume was increased until there wasn't a heart that did not keep the song's rhythm.

Miryam and Rohan watched their friends kick up their heels while holding hands on the sidelines. Jon was quite the dancer as he twirled his partner around the floor. There were quite a few girls who waited hopefully for a turn around the floor with him. His parents shared smiles as they recalled bits of his childhood to each other.

"Remember when he was too shy to stand up in the Christmas program at the kirk to read the angel's greeting from your scriptures?" recalled Miryam.

"Aye, an' I recall when he got so tall tha' one year. His feet couldna keep up wi' his knees. He tripped o'er e'rythin'!" Rohan grinned from ear to ear.

The tune ended with a hearty round of applause. Then a ballad began, no doubt written by a pioneer, telling of new love, and of leaving home to travel to new places. Rohan rose and bent from the waist to Miryam. "May I ha' this dance, *mo anam cara?*"

"My, my! Have some of Ralph's manners rubbed off on you?" teased Miryam. She had expected a dance or two tonight with her husband, but not such an affectionate and gentlemanly request. Who knew that he still had it in him? She accepted his hand with delight. Together they moved gracefully in the crowd, hardly impaired by the roundness of her body. It occurred to them both that this was where their love had first blossomed, on a dance floor.

"Rohan, let's remember this time. Keep it fresh in our hearts?" whispered Miryam.

"Aye, Miryam, I shall." Rohan spoke into her hair as he breathed in the fragrance of her lavender bath. It was the sweetest scent he knew and the most ease he'd felt in many months.

The music ended, but did not begin again. There seemed to be much discussion among the folks near the stage. A loud voice then rose to address the crowd. "Say, is there a body here who can hold his own with a fiddle? Ol' Whiskers' rheumatiz has gone and acted up again, and he can't play anymore tonight."

Miryam and Rohan exchanged a look, and a smile. As he walked forward he spoke out, "I'll ha' a go."

"What a perfect evening!" Miryam thought to herself, "I can watch him play 'til my heart's content." She took up a seat near the musicians, settling in for a night of watching Rohan do what he used to love best. Their friends came to spend a song or two visiting with her, bringing her refreshments as the time passed. She couldn't remember when she'd laughed so much in years. Something in her soul began to heal.

Rohan was in his glory as he drew the long-silent melodies from his memory. The music flowed from him as easily as if he's never put his fiddle away. His heart swelled with something he'd forgotten. At first it was an ache, almost like when a body has run hard for a long time and can't catch its breath. But it was not a need for air. It was surely a need for something though.

Did he need to be filled - or emptied? He didn't know. He only knew that this ache was necessary, like a sore muscle that needs a good stretch. As he played on, the need became like that of a drowning man, so desperate! Joy and pain fought within him. He struggled not to let all these emotions show. Song after song, he could think of nothing but to play as if his life depended on it. Finally he prayed, "Oh God! If ye be here, release me, please! Ta'e this pain awa' from me! I'll try t' set my heart upon ye from noo on."

It was as if a caged bird in Rohan's chest was set free, wings flapping, with wind lifting the feathers in flight. He knew then that God was indeed real. He could feel the strength of his youth returning to his spirit. But he still didn't know what God wanted of him. Perhaps that would come later as he shared this feeling with Miryam. For the time left of the social, though, he would play with all he had in him, in a sweet release of all that he had borne, so painfully and suffocatingly, deep inside.

But later, on the way home, he was able to dismiss the miracle. It was as if it had been stolen away and Rohan could not quite determine whether the lifting of his burden was more than just a trumped up bit of excitement because he'd had the chance to fiddle again, or if something supernatural had occurred.

Da told me that he wanted to hope, but was afraid to step out and believe that something good had happened. What could he hope for? Love? Peace? Security? In past troubles he had occasionally sought refuge in God, but lately he had all but lost the ability to try.

Then again, what if he had just that night been given a powerful hope to hold on to? What if real love had actually sought him out and was now actively holding on to him?

They say that faith comes by hearing something so many times that you then can believe it. Why else would people repeat "I love you" so many times during courtship? We say it to make it real and secure it in our hearts. We repeat it because it's so important to lift up our loved ones and establish the bond of love between us. Da was hoping that the love he searched for was greater than his need, because to him, his need was insurmountable.

God's own heart longs for us to be in a loving relationship with Him. The safety of His embrace is what we all long for. God has designed each person with an almost indescribable yearning for Himself. We try in vain to fill that yearning with human relationships and material things. We crowd out God. But only God can fill the deepest abyss in each heart. He knows that we are broken by hurts accumulated over a lifetime, needs not met, lies believed, fears that enslave us, anger that consumes us. These burdens turn us inward and grow into resentments that become sin. And that sin is a painful separation from God.

We all know we are lacking something, but we are not sure what we are missing. We spend our lives searching in vain, clinging to many substitutes during our journey. Yet Adam and Eve once had it, this friendship with God. It was theirs at creation, but was lost with the first sin. They could not pass it along to their children because it was beyond remembering. They were utterly bereft. That place within us is still void... until we surrender our lives to our Creator – until we cry out to God - and He answers!

Hanukkah arrived in a deep snow storm. The *Shammus* candle was lit, and the prayer began with the same words Miryam used every *Shabbat*. "Blessed are You, Lord, Our God, King of the universe..." Each succeeding night another candle was added, from right to left until all burned to glorify the miraculous Lord who had kept the oil in the ancient lamps burning. Miryam was getting somewhat uncomfortable in her pregnancy, and irritable. The letter from her mother had reminded her of Mama's need to always do everything perfectly. What would Mama think if she knew of the stain upon Miryam's life because of the rape? Would Mama and Papa accept this baby as a grandchild if they knew?

The old insistent fussiness was in her to "do everything right," to earn the approval of others, and maybe of God. She wondered, "Perhaps if I observe Hanukkah properly, God would have mercy on us and fix everything – a safe delivery for the baby, a peaceful heart for Rohan..."

The memories of the miscarriage she had suffered had begun to haunt her. The child she carried was moving regularly and she remembered how the previous pregnancy had ended abruptly with a lack of movement at the death of the baby. She worried about this but could not share her concern with Rohan. Talking with him about this child, who was not his own, always resulted in a sullen, if not angry, spate of days after such a discussion.

Of course I wasn't there for that Hanukkah, but I was every year since then. When I got big enough I was given the privilege helping Mama to light the candles. She would let me hold the lit piece of kindling, covering my small hand to guide it with her own soft one. I always loved the way her skin felt, so smooth, so gentle. The light would shine on our faces as we carefully lit the menorah.

"Miryam," Rohan asked that night in the darkness of their bed's corner, "tell me aboot your God. Wha' do I need t' ken aboot Him? Wha' am I missin'?"

She was taken aback. "You're missing something?"

"I dinna ken who God wants me t' be."

"You don't think I could know do you? I only know what I was taught as a child, some prayers that I memorized. A *broche* for special feast days. Some certain words to say at certain times. As for you, well, I think you're doing a fine job of being a husband, and a horseman. I think that's what He wants of you." Then she took a risk and ventured, "Maybe you might try to be a father more…"

Rohan didn't flinch. His mind was elsewhere. "But do ye recall at the dance when I was fiddlin'? I kent I'd die if I didna keep on. I had t' do it! It hurt me nae t' play. Takin' the break for refreshments was torture for me. That's the reason I went flyin' so fast ootside the door for some air. I e'en prayit God t' let up on me, 'til all o' a sudden He did just tha'! Twas like my life's blood was pourin' oot o' me an' then God just turnit in t' honey. Then, when I played, twas just for the joy o' it. What aboot tha'?"

Miryam was amazed at the length of his speech. "I had no idea you felt that way. I do remember that sometimes you looked very full of the music. Do you think maybe He wants you to be a fiddler more?"

"Nae," whispered Rohan, "… I ken He wants me t' be prayin' more."

Da knows now that at some point we all must step out into the unknown and leave ourselves behind if we want to grasp the meaning of our hopes, and our longings. When something within us is so strong that we yearn for its fulfillment, and at the same time, so beyond us that can't even express it - it is then that we have approached the edge of faith. But only the faith that is actually tried can be grasped. If we do not step beyond our own human knowledge, we will never know the absolute freedom of belonging to an infinitely good and sovereign God.

Mama sat most evenings in the lamplight sewing tiny garments for her baby. Jon came down to rest on one knee next to Miryam's chair, marveling at the size of them and asked whether he'd really been that small. "You were just a little bundle," she replied. "Your baby nose was no bigger than a flower bud. "Oy!" Miryam startled. "He moved! He moved, Rohan! Come feel it!"

Miryam stared intently at her rounded form, smoothing her dress flat against her to see where the baby lay. Jon timidly stretched out a hand and let it hover just above the cloth. She laid her hand over his and gently placed it where the kick could be felt easily. They waited, nervously glancing at each other, holding their breath. Then a swift movement caused both mother and son to laugh aloud as Jon pulled his hand away in amazement. Rohan, however, got up from the settle, almost upending it, snatched his coat from its peg and left the house.

After church that Sunday, Gus stopped in at the MacVoy's to borrow a tool that his handyman, Dan, needed. Rohan asked him about the man. "Och, he a guut man iss. A kind man, unt to me a great help de repairs vitt," Gus replied. They found the necessary tool and visited a while, Gus talking the most as usual.

"Mr. Himmel sure can keep up his end of a talk, can't he?" Jon remarked after Gustav had finally left.

"Goose mun e'en talk t' his dog when nobody else is 'roond," chuckled Rohan. "It may be the only dog tha' can talk an' we'll ne'er ken it, because Gus's alwa's interruptin' 'im!"

"That reminds me of a story they read at Sunday school from the Bible," Jon said thoughtfully. "The people were so happy that Jesus was coming to the city that they were shouting at the top of their voices. It made the Pharisees angry. Jesus telt them that if the people stopped shouting 'Hosanna!' that the very stones would begin to shout it. Mr. Himmel could maybe get the stones to shout, too."

Roh had a good chuckle at that. Gus most always raised his mood to a better place. He wondered about Jon's comprehension of the Bible. "Ye remember all them stories, do ye?" he asked.

"Sure. Lots of them make more sense to me now that I'm grown, some still confuse me though."

"Me, too. P'raps I could use some o' tha' Sunday schoolin' as weel," admitted Rohan. It was the first time he had willingly said that he wanted to know more about God. The thought had been on his mind since the winter social. He didn't know if Miryam knew more answers than he did, but somebody must!

With Hanukkah past, it came time for Jon to travel east to his grandparents. Preparations had been made. Small parcels of biscuits and dried meats and fruits were packed for the long train ride. He was eager for the adventure but hoped to be home in time for the baby's arrival. Miryam watched him as he moved around the sink, putting the clean dishes back on the shelf for her. She called him to her, drew the tall lad close, and in a moment of mischief said, "I've no room on my lap for you right now so will you sit down here and I'll sit on *your* lap?"

He laughed and did as he was told. Shaking her finger under his nose playfully, Miryam warned him, "You'll be going too far away from me for my comfort, you know. Don't go keeping company with strangers! You must be polite, but when you get on the train, don't leave it, or get involved with any goings-on! Watch out for those made-up women, and for any *shnorrers*. There are people who ride the trains just to see who they can cheat! Don't you think they've got trouble in mind? Just mind your own business and you'll do fine." Then she began to tear up. "I'll miss you, you know. You must write every week, do you promise?"

"I will, Ma. And it's not forever. I'll be home soon."

Miryam continued, "Now then, you must call your grandfather *Zaydee,* and your grandmother *Bubbee.* That's the Yiddish way. They'll like that a great deal. You know they've never really been happy that I married a *goy.* Jews are supposed to marry Jews you know. Listen to what they say with a grain of salt thrown in. Don't argue. It won't do much good. Just listen. Now give me a *kush*." She held his face in her hands and kissed him.

Rohan had brought the wagon up from the barn and called through the doorway. "Tha' stage willna wait for ye. We mun gang!" When he saw the carpetbag stuffed full, he chuckled. "Did ye pack e'ery blame thin' he owns?"

They spent the trip into town talking over how things used to be in the east, and how they may have changed since then, and what to do when *Zaydee* had one too many glasses of wine, and how to put up with *Bubbee*'s fussy housekeeping. Saying goodbye at the station was a tearful affair but the coach was on time and it was over all too soon. It was Jon's first time going anywhere at all, ever, and he suddenly felt a pinch of fear. Miryam noticed and didn't hide her feelings a bit. Seeing her only child leaving was harder than she expected it to be. And Rohan's eyes welled up, too, in spite of himself. He felt such a bitter sweetness - here was his son, fully grown, traveling so far away, and now he wanted to hold him close as if he were still a *wean*.

Ralph came to the station to see Jon off and handed him a packet of letters. Miryam and Rohan listened and laughed as Ralph explained his plan to have Jon mail them a few at a time along the way to Ralph's cousin in Boston, who would think that Ralph himself was headed east to Kentucky! The old prankster brought a much needed frivolity to the departure.

"You won't feel too bad about not being here for Christmas?" Miryam asked Jon.

"No, Ma. We had a good Hanukkah together. That's enough."

After the farewell hugs, and several kisses that Miryam could not hold onto, the boy climbed into the stagecoach and waved until he was out of sight. His parents didn't talk much on the way home, but held hands while Miryam sniffled and leaned against Rohan.

Chapter 13

Gustav and Ava, Ana and Rose spent much of Christmastide with the MacVoys, decorating each other's houses and sharing large holiday meals. They were good for each other, especially for Miryam to have other women to talk to. The laughter she had needed so much came in abundance and spilled over onto each and every one of the family members. Whenever the Himmels invited the MacVoys to visit, they also invited Dan to join them, but he always found a reason to be elsewhere.

Rohan and Gustav got along famously, mostly because Gus talked a lot, and his friendliness brought out a side of Rohan that Miryam had never seen before. Apparently Rohan could talk nearly as much as anyone else when he was with the right person. His sullen moods seemed to dissipate for the most part.

On Christmas Eve, Rohan greeted the Reverend MacClure, a fellow Scot, *"Ciamar a tha thu?"*

"Tha mi sona gu leor," replied the vicar, as several jaws dropped in confusion. They both had a loud guffaw at the befuddled expressions of the bystanders.

"For the sake o' these fine folk 'roond us," the good reverend grinned, "Rohan has asked me 'How are you?' and I have said, 'I'm happy enough.' And that I am! Tis guid t' see ye Rohan, an' your dear family as weel."

The Reverend attempted the impossible for his sermon, in Rohan's way of thinking. He tried to answer the question Rohan had been asking himself ever since the first carol was sung in this Advent season. "Why would God be born a babby?" was his topic. Rohan sat on the edge of his seat as the reverend explained. If the man could answer that question for him, he would be a fine fellow indeed.

"Noo e'ryone o' ye kens," MacClure began, "tha' if a body punches ye in the nose, your first thought is t' punch him back. We ha' all got a need for justice. But God, Who is the creator o' all human life, says tha' decidin' right from wrong, an' givin' oot justice, is His job, an' tis His job alone! Tis nae for us t' judge each other an' carry oot punishment any which wa' we may choose.

"Noo when Adam an' Eve disobeyed God, they started us all doon quite a slippery slope. It made for the whole lot o' us livin' withoot regard for God, hurtin' one another t' get wha' we want, an' then dishin' oot oor own kind o' justice hooe'er we see fit. Tha', my friends, is sin. Life wi'oot God is a poor life indeed!"

He paused to let his words take effect. Believing he had everyone's attention, he continued.

"When the man an' the woman in the Garden o' Eden ate o' tha' forbidden tree, twas as if a part o' their verra bein' was removed from 'em, likened t' a ship wi' a faulty rudder. Tha' rudder might keep right for an hour or twa, but sooner or later, it'll get loose. This makes it unreliable, an' if nae constantly corrected, most useless. The piece o' the works tha's missin' in us humans is the relationship we once had wi' oor Creator!

"Since then, man has lived in this cycle o' sin, needin' constant correction t' remain on course, an' since a human started this cycle, twould ta'e a human t' stop it.

"God had t' tell those first people t' leave the garden so they could nae have access t' the tree o' eternal life while in a state o' sin! God ga'e 'em rules t' live by, so tha' they would recognize their sin an' choose t' live rightly, but God knew twas nae possible.

"For thousands o' years, God taught men t' come right t' Him wi' their offerins an' animal sacrifices. Twas the way He chose t' let 'em ken that sin's a serious business. He telt 'em in His Holy Book tha' only the sheddin' o' blood could make up for their debt. So He let 'em use the blood o' sheep an' kine t' pay for their sin, but He kent tha' all tha' twas nae gang t' be enough. The blood o' animals could nae pull humanity oot o' the muck an' mire. Twas a human who sinned, so only human blood could do tha'.

"Noo, ye see, God didna want t' step in like a bully an' send e'ry one o' *us t' oor deaths. He already had t' do that in the time o' Noah, an' He chose only eight people t' survive it, eh? Twas the flood o' His complete heartache o'er all that mankind had done. But His mercy stood strong, an' so, t' release us from the life o' slavery t' oor own vengefulness, God dressed His own truth in human flesh an sent Jesus, His Son, His Word o' peace, directly t' us.*

"That's what those Christmas angels meant when they were singin' 'Glory t' God in the highest, an' peace t' His people on the earth!' God was sayin' tha' He was gang t' come amongst us, an' live wi' us, an' show us hoo much He loves us an' hoo we are t' love Him back. When we live in His perfect plan, He'll hold oor sins agin us nae more!

"Noo in the second book o' Chronicles, tha' means an 'istorical account, you know," he added parenthetically. "King Solomon asks an interestin' question. He says, 'Will God in verra deed dwell wi' men on the earth? Behold, heaven an' e'en the heaven of heavens, canna contain Thee.'[7] The Hebrew prophet, Isaiah, telt it all many long centuries before it happened when he said in his book, chapter 4, that God would send a branch o' Himself,[8] an' again in chapter 9 by explainin' tha' this branch would come as a child, a son o' God. He even telt wha' this son should be called: He was to be named the Prince o' Peace.[9] Later he telt o' Jesus' family tree. He was called a root o' Jesse, bein' from the family o' King David. The prophet said tha' Jesus would be a 'light for the gentiles.'[10] That's us right here today.

"Weel, tha' Isaiah fellow was right in his foretellin'. Tha's just what God did by sendin' Jesus doon here t' us at Christmas. Almighty God came t' us as a wee bairn. But then He grew, an' when He became a man, Isaiah telt aboot tha', too. He said he would be a man o' sorrows, despised an' rejected o' men, an' tha' all the cruelty he endured was really the punishment we should have endured for oor sins. He lay doon His very life on oor behalf, like a lamb led t' the slaughterhoose. An' then o' course, ye ken the rest. He didna lay in the grave verra long, did He? He rose up from it an' He lives!

"Each one o' ye need t' ha' your own conversation wi' God. Tell Him tha' ye understand wha' He's done for ye. Ye need t' tell Him tha' ye truly know why Jesus was born on Christmas Day. Tha' fellow, Isaiah, said tha' Jesus was the Word o' God, which would proceed from His very own mouth an' would accomplish wha' He desires an' achieve the purpose for which He sends it.[11]

Reverend MacClure paused to let the gospel sink in.

"He can gi'e each one o' ye the peace you're lookin' for. Our God, took on the form o' man an' was born in Bethlehem. His Name is Jesus, fully God an' fully man. He loves us wi' perfection an' humility an' e'en sacrificed His earthly life through undeserved torture an' a cruel, verra painful death - in order t' free us from oor sin, oor inability t' surrender ourselves t' God. He loves us still today, because death canna hold Him. Because o' His obedience t' God's plan for Him, He was raised up from the grave in triumph! We celebrate His birth, His life, an' His resurrection, which God had planned before the foundation o' the world. In oor worship an' 'umble thanksgivin' for this Christmas gift from God, we KNOW, finally, tha' we belong t' Him – tha' we are fully an' completely LOVED!"

Chapter 14

The days grew longer and Miryam's child grew with them. She let out two of her dresses, to wear whenever she went to town, but decided to just leave others unbuttoned in the middle, covering the opening with her heavy apron. It wouldn't do to have everything too big after the baby was born! After months of the bedrest Ava had advised, she felt well enough to do light housework, only slowing down now and then because her cumbersome shape made certain chores awkward to do. Milking Wilhelmina was certainly no longer a favorite pastime. So her daily conversations with the little cow were now held while she put fresh hay in her trough. She stroked the gentle creature and talked softly to her while Roh did the milking.

Cooking was still easy enough to do, except for bending to put anything into the oven. Miryam asked Rohan to take word to Ava that they should try to arrange a day together. They could catch up on their visiting and get pies and breads made at the same time. Miryam wondered how to tell Ava about her baby's conception. It was going to be apparent that Rohan was not pleased about this pregnancy, and she knew Ava could be trusted to keep the story to herself. She had become her dearest and closest friend. Today they were going to make doughnuts from a recipe handed down in Ava's family. It was a rhyme and a recipe both.

Mr. Pitt's Doughnuts
One cup of sugar, one cup of milk,
Two eggs beaten fine as silk,
A little nutmeg or lemon will do,
Of baking powder, teaspoons two.
Lightly stir the flour in,

Roll on a pie board, not too thin,
Cut in diamonds, twists or rings,
Then drop with care the doughy things
Into fat that briskly swells evenly the spongy cells
Roll in sugar, lay to cool,
Always use this simple rule.

Over the past months Gustav had brought his family to visit often and the two women had taken to each other like kittens to cream. Ava was a sweet, woman with a voice that reminded Miryam of a flute she'd heard back in Kentucky, high and melodic. Though she was still young, she was roundish, tender and motherly. Whenever they met, whether in the kirk, on the street, or in the mercantile, Ava would hug Miryam with such a warm embrace that it made her want to stay there forever. Ava was like family. Whenever she visited it was a special occasion for Miryam. She also became quite fond of the quiet daughter, Ana, whose face always shone with eagerness to please.

As Gustav drove into the yard Rohan went out to greet them and to help unload the tins of flour and lard, and baskets of fruit. Ava had also grown three huge pumpkins that would easily fill as many as five pies. Their land seemed suitable to grow apples and berries, so there was much ado about the plentiful fare. The men retired to the barn to talk after getting everything in and little Rose settled down to play. Ana had not come, but chose instead to work on her sewing at home.

The women took to washing and cutting up the fruit, apples twirling as the peels fell in ribbons to the table. There was so much fruit that they decided to save the dried currants for another day when they would make jelly. The house was cozy as the pumpkins steamed in the oven. Rose watched the progress and gurgled her delight, then slept until she became hungry. She could sit up by herself now.   "Mine mudder said alvays dat ven de bebees vear de roundness from der bottoms off, dat iss ven dey guut sit up," Ava giggled. She scooped up Rose to feed her.

While Ava nursed her, Miryam broached the subject of her own baby. "Do you suppose I'll remember how to be a new mother again? It's been fourteen years since I fed, or bathed, or took care of a baby."

"Ach, not to vorry," reassured Ava in her heavy accent. "You for sure vill yust vat to do remember. It all vill to you natchurrly come back. You vait unt see."

Miryam loved to listen to the sucking and swallowing sounds of Rose's nursing. The swell of Ava's breast showed from her open bodice and revealed the bounty of motherhood.

"Ava?" Miryam summoned all her courage.

"Yah?"

"I need to tell you something. It's very hard for me to talk about it... but I have to tell someone." Miryam's voice broke as she said it. She struggled to keep her composure.

"Mine dear friend, you know dat I here to listen vill alvays be," comforted Ava.

"Last summer," Miryam began, "the day Rose was born? When Rohan was at your place?"

"Yah?"

"I... I was out in the yard doing the washing, and someone rode over the hill and I thought it was Rohan... But it wasn't." Miryam's face burned with shame at the thought of the ordeal. Tears welled up as she looked into Ava's face. What would Ava think of her? She turned her face to the wimdow and stared out as she spoke.

"He tied Jon up, and ... and ... he..." Her voice fell to a whisper, "... raped me." She clenched her jaw and closed her eyes tightly against the flood she knew was coming.

Her hands smoothed the tablecloth again and again, as if to clear away the words she had spoken, as her eyes flowed with tears. She turned her face down. She could not bear to face her friend. Ava slowly lifted her sleeping child from her lap to the cradle. She came to Miryam's side and laid soft hands on her friend's trembling shoulders. At Ava's touch Miryam's fear melted away. She buried her face in her friend's apron. At length they held each other close, weeping together for the loss of dignity Miryam had suffered.

"Och, mine *liebchen*. I so sorry am," crooned Ava. "Ve vill together through diss walk. Yah?"

Finally Miryam lifted her face to Ava's. "That's how I conceived this child, Ava. Rohan is not the father."

There was a sharp intake of breath. "Iss he diss knowink?"

"He knows. We hadn't... He was away from home often then."

"Vat about it doss he say? How he feels?"

"He's angry. But do you think he will talk to me about it? No! He doesn't talk about anything anymore."

"You vill have to all de more love him, den. Love him until he can your love return to you... unt to de bebee, too. You can pray... I mean... *can* you pray? I don't much know about de Jews, how you to your Gott talk."

"I'm ashamed to say I don't know much either except to say the same words over and over. The words my parents taught me."

"It a place to start iss. You can your vords say, unt den I vill sometink say, unt it vill enuff be. Enuff to tell Gott dat ve need Him, don't you tink?" Ava realized that this violence had also affected the whole family. Somehow she found words to pray that were for all of them. Miryam spoke a few phrases she remembered the *rebbe* had used in her synagogue.

When they had finished, Ava counseled, "You must remember dat evil iss not a matter uff how bad, but dat not uff Gott it iss. Any vord dat hurts iss like you a beatnik suffered. Any broken trust iss to de body like a vound. Dat man no more evil iss den you or me. He yust more dangerous iss. He doss not uff vat iss evil understand, he no shame to rrrrein him in hass!" Ava rolled her 'r' with conviction. "He like an animal iss. An animal dat sees his prey unt after it rrrruns, kills, unt devours!"

"What about the next homestead he comes to? He'll just hurt some-one again! He'll... he'll..." Miryam burst into tears. "Oh Ava, I have such an ache in my heart. I don't know what to do."

Ava spoke on, "We must for him to pray. Dat dis man vill vake up from de evil he hass done! Unt to hear de voice uff Gott to him callink! Ve here might de only vons be to effer pray for de likes uff diss man. Ve may de only vons be to see dat he iss yust a man. He all wronk hass gone. But no man lost iss, as lonk as he still livink iss!"

For a bit, Miryam and Ava were each quiet with their own thoughts. Then Miryam spoke of what she knew was true. "Anger never helps," she whispered in the stillness. "It kills what's good inside us." She let the words sink in. She knew that this day would live on in her mind. She searched her heart for something to hold the terrible memories, surrounding her like a pack of wolves, at bay.

"You must try, as de Bible says, to for your enemies pray."

Miryam certainly did not know how. But she knew that to do otherwise would be to set herself up for even more pain than she had already faced.

"Let Gott de judge be. He vat to do knows to brink dis man to his senses back. Yust let him go, unt hate him not, or you vill inside your soul a bitterness get dat vill you like a stone harden."

"I'll try Ava. May God help me, I'll try." whispered Miryam.

Mama told me that at time of her life she had not slept well for months. She relived the day that the stranger came in her dreams and then her mind refused to give her the nightly rest she needed. A person can be caught in the undertow of hurts and fears. One would think that understanding and accepting the past would heal the soul, but Uncle Ralph told me once that he had read something by a man named St. Augustine of Hippo. It said, "Our hearts are restless, O Lord, until we find our rest in thee."

One day Mama told the reverend MacClure about this constant reliving of her fears and he read a prayer to her from the prayer book they used at the kirk. It was written by St Augustine as well.

"Keep watch, dear Lord, with those who work,
or watch, or weep this night,
And give Your angels charge over those who sleep.
Tend the sick, Lord Christ; Give rest to the weary, bless the dying,
Soothe the suffering, pity the afflicted,
Shield the joyous; and all for Your love's sake. Amen"[12]

Then he gave her a short verse from his Bible to read before going to bed each night. It was Psalm 3:5,

"I lie down and sleep; I wake again, because the LORD sustains me."

Mama began to sleep peacefully again.

Chapter 15

Dan found work often enough to keep some money in his pocket, as well as to pay Gustav a bit for his room and board. Gus tried to refuse, but Dan insisted. The many repairs to the Himmel property had finally been accomplished for the most part, and Dan was mostly doing odd jobs for other people. Folks liked his polite ways and his workmanship was trusted. And, he reasoned with Gus, if he was living anywhere else he would be paying rent.

He made the rounds of the village people and then the outlying farms, but avoiding those close to the MacVoys. He mended broken furniture, or replaced a cracked windowpane, chopped wood, or put up a fence. The work was varied and thus always interesting. He had whittled some toys to sell during the Christmas season, and Bettina had agreed to sell more at the mercantile throughout the year. He was enjoying his new life. He'd met the preacher when he'd replaced some floor boards in the vestibule where the snow and rain came in under the door and rotted the planks. It was a long job so Reverend MacClure used to pull up a chair and pass the time as Dan worked.

The Reverend MacClure was a laid back sort of fellow and didn't ask many questions. He just whiled away the time as if he'd known Dan forever and there was no real need for Dan to respond. At first it had made Dan uneasy, as if the man was inspecting his work to find fault, or maybe, being a preacher, the reverend wanted him to do this for free. But soon he came to realize that it was just a comfortable way to spend an afternoon. They began to exchange bits of their lives and their travels in the world, and became companions.

As the weeks passed, with the work long finished, Dan and MacClure often made time to just sit and talk. They eventually came to the realization that Dan had no idea who God really was, that he was hungry to know Him, and that the reverend was in a position to make the introductions. Dan drew in the knowledge like a thirsty man pulls a bucketful of water from a well.

One day as they took a walk in the country Dan spoke up. "Do you mean ta tell me that every wicked thing I've done has already been forgiven? Paid for?" he asked incredulously.

"E'ery bloody thin' ye ha' e'er done or will e'er do. Aye! Tha's the wa' it works. God knew we couldna e'er pay back the debt we owe, so He sent Jesus t' do it for us. Tis finished. But the catch is, ye have t' admit wha' ye done."

"I have ta tell ya what I did?"

"Ach, nae me," chuckled MacClure, "an' t' be sure, God already knows it all. Tis just tha' ye need t' tell Him, so tha' He knows you're confessin' it. Ye see, God mun judge 'tween guid an' evil, 'tween givin' hearts an' selfish hearts. His perfection is the standard for all morality. For His justice t' reign, righteousness must be blessed an' evil punished. If we're honest, we mun acknowledge tha' in oor hearts an' attitudes, we're nae perfect. We're found wantin' e'ery day.

"We're all self-servin'. Each day we step o'er, or aroond, or onto the hearts o' oor fellow man. We sin by committin' wrongs an' also by leavin' righteous acts undone. We may feel righteous in oor own eyes, but God knows oor e'ery unclean thought. His wrath is justified, but He doesna desire t' punish us. His mercy toward us is a deep, deep well."

Dan took this in slowly. "But what if I done somethin' truly awful?"

Reverend MacClure shook his head and suppressed a chuckle. "I dinna mean to make light o' your sin, Dan, but ye surely are not the first t' come t' Him wi' a full load."

Dan tested this again, looking the good cleric straight in the eye. "I am more guilty than I would ever want ta say aloud."

"An' God knows it all. His punishment for sin is severe, requirin' the sheddin' o' blood. In the ancient times God telt men t' sacrifice an animal's life, t' shed its blood t' cover his sin. An' not just any animal would be acceptable, but only a healthy, clean animal. When that bright red blood o' the offerin' was spilt, e'erybody who saw it knew the reality tha' God canna o'erlook sin.

"The total o' the sin o' e'ery person who has e'er lived, an' those who'll someday live, is an unfathomable weight for oor understandin', but God has calculated its exact measure - a death sentence for all."

Dan shook his head, "I know it. I feel it!"

"In order t' establish true peace He mun exact true justice," MacClure continued, "but wha' man could pay such a heavy price? Only a human bein' could legally pay the debt incurred by humans. But no blameless human has e'er lived. Except Jesus. Nary a one has e'er been worthy t' qualify for the sacrifice. No immoral man could pay the ransom for e'en his own life, let alone the price for the selfishness o' all mankind. So God clothed Himself, His own glory, with mortal flesh t' do the job for us all."

"How can I know I'm really forgiven?"

"Ye say you're sorry, thank God for sendin' Jesus t' ta'e your sin awa' on the cross, an' keep your face turnit toward Him so ye willna fall prey t' those sinful ways agin. That's all there is t' it."

"Well, do I have to be in the church to do it?" Dan had been attending services for a long while and had grasped that God's presence was sometimes more palpable there than in other places, perhaps, but he was a bit threatened by the formality of the setting.

"Nae, He's alwas aroond, ye dinna ha' t' go anywhere special t' talk t' God."

Dan thought this over. There was so much that he carried that burdened him. It would be a great relief to know that he was forgiven of all those drunken rages and to be released from the hurts he'd caused so many people. The thought of possibly making reparations scared the daylights out of him, but the price would be worth his peace of mind. The knowledge of what he had done to Miryam and the whole MacVoy family was a huge enough burden to begin with. It had weighed heavily on him for months. Then there were those who he must have traumatized without ever knowing, while raging, roaring drunk, somewhere out in the world. Confessing it all would be a huge step, but he believed that if forgiveness was possible, he needed to get it done, and soon.

"Is this here a good enough place? Right now?"

"Aye, any where an' any time is just fine wi' Him."

"Will ya stick close by in case I don't git it right?"

The reverend answered softly, even though no one else could hear or see them, "I'll be near enough, Dan. But once ye actually decide ye want t' talk t' God, tis easy from there. Ye'll surely do fine."

Dan looked around for a suitable place to have his conversation with his Creator. A rocky projection offered a kneeling place. Reverend MacClure strolled a bit away to give him privacy.

Dan didn't know just what to say, but after several minutes of frustration he realized afresh that God knew it all anyway. So he just burst out, "I'm sorry!" Then put his head down on his crossed arms and wept into his shirt sleeves. After a time he began to recount all the vileness he had lived and the suffering he had caused. As each offense came to mind he repented anew and wept more. He also asked for Etta to be forgiven saying, "She don't have any idea what she's doin' with her life."

Many, many long minutes passed. Almost an hour later, MacClure saw him rise to his feet and lift his hands to the sky. He jumped up and down twice and then ran full tilt at the reverend, jumping on him and knocking him off his feet. They laughed and cried together as they lay on their backs looking at the clouds from their "holy place" in the meadow. God was as near as He'd ever been.

As they lay there Dan choked back his tears as they flowed again, saying, "I thank ya, friend, for yer patience with me an' fer settin' me on the right road."

MacClure, who was choking up a bit as well in empathy, replied, "I ha' been there too, ye ken. An' I think ye should call me Jamie outside o' the kirk of a Sunday mornin'. Aye?"

The reverend walked back to town with Dan and asked him to wait a moment as he went into the church. He came out a moment later with an envelope in his hand.

"Twas written by my late wife when she was verra ill. She was a woman who loved poetry an' God both. She wanted t' tell me what twas like t' know God's love. I didna know Him then, an' I never got the chance t' tell her that this scrap o' writin' she did helped t' bring me in t' His arms. She died that night.

"After ye ha' thought on it, please return it t' me. Tis mostly all I ha' left o' her."

"Thank ya... Jamie," Dan said as he met MacClure's eyes. "I'll take care with it." He tucked it safely into his vest. When he reached the Himmels he went to his room in the barn, sat down on the bed, and pulled the paper out. The words on the envelope were written in a weakened shaky hand, but bore witness to a strong truth.

"Dearest husband, I hope you understand what I'm saying here. If you don't today, I pray you will soon."

There was a poem written on the stationery inside:

"You've been there, haven't you? Or perhaps not.
I've been there in dreams, and awake.
It's a place where the tears run down my cheeks - hot,
but not one complaint I'll make.
God's truth is so vivid, so wild and so free
that I wonder I didn't know
that there is a place where I'll always be,
though I'm not sure when I'll go.

My love, and my master lives there, does He,
and I'll stand secure at His side.
The horizon's so far I can't clearly see,
the distance is so far and wide.
Yet close is His touch and His Word in my head,
and there's music that makes me dance.
Close up is the wonder of life-giving bread,
and red wine that leaves nothing to chance.

That place is a home where dreams are real
and all that we hope for is true.
Have you been there, I wonder? Do you feel
His heart, beating and calling for you?
If you don't hear His voice, don't worry or fret.
He's not far away, but quite near.
He made you, and knew you, and knows you still yet
and He's nigh when you ask Him, "Come here."

He's waiting and watching and wondering when
I'll lilt to tune the He plays,
Oh, He'll pluck me from this world, and then

I'll dance for the rest of my days
You've been there, haven't you, or perhaps not...
I've been there in dreams and awake.
If you like, I'll tell you the gift He has brought
and I'll share all I know for His sake.

From your wife, your Christina, with much love, I hope you will
share this faith with me. I don't want to miss you when I am in heaven."

Dan went to sleep with a smile on his face for the first time in as many years as he could remember. He dreamed of being with his family and celebrating a grand happy occasion with them. There were no distinct faces, but much joy and an enormous sense of belonging. He woke with a start, looking around him to see what had interrupted his dream. The patch of light from his window illuminated his trunk and the tablet and pencil he used daily to keep track of his chores and his paying jobs. He lit his lantern and began to write with fervor what was swirling in his head.

"I was startled in the darkness as if I'd heard my name.
No one was there yet as I listened, I heard it once again.
A voice was singing, and then I knew.
The voice was Yours, the song was true.
I rose to follow but could not see
the One who wooed and beckoned me.
There were no words and still You spoke.
My spirit yearned, my heart awoke
to the joy and the pain of the bittersweet refrain.
O LORD, sing to me!

Sing me a song to lead me onward that I may never step aside.
Keep me in tune, Lord, with You only,
that I may stand against the tide
of drums and bugles, of marching feet,
that bids my heart to take its beat,
calling my life to keep repeating

all the steps I've made so long.
I've been so wrong.
Teach me Your song!
I want to dance, Lord, to Your music,
to each sad and happy strain.
I want to move at Your direction, in the sun and in the rain.
For You alone call with mercy in the fragrance of Your dawn.
You give me light to change my darkness,
teach me, Lord, to sing Your song!"

Chapter 16

"Ralph," called Bettina from the back door. "Here's a letter for Miryam and Rohan! It's from Jonathan! Come quick! You need to take this out there right now!"

"Coming, my flower!" replied Ralph in his jovial manner. He loved Bettina, but teased her constantly with his pet names and his bookish language. She couldn't read a word and was always amazed as he read aloud to her when they sat down after supper by the fire. Perhaps this was why she was so interested in other people's mail.

Ralph had just taken some foodstuffs to the rooming house and was stomping off the February snow he'd brought in. "You always seem to want me to go out as soon as I come home, Madame! Are you tired of me?"

"You're a scoundrel, mister! And I'll thank you to just do as you're told. You didn't give me any children to scold so it will just have to be you! Now along with you!"

Bettina planted a wet kiss on Ralph's forehead and patted his chest. "Stay warm and hurry home for lunch."

"As you desire, lovely bride," grinned the elderly gent as he accepted the letter to be delivered. "Tis a beautiful day for a ride, would you like to accompany me?"

She thought for a minute, maybe two. "Yes, but I won't. Miryam would feel that she should put on tea and all, and she's probably not up to it. So don't you stay too long either. Just long enough to get the gist of that letter, though. I'll stay here and get Reverend MacClure's groceries packed up for this afternoon. He's coming around after them."

"Very well, my sweetness. I shall not stay long from thee." Old Ralph bowed low, doffing his cap as he backed through the doorway. Replacing his cap he strode across the alley to the livery to get a buggy for his trip to the MacVoy's.

When Rohan saw the buggy come over the horizon he knew there would be mail. Ralph seldom made social visits unless there was mail to deliver. He didn't like to have to rent a buggy too often without a good reason. But when the mails came, he was happy for the excuse to go "visiting."

"Miryam," Rohan called from the porch, "Ralph's on his way, put on the kettle!"

Ralph was fairly carried into the house by their enthusiasm, hardly getting his coat off before they ripped open the letter. No one noticed the kettle steaming until every word had been read twice. Jon had promised to write regularly every week but he had not done so. This his first, so each word was relished and read over and over again.

"Dear Da and Ma,

I'm not sure I should be saying this, since they're your parents, Ma, but I really don't want to stay here much longer. I've never felt so alone! They don't say good morning, or good night, or hello or goodbye, except as a formality. Does Zaydee always watch everything to see that it's done his way? Does Bubbee ever stop washing things? Nothing is ever clean enough for her.

How did you ever learn to laugh Ma? I guess it was from Jasper, he still thinks fondly of you. He and I get along. He's teaching me even more about fine horses and racing. Though I reckon there's not much need for race horses at home. Jasper's dog had pups and he gave me a girl. I named her Sass because that's what she does. I tell her don't sass me and she yips right to my face but she obeys when I call her, or when I tell her to sit and all. I hope you don't mind but I plan on bringing her home with me when I come.

Zaydee's doctor will be letting him start heavy chores again soon and I'll be ready to go whenever that happens. Thanks for all the noshes you packed for the train ride here. Bubbee says she'll make sure I have lots to eat on the way home and for the stage coach as well. I liked the train enough but the noise and the smoke from the potbelly stove got to me on the second day, so when I come home I'll ride in the cattle car again. The cows and horses kept me warm enough and were not so nosy as the old lady noodge who sat next to me was. Travel was not quite as much fun as I expected, so don't ever worry about me running away and joining the circus!

Just expect me anytime after March 1st. I'll ask Ralph to bring me out unless I see Da in town when I pull in. I hope you are well, and that the baby hasn't come yet. I want to be home to see him, or her, as soon as he's born. Bubbee did tell me that babies are especially beautiful then. I'm surprised she said that, but she did.

Love, Your son, Jon"

"Well, young Jon will be bringing home a puppy!" Ralph remarked. Figuring that it might make Miryam uncomfortable, he decided not to touch on the subject of Miryam's parents. "I suppose I should be on my way. Bettina will be fixing to have kittens until she hears about this letter." Everyone knew that, as the one who delivered the post, Ralph also shared what he learned with Bettina. And that meant the whole town would know. But they all knew, too, that he only shared what was common fare. Personal heartaches remained sacred. Ralph would let everyone he met hear about Jon MacVoy's new pet, but nothing more.

The primroses alongside the road woke up to the late winter sun and brightened the trip to town. Miryam wondered if they would soon be covered by another snowfall. Rohan and Miryam had some errands to do before the baby arrived. There was material to buy for more nappies, some of the newest things to fasten them – called safety pins, and they decided to get a store-bought mattress for the crib Rohan was building. The cradle would do for a few months, but the crib Jon had used as a small child had long since been passed to another family. No one had expected that Miryam would have another child after her miscarriage.

They met Gustav and Ava in the mercantile. "Vat a nice surprise! I for you many a tought haff sometimes," Ava said to Miryam. "How you are doink? I mean vitt all?" The ladies moved further into the store to look at the material and to talk away from the men. "Rohan better iss, yah? He seems to be yet not so ankry?"

"I think he is thinking of answers now, and not questions so much. His moods are not so black now."

"Iss guut. I pray, too. Gott de hearts uff men vell knows. He to dem talks yust so, dat dey vill hear Him." Ava went on, "He eefen vat iss not spoken uff knows. Unt He, in a lankvich dat iss not spoken, answers. But our hearts hear Him ven ve listen."

"We will see," replied Miryam. She put a hand quickly on the baby as it moved in her womb. "Oh! The baby hears us talking about him!" The women laughed, hugged and went on with their shopping.

Gertrude Lubbock stood in the next aisle and scowled. There was fodder for her gossip mill.

Bettina was beside herself waiting for Ralph to come back from his daily errands. Another letter had come for Miryam and Rohan. Jon must be lonely. "Now don't fret," she told herself. "It doesn't mean it's bad news."

Ralph came through the door in a blustery gale. "The day is colder than it looks!" he puffed. "Beautiful to see, but much too cold to be out walking in!"

Bettina rushed up and thrust the letter at him. "Hurry, it must be important! It's only been a day since the last letter!"

"Oh my dear," chided Ralph, "you look as if you've got St. Vitus's dance! Give me a bit to warm up."

But Bettina was already putting a loaf of bread and some preserves in her basket. "I'm going with you this time."

"But…" Ralph's objections were useless, he knew. "All right then. Get your bonnet and your extra warm duds on."

She had her coat on and was out the door before He could say another word. "For an old woman you can move pretty fast," he called ahead. "Mind you, my dearest, I still love to see you kick up your petticoats!"

"Ralph! Someone will hear you!"

As expected, the arrival of a second letter from Jon caused no small stir at the MacVoy household. Miryam again insisted that Rohan read it first, "just in case there's bad news."

"Tis all well. Get on wi' ye an' read it," he said, handing the paper back to Miryam. She read aloud so Ralph and Bettina would hear as well.

"Dear Ma and Da,

Bubbee is all in a fidget. Zaydee told her that Jesus is a Jew! He says Jesus is the Messiah! Her whole world is what she calls ongepotchket, turned upside down. She says he has become goyim. Now Zaydee can hardly get a word in edgewise. It's funny to watch them argue. I know I shouldn't make light of it, but there has been more lively conversation in the past two days than in all the rest of the time since I've been here! She says to him, 'Now do you want to go to market and bring home a pig for supper? You bring a shanda to the family! What will people say?'

It seems that Zaydee has found a packet of papers in an old trunk he had in the attic. He thought it was empty all these years because it was so light. He was going to give it away to someone who needed one and thought of checking inside just to make sure it was empty. It seems that all these papers were a collection of writings that were hidden by Zaydee's own father because he had secretly become a Christian!

There were things written down from what is called the Old Testament and some from the New Testament. Zaydee was surprised that there's a New Testament now. Well that made Bubbee madder than a hen out in a rainstorm.

She told Zaydee that he has taken leave of his senses, and he must never say such a thing again. But he does! He's so full of sand he could hold back the ocean. Bubbee says he's meshuggeh, crazy! If Da were here he'd say Zaydee was right gowky!

They don't have one of those Old Testaments here so I can't look up what he's talking about so I'm sending you the name of it so maybe you can find a Bible at the kirk and see why all the fuss and bother. Zaydee says it's from a prophet called Isaiah, in the 53rd chapter.

Otherwise, I am training Sass to fetch a ball for me. She does it pretty well, but then, she won't let me have it when she comes back to me. She's getting big fast, and she loves the barn cats. They don't see it that way though. She tries to pick them up by the head like they're her pups. They don't like it one bit!

Love, Jon"

"Ralph, you are the one who knows the books," Miryam began. "Do you know what Jon is saying? Who is this prophet?"

Ralph harummphed, which caused his mustache to flutter briefly. Bettina knew he was getting ready to expound upon this weighty matter. "Well, yes, I've read this book of Isaiah. He tells about how the Hebrews, that was what they called the Jewish people back then, were not faithful to God, so God would send a servant to bear away the iniquity of men... and of course women, too." He looked sideways at Bettina, who scowled at him.

"Yes...Ahem!" he continued, "This servant would have to suffer on behalf of the people. Isaiah said that he would be tortured, and finally led to slaughter like a Passover lamb. And even though he was innocent of any wrong at all, pain and death would be laid on him by God as payment for the sin of the world."

"But what does Jesus have to do with this? Why would Papa say Jesus was a Jew?" asked Miryam. "Jesus is one of the gentile gods isn't he? I don't understand."

"Well, He was born to a Jewish family. So that makes Him a Jew."

"Ach, noo wait up a bit here, tha's daft!" Rohan interrupted. "Hoo can tha be? My family has been gang t' the Christian kirk for generations an' prayed t' Jesus the Christ. He canna be a Jew!"

Bettina, without ceremony, began to gather her things, handing poor Ralph his coat. "I think we must be going now, or it'll be dark before we get home. Come now Ralph, there'll be time for more talk another day."

"But," Ralph sputtered. He looked at Bettina, but she was bustling and ready, so they took a hurried leave.

They said their fare-thee-wells at the door, avoiding the questioning looks of Rohan and Miryam, and climbed into the buggy, bundling themselves against the cold.

"Why do you race off so, woman?" Ralph questioned once they were on their way.

"Because I know you. You'll start to wax poetic, then you'll begin to drone on and on, and then you'll find yourself the object of your own admiration. God doesn't need your orations. He has ever so many ways to work that do not include your own wisdom. You're a fine man, and you surely are wise. But right now I truly think is not the right time to speak more. The seed has been planted. Let's let God water it, and let His love shine on it, and it will grow."

It was February. Ralph and Bettina drank their tea in their cozy rooms behind the mercantile. Dinner was a pot pie made of her winter vegetables and a bosomy chicken someone had traded for their weekly supplies. The root cellar was still well stocked from Bettina's fall garden, so they never worried for food, but the addition of a chicken was a delightful surprise. A fairly heavy envelope had arrived from Kentucky, in an unmistakably fancy script. It was too late in the day to take it to the MacVoy's, so they had time now to speculate.

"What do you suppose it could say this time?" Bettina queried. "And what's all the dither about Jesus being a Jew? We never did get to talk about it since we were at the MacVoy's. The Jews don't believe in Jesus, do they? …Ralph? What about…"

"If you ask more than one question at a time I don't know which one to answer when. Start somewhere and then we'll go one step at a time."

"You know, sometimes I think you like to hold it over me that you've learned so much from your books… and that I can't read and you can."

"No, lovey! I never think of you as not knowing how to read. You're the one who does so many things that I myself cannot do! I could never take care of myself the way you take care of me. Just because you can't read does not mean you have any less love in my heart!"

"Very well…" This admission pleased her to no end. "Let me ask something then." Bettina reviewed in her mind all that she had heard over the years about God. Since she was unable to read the Bible, some things just hadn't come full circle yet. "Why don't the Jews believe in Jesus?"

"Well…" Ralph always opened any discussion that way - with hesitancy, warming up as he journeyed along the shiny rails on his train of thought. Bettina wondered though, after quite a few moments had passed, whether his train had lost a few cars.

At last he began, "They always believed that the reason they were chosen by God was because He liked them best. To them it meant they were special. But truly, He loves all people, He was just working through the Jews to make an example of the relationship He wants with us all. He chose them to belong to Himself. But they kept disobeying Him, and He had to keep taking His hand of protection away from them so they would call to Him for help. So they'd learn to stay close by Him.

"It's like when a child is learning to walk on his own. The mother lets go of his hand and he takes a hesitant step. He may succeed, or he may fall, but the mother is there. If she doesn't let go, he will not learn to walk. God let go of the Jews to let them learn to trust in Him, but they were not submissive to His leading. Their sin put them continually in opposition to God's plan, and instead of walking with Him, they went their own way. So God solved the problem by sending Jesus.

"Of course God knew it would happen that way from the very beginning. He had created all of mankind to belong to Himself. But when the first man and woman disobeyed His command in the Garden of Eden, their relationship with God was severed. The serpent in the garden was really the devil, and when Adam and Eve disobeyed God, their ownership of the earth was lost. There was no way to restore it short of repentance and complete obedience.

"But they couldn't do it. No one can! Not one person, from that day on, has ever been able to fully obey God. The breach between God and mankind remained. So the plan which God had set in place before the foundation of the world was put into action. He chose to actually be born as a human in order to bring humans to Himself. That way He could speak with them, and interact with them to show them how much He loved them."

"So why don't the Jews believe this?"

"Because theirs is still a religion that is based solely on doing the right thing. It's all based on strictly keeping all their laws. They don't think they need a Savior. They think that following a prescribed way of life will be enough to please God. But nothing could be further from the truth."

"I'm not sure I understand, Ralph. I think that following God's way is very important."

"It is, but what if we followed all the commandments but did not have love for God, or for our fellow man? It would be like knowing how to read and write, and how to use eloquent language, but never being able to say anything that was edifying or helpful."

Ralph continued, "It's the way I used to be. I thought I was a pretty wonderful person." He waited for a response. "You could reassure me here…"

"Yes, I could…" Bettina said quietly, holding in her smile.

Ralph gave her a sidelong glance. "I'd never done anything very bad, in my own humble opinion, of course. Then one day I realized that I had never given even the smallest part of my life to God to control. I had always felt that I was in charge of my life, and suddenly I saw that I had denied God even the smallest courtesy of acknowledging that He had made me.

"You know how everybody has someone they must answer to, whether it's their parents or their employer or their spouse or the community? But at that time in my life, I thought I was an authority unto myself. Too independent for my own benefit."

"Too big for your britches?" Bettina chuckled. "But you know better now? God's in control. - And He made me second in command!"

Ralph laughed out loud, "You always were a rascal. You led me right down the garden path, didn't you?"

Chapter 17

Ralph and Bettina arrived at the MacVoys' the next day as early as it was acceptable to do so. Of course they brought some fresh scones and jelly with them so they would be invited to stay, and would not feel guilty about Miryam having to go to any trouble this late in her pregnancy.

"Oh dear, what can it be now?" Miryam puzzled over the letter. "Open it for me?" she said, handing it quickly to Rohan.

He had made the habit of late to keep his eyeglasses close at hand, so he quickly scanned it and passed it back.

"'Tis just *drammach*," he said, and sat down to his coffee after plucking a scone from Bettina's basket. "Naught but more *blether* aboot God!"

Miryam ignored Rohan's comment, turning instead to Ralph. "I'm so glad you're here then. Maybe you can help me understand it. After that last letter, I'm even more unsure of religion than ever!" Then Miryam read it aloud.

"To my dearest Daughter,"

"Oh my!" she exclaimed. "Papa has never addressed me as being his dearest!" She continued.

"I know Jon has written you about my new belief, that Jesus is our Messiah, the true Savior of our people. Please bear with me on this. I do believe it may be true! Yes, you could probably say that I'm just a foolish old luftmensh, following a dream. But this is important to me. I have some feelings that are very strong and I want to share them with you. I don't know if I can say this without alienating you, but I must try!

I want you to know how much Jesus loves you. This isn't a plea for you to 'believe as I do.' It's a plea to believe as much as you can, and take the time and effort to search out the truth even where it might be hard to find. There will always be questions in your mind and quite often questions in your heart. That will always be the case. It is the same with me and truly with everyone. But now I believe that there actually are answers. The answers can be elusive, but worth pursuing.

In my mind, the fullest life possible is lived in an abiding relationship with God. I'm so sorry that I seem to have painted a wrong picture of Him in your childhood. I never meant to misrepresent Him. I look back and see that I have been a hard man. I have acted more like a businessman with you than a father. I must have portrayed God to be a judgmental and hard-to-please taskmaster.

But that's not who He is and I am so sorry I gave you that impression. From now on I promise not to say judgmental things and I will be supportive of you and respectful of you. I ask you to do the same for me. What do you say?

Your Mama is, of course, furious with me, but I have to just let her be. God has shown me that I cannot win her to Him. He can do it well enough without my bumbling attempts.

Jon is well and happy and we are fast becoming friends. My shoulder is nearly mended now and I will be sending him home when all the arrangements have been made. I hope it's not a problem letting him bring the dog home.

Your loving Papa

Post Script – Please find and read the enclosed missives which were found by myself in an unused trunk.

They were wrapped in a large piece of vellum and tied with a purple cord. Written on the outside were these words:

Shadows are but a reflection of what God has made,
a seemingly perfect reproduction, yet without substance.
No reality, no strength.
Let Your life be a real acceptance of your Source of light.
Do not be only a shadow,
bearing shallow witness to what you could be.
Be filled with the Light of the Lord.
For there is no darkness where He shines in His glory.

I have copied those found documents and I enclose them for you. I found that I could not part with the originals as they are far too precious to me since some are in my own father's hand. They have been carefully kept for the time that someone (I thank the Lord God that it was me) should find them.

Again, I send my love, Papa."

Miryam sat back with tears in her eyes. "This is the first time my father has ever called himself Papa to me." She blew out a long sigh. "I always called him that, but he never referred to himself by anything but Father. She drew the large packet of writings from the envelope, all in her father's unique script.

The first was an explanation of part of the temple of worship in Jerusalem.

The curtain, or veil, in the temple before the Holy of Holies
separated the inner room from the outer room.
It was sixty feet tall and thirty feet wide.
No one could go into the Holy of Holies but the high priest.
Once a year on the Day of Atonement, the high priest went in
to offer blood sacrifices to God to atone for
the sins of the nation of Israel.

The next was shorter and carried three references from the Christian scriptures, with her father's comments concerning each one.

"Jesus, when He had cried again with a loud voice, yielded up the ghost. And, behold, the veil of the temple was rent in twain from the top to the bottom; and the earth did quake, and the rocks rent." Matthew 27:50-51 (No human could have torn that curtain, and certainly not from the top to the bottom!)

"Neither by the blood of goats and calves, but by His <u>own</u> blood He entered in <u>once</u> into the holy place, having obtained eternal redemption for us." Hebrews 9:12 (Jesus' blood was pure because He is the Son of God, so He had only to shed it one time instead of the repeated sacrifices made by the priests.)

"Having therefore, brethren, boldness to enter into the holiest place by the blood of Jesus, by a new and living way, which he hath consecrated for us, through the veil, that is to say, his flesh." Hebrews 10:19-20 (My dearest Miryam, we are now free to enter the Most Holy Place without fear. His sacrifice is not ended in death but He is a living way, with His own body being the open curtain into God's presence.)

On the next several sheets were poems written by her grandfather.

"O Master, Who has called to me,
Who carved each mount, Who filled each sea,
You came to me a tiny babe,
my Savior in a manger laid.

O Maker of eternity,
Whose stars fill space with pageantry,
Whose plans are made with perfect care,
You put on flesh, my heart to share.

You entered this dark world with love
on quiet wings, a heav'nly dove.
Your mission sweet; my life to save,
to pluck me from a certain grave.

Your bravery true, Your noble quest
did lead You from Your Father's breast
to dwell among the base and low,
the lives of men to fully know.

You did not wish to seal my fate
in punishment outside Your gate.
Instead You came to take me in.
You bore away my debt of sin.

O bright-lit mystery, life profound,
in freedom stood, divinely bound
to foreign guilt and unearned shame –
You've paid my debt, I will bless Your Name."

Asa Gold - 1813

~~~

"O Lord, I'm safe in Your harbor,
a refuge You've made for me.
Yet somehow, I feel a great stirring,
this is not where I always will be.
This quiet is surely a blessing,
but You call me from still waters now.
O help me to cut my moorings,
to look with Your eyes out over the bow.

I know that the waves will crash over me.
I know that the storms will rage all around.
But I choose to trust You, O Maker of these.
I carry Your anchor, to Your promise I'm bound.

O Lord, though I rest in Your harbor,
You're my refuge wherever I sail.
I'll travel on high seas, through danger.
You hand will sustain me, Your love never fail.

O help me to cut my moorings,
to sail from these still waters now.
For somehow I feel a great longing
To look with Your eyes out over the bow."

Asa Gold 1815

Behold the Bridegroom comes for His own.
Fall, O bride, before his throne.
Blameless and spotless in His sight,
Clothed in His blood and fine linen white
Bow before the Lamb, worship His Name
Yesterday, today, and ever the same.
Worthy is the Lamb of God
Mighty is the Lamb of God
Holy is the Lamb of God."
A.G. 1815

~~~

"Abba, please send the sweet wind of Your Spirit
to stir the broken pottery of my life.
Abba, please send the sweet rain of Your Spirit to
soften the hardened clay of my life.
Restore me to a workable lump in Your skillful hands.

Abba, please shape me to hold Your desires within me.
Mold me to be of service.
Gently place me in the kiln of Your consuming fire.
Burn all my dross away. Try me and test me.
Make of me a working vessel in Your skillful hands.

Abba, I commit my usefulness to You.
Engrave Your law and Your name on my life.
Please fill me with the gift of Your living water
to pour out in accordance with Your sovereign will.
Abba, I am Yours. Spirit I am Yours. Jesus, I am Yours."
A.Gold 1816

On the next paper were two scriptures taken from the prophet Isaiah's writings.

"Therefore the Lord himself shall give you a sign;
Behold, a virgin shall conceive,
and bear a Son,
and shall call his name Immanuel."
Isaiah 7:14
(Miryam, In Hebrew, Immanuel means "God with us.")

"For unto us a Child is born, unto us a Son is given:
and the government shall be upon His shoulders:
and His name shall be called (Vayikra sh'mo)
Wonderful Counselor (Pele Yoeytz,)
Mighty God (El Gibbor,)
Everlasting Father (Aviad,)
Prince of Peace (Sar Shalom.)"
Isaiah 9:6
(Miryam, please note that a human child was to be born
who would be the Mighty God!)

Another was a sort of memorandum.

I AM YOUR FRIEND FOREVER.
I WILL ALWAYS TAKE CARE OF YOU.
I WILL WATCH OVER YOU
AND SHELTER YOU IN MY ARMS.
I WILL NEVER LEAVE YOU.
I WILL GIVE YOU EVERYTHING YOU NEED.
I WILL HELP YOU CARRY YOUR BURDENS.
I WILL DEFEND YOU WITH MY STRENGTH.
NO ENEMY CAN TAKE YOU AWAY.
I WILL HEAR YOU WHEN YOU CRY.
I WILL ANSWER WHEN YOU CALL.

I carry these words in my heart.
I have memorized them, and I am certain that they are true
because they have been proven time and time again.
A.G. 1819

The next was another Scripture, this time from the Christian Bible.

"For I am convinced
that neither death nor life,
neither angels nor demons,
neither the present nor the future,
nor any powers,
neither height nor depth,
nor anything else in all creation,
will be able to separate us f
rom the love of God
that is in Christ Jesus our Lord."
Romans 8:38-39

Miryam looked up from reading, her eyes brimming with tears. "Whatever this change in him is about, he is a new man."

Bettina tapped Ralph's knee under the table.

"Do you want to write back today?" asked Ralph, knowing that Bettina would want to know what would be in the outgoing mail.

"Not today," answered Miryam. "I need to think on this."

Chapter 18

It was coming on dawn. The morning serenade of the first of the spring birds had kept Miryam company for quite some time. The pressure at the small of her back had begun hours ago, but was not enough to keep her from dozing off in between the twinges of labor. But now the level of discomfort had increased. She decided to wake Rohan.

They had arranged a signal with the next neighbor that if two shots were fired, then repeated soon after, someone must ride for the doctor. Rohan would not have to leave Miryam alone. He ran to the mantle and took down the rifle. It was loaded and ready as always. The shots were fired while Rohan stood in the doorway clad only in his altogethers. After donning his *breeks*, he ran from the stove to the bedside, from the wood box to the bedside, from the fireplace to the bedside, briefly to the outhouse, to the well for more water, and breathlessly back to the bedside.

Her labor seemed harder and faster than the last time, the child she'd lost. Miryam worked her way through each contraction, mentally noting their length and intensity. She could wait no longer and called Rohan from his awkward attempts to keep himself busy with breakfast in the kitchen. By this time he had hastily pulled on his shirt and had one suspender over a shoulder, the other dangling. He was both nervous and angry that this child was coming.

"I think… you'd… better deliver… me," she said softly, her breathing fast and uneven. "I'll tell you… I'll tell you … what… to do."

The impact of her words struck him like a fist. It was not feasible to him that this could happen. He was bound up inside with fear that in this, too, he'd fail her. Here was the end result of that day when he'd come too late, and he just knew he'd fall short again, but with even more dire consequences this time. He may lose Miryam in death. He'd heard all kinds of stories about women who had died in childbirth. Folks always wanted to tell these gruesome tales though no one ever wanted to hear to them.

Rohan cared little about the welfare of the child, who in his mind would always bear the mark of his shame at not being here when he was needed. It would only remind him of his guilt. He could not carry this burden even now, before seeing the child. What would it be like when there was a daily reminder to him at every turn? He did not want this child delivered at all except for Miryam's sake.

He heard a commotion in the yard. Hoping it was the doctor, he left her to see. An elderly gentleman was alighting from a fancy carriage with his Negro manservant a step behind him.

"I say, can you direct me? I am looking for..." The words were lost in a cry from Miryam in the house. "What's the matter here? What can I do to help you?" asked the old gentleman. His concern was quite genuine. He looked to his servant as Rohan told of his dilemma.

"Ezra here can deliver her," the gentleman said. "He's had training in all manner of medical procedures."

"Please, I'll do whate'er ye say. Come in, both o' ye."

Ezra bounded up the steps and disappeared.

"I shan't, for it's not my place," the gentleman said to Rohan. "The weather is fairly mild today, I shall stay outside and wait unless you call for me."

"Ezra's grandmother, Damie, can help as well. Damie, will you come please?" A strong looking woman with the darkest skin and the whitest hair Rohan had ever seen emerged from the carriage. Her bearing was elegant and authoritative. "Certainly Edwin. What is it?"

"The lady of the house is about to bring forth a child. Will you assist Ezra please?"

"I'd be most delighted," she replied, as she swished her silken skirts into the house.

Mama said that I was in quite a hurry, and that she was, too. She said it surprised her to remember that labor was so painful.

Another cry pierced the air as Rohan hurried into the house. The manservant gave directions for Rohan to bring clean cloths, hot water, and a sharp, clean knife and a needle and white thread just in case. He introduced himself to Miryam since her husband was not in his right manners at the time, and reminded her to relax.

Mama said that she had stared at Ezra as if the roof had just opened and he had descended through it. But she was in no condition to be choosy about who could help her.

She struggled even to take a decent breath, panting heavily. She could not seem to get enough air.

"You must breathe more slowly, the baby is not in such a hurry as you think. He will come only when he is ready, not before."

Another contraction came and Miryam tensed and grimaced.

"Look at me," coaxed Ezra. "Take a breath and let it out slowly." He demonstrated, making his cheeks big and puffed up like a bullfrog and then blowing out with a high pitched whistle. In spite of her pain, Miryam responded with a nervous laugh.

"That's better! It is best not to hurry babies into this world. There will be plenty of time to rush later when he cries for his supper. Eh?"

Another contraction began, and Miryam stiffened.

"Wait, wait!" Ezra instructed. "Breathe in, and then breathe out slooowly,"

"I can't… I can't get away from the pain," Miryam gasped.

"You must think beyond it, think of the place where the baby will lie down for his naps. Think of his warm breath on your cheek as you hold him. Think ahead to the sweet smile on his face as he dreams of milk. These are the thoughts with which you must fill your mind when the pain is strong. Cry out if you must, but do it sloo000wly."

Then Ezra left the bedside to remove his coat. He rolled up his sleeves, went to the sink and asked Damie to pour hot water into the basin from the kettle where he diluted it with a dash of cold water to wash his hands. Rohan had never seen anyone wash so long or so thoroughly.

Damie handed him a clean towel she found folded on the shelf under the basin.

Rohan found the things the man requested. He thought about the words Ezra had spoken to Miryam. He remembered the soft infant smell of his son, Jonathan, and the wonderment of holding so fragile a life in his strong arms. As of yet, he'd pushed the reality of the soon coming child far away in order to feed his guilt and anger at the circumstances of its conception. Now it was fast becoming an entity that must be reckoned with.

He'd watched after supper each night for a week as Miryam knitted the last blanket for the baby, hatred rising in him like the howl of a coyote. He wrestled now with reality. Jon was not so dependent now, or so he thought, on the nurturing of his father. He felt that his parenting was nearly over as far as the young man was concerned. Yet in his mind he knew he could not ignore the need of this new child for a father to teach him how to grow. He argued to himself that the nurturing of this bastard child was beyond his ability.

Damie went to Miryam's bedside and knelt down. "Hello, dear," she said softly, "my name is Damie, and my grandson here is a real doctor, so don't be afraid. He knows what to do, and I'll be right here with you, too." She held out a hand which Miryam was only too glad to grasp and hold tightly. Another woman was a welcome sight.

Another pain came quite quickly after the last. Miryam grimaced, fighting it with all the might she could muster up. Damie touched her face and said, "Listen to my song, girl. Hear it carefully, don't let it slip from your grasp. Let the pain fall away."

Having Miryam's attention, she kept eye contact with her as she sang softly in a tune that wove around Miryam's pain, insulating her from it.

> *"Through trial and cares, hatred and snares,*
> *I wait for You, for only You.*
> *Mid conflict large, I will sing Your song,*
> *I will wait for You, O Lord.*
> *As a woman cries out in labor*
> *for the promise of life to come,*

I yearn for Your fulfillment Lord,
for the harvest has begun.
O let They will be done."

Miryam let herself melt into the deep brown eyes of a woman she had just met, feeling a well of strength there that she had needed for so long. As another pain began she remembered to cry out slowly, but stronger than ever.

"That is fine," assured Ezra. When the contraction was over he helped Miryam position herself for the delivery, then draped her with a sheet. Kneeling on the floor he looked at her with great compassion.

"I must reach under your nightgown." He spoke softly. "I'm going to touch you now, to see if the time is near. It will hurt some. Shout if you need to and let the pain ride away on your cry, but do not be afraid of it."

He determined that the baby was ready, then turned to Rohan who was across the room at the fireplace, watching and wishing he was elsewhere.

"Come here, sir, you must help me now. Help her to sit up more. She is crowning."

Rohan crawled up behind Miryam as instructed and helped her to a sitting position at the side edge of the bed, her feet propped, one on a small footstool and the other on an upended bushel basket.

Ezra then spoke to Miryam. "Now, at long last, you may hurry, ma'am. Pant when I tell you, and then – but only when I say so - you must hold your breath and bear down to push the child out. He is waiting for you to do it, so you must!"

He spoke firmly, but gently, leading man and wife through the birth of a son.

She waited until I was old enough to hear the full story to tell me these things, but she recalls that, all in all, it was a pretty uneventful birth… until she saw me. I was not who she expected. I was small but sturdy and olive skinned with "hair as black as the inside of a black cow." She said that I was as out of place as a donkey at a steeplechase.

When he turned his attention to the babe, Ezra noted that though Rohan was pale, freckled, had curly red hair and blue eyes, and Miryam had wildly unruly light brown curls and blue eyes, the tiny boy was ruddy and had straight, black hair, and jet black eyes. He began to understand that this was a more meaningful birth than those he had attended before. The boy cried weakly. He cut the cord and handed the child to Damie who took him to the table where she had laid out toweling and the basin to wash him. Miryam cried her tension away. Rohan bit his lip 'til it bled.

Ezra caught the afterbirth as Miryam pushed it out. He saw that all was well and removed the blood and water soaked cloths from the bedside He nodded to Damie that Miryam was medically sound, and the older woman helped her ease back onto the bed fully and brought the clean swaddled baby to her. Miryam held him with wonder on her face. She had prayed and God had given her another child.

Damie brought another basin of warm soapy water to the bed and washed Miryam tenderly. Having done so, she took the soiled things onto the porch, then moved into the kitchen area to prepare some food. She found tea and bread, and brought a tray to the couple at the bed, then donned her coat and went outside, leaving them alone. She had noted a marked lack of conversation when there should have been much excited counting of fingers and toes.

Even after Ezra and Damie left, it was too quiet for too long a time.

"I've prayed for another baby for a long time," Miryam said at last to Rohan. "Ever since we lost our little girl I've wanted another child. I didn't think it would happen this way to be sure, but God has answered my prayers."

Rohan didn't want to talk about answered prayers, and certainly not about the absurd and seemingly irresponsible manner in which God had answered them, so he held his tongue and just watched Miryam with the newborn child.

Mama said that, even then, as strange as I was, I was holding on to her heart. She saw something in me that was saying to her, "Love me, mama. Please fall in love with me."

138

Outside, the old gentleman had wrapped himself in the coach blanket, had made himself at home in the rocking chair on the porch, and had fallen asleep. Damie sat in the other rocker and closed her eyes. Ezra unhitched their horses and put them to graze in the paddock. Breaking out their supplies, he made a meal of various items found there. Having laid this out on a large ornate tray with four plates, four napkins, and four drinking glasses, he drew some water to drink from the well and then sat down to eat and rest on the porch.

Shortly, Rohan came from the house and sat down near him. "I canna begin t' thank ye. I didna ken wha' t' do, an' I was beginnin' t' panic. I didna e'en put on my *shoon*," he remarked, looking at his bare feet.

"But they're both sleepin' noo," he said motioning toward the door.

He mentally noted all that the servant had done to care for their horses and for his master, and that it was all done with great attention to detail. His question burned in him until he finally voiced it. "Why are ye nae a free man like the others? An' why hav' ye put out four plates?"

"I am quite free in every way, and there are four of us traveling together." he replied.

"But ... Are ye paid?" asked Rohan awkwardly.

"There is no need for pay, I am his son," said the stranger, looking into Rohan's face.

There was a silence born of shock which lasted several moments. "Hoo can that be?...

"No, I'm sorry. I've nae right t' ask aboot your station. Forgi'e me."

Rohan rose, utterly embarrassed to have asked such a question. But Ezra stopped him.

"Wait. There is no need to be sorry, sir. As to your question about the four of us, there is a young boy asleep in the carriage. We have been on our way to see the vicar here, a Reverend Jamie MacClure, to find a placement for him. He was found on the trail where a wagon train passed a week ago, abandoned and weeping."

"I'm sorry t' hear that."

"Yes, we shall be glad of the vicar's advice," Ezra replied. "As to my own situation, I am Mr. Dennis' son, and Damie is my grandmother."

The surprise of this revelation must have shown plainly on Rohan's face, for Ezra broke into a boisterous laughter. "I never tire of seeing the expression on people's faces when I say that!" He held his sides as if he was about to explode. "I know I shouldn't be so bold about it but I just can't seem to help myself!" He shook with laughter again.

Finally he was relaxed enough to tell the story. "I was born to Mr. Dennis' wife. Of course I call him Father. And since then he has called me his own, his son. There were papers that were signed, but to Father they were a mere formality.

"You see, he is a rich man and a lawyer, and since I am obviously a man of color he knew that there would be a question one day of his substantial inheritance coming to me.

"Mr. Dennis, formally adopted me and saw that I was trained for the profession for which I showed an aptitude, that of medicine. I have always been fascinated by it. My paid services are not accepted often because of my color. People do not believe that I could be skilled. Still, when I am needed, I can be of help."

Ezra paused. "May I now tell you more, sir?"

Rohan nodded, preferring listening to speaking.

There were a few moments of hesitation. "I have been able to learn a little of your circumstances here." Ezra said delicately. "Seeing the child who is so different from you, reminds me of my own birth. May I be so bold as to explain to you my history?"

Rohan did not wish to speak of this subject to a stranger and in his mind he struggled to avoid the issue, but found he could not. Ezra had seen the infant born to his wife and surely could guess that there was somewhat amiss in his parentage.

He answered at last, "Go on if ye feel I need t' hear it. I sorely need some wisdom."

Ezra continued, "My mother was a white woman of some means. She was brought up with every luxury and felt completely worthy and deserving of all that she had ever received. Her family was above the salt, as they say. There were many suitors, my father among them. There were parties and flirtations, each ending with a different beau in favor. She kept them vying for her attentions, and they all fell at her feet.

"Then one day, out of the blue, she indicated to my father that she wanted to marry him. He was amazed since he never thought her favor to rest upon him, and had not dared even to think of asking her! It seemed she had even worked out all the details and asked him to agree to them, which he did. He was enthralled with her, thinking himself to be among the luckiest of men.

"And so they were married, quietly and quickly, with few in attendance except their family members. People thought it odd, but then they were used to her impulsive nature and her vain eccentricities.

"Too soon, she began to grow heavy in spite of her corsets and it was apparent that a child was coming. My father was crushed. He had adored her and now he knew that their marriage was a sham to cover the 'early' birth of her child. They'd been married five months when I was born in secret, a black boy to a white woman. He soon learned that I was fathered by a slave from another estate.

"I was whisked away in the night to the servants' quarters and very few knew the truth of the situation. My mother and her attendants circulated the story that her child had been premature and had thus been too weak to live.

"My father was aware of their efforts to hide me, but as an infant I was not easy to keep quiet. He soon found me in the cook's pantry and knew he could not abandon me. He kept me away from my mother by placing me in the loving home of a servant, who was known to be a wet nurse, and her family. He then located my true father who was unfortunately married, but his mother, my own Damie, was willing to come to live on our estate. He was able to purchase her easily since she was growing old and was considered to be less useful. He set her up in her own beautiful home and I with her. She has cared for me ever since. Father went about his daily business, keeping up appearances for the most part, but he became my father in every way that he could, spending all his waking hours with Damie and me, determined that I would not be scorned and rejected, as he had been by his own wife."

Rohan stared at the ground and let Ezra speak of the things which had been so instrumental in shaping his very life. Could there be a way for him to send this newborn away? But where to? In spite of Miryam's emotional statement that she thought the baby was an answer to her prayers, wouldn't it be better for them if he could whisk this child away - to a safe place, of course? What gain could come of this obvious remnant of Miryam's rape?

But Ezra's story continued in a new direction. "My father left my mother to her social engagements, sharing the same name, nothing more. She never acknowledged me in any way, yet my father knew that she was greatly disturbed by my presence nearby.

"So Father offered her an agreement, proposing that she sign a legal document relinquishing all parental rights and giving me into his custody permanently. He then accomplished a legal adoption for me. In return for relieving her of her parental responsibilities, he would take his leave from her and make a new life for the two of us as father and son. He would not scandalize her by divorce, neither would he free her by it. She agreed and we left her there.

"Since my birth he has called me his own. We have had a few brushes with those who could not accept us, but we are happy and most often free of the bonds imposed by society at large."

"He mun love ye considerably," Rohan reflected.

"He has given his life for me. You see, he is no longer able to practice law because of me. He was disbarred when my adoption was made known in the gossip of the legal community. A local judge was so strongly opposed to the idea, being a friend of my mother's, that it became a project of his to see my father discredited, thereby protecting the reputation of my mother. He invented a grand series of infractions which he accused my father of. He was successful in bringing my father before the bar and removing him from his rightful place as an attorney at law."

"Hoo ha' ye made your livin' then?" Rohan wondered aloud.

"My father is still a very wealthy man and we both employ a great many talents. By the grace of God we have lived quite well."

"Are ye nae bitter toward your mither?"

Ezra shook his head slowly, looking down at the ground at his feet. "She is a woman who does not know what love is. I cannot expect her to give me something which she does not possess." He paused for a time, then added, "One must know love to be able to give it."

Rohan looked down at his bare feet. "I thought I kent aboot love. I ha' felt it in my heart – an' I ha' tried t' be a guid man. I see noo, tha' in sae many wa's, I'm anythin' but tha'."

"I think you know more than you admit. It's love that holds a family together in spite of difficulties. It's love which commits one person to another, whether he deserves it or not. You have had something happen in your family that could have torn you apart but you've stood by your wife. And you will care for this child. You will choose to!

"I had done nothing to deserve my father's love, yet even as an infant he cared for me as his own. He has dedicated his life to my welfare. He has not sought any recognition or payment." Ezra reflected thoughtfully, "I have not always been a good son, but I have learned from him about growing into a man of conviction. He has kept no account of my failings. That is part of love – and to give and forgive unconditionally."

Rohan balked at this idea. "I canna see hoo. Hoo can I forgi'e someone I hate?"

Ezra was taken aback, "Do you hate this child?"

Chapter 19

The old lawyer stirred, then awoke and looked about him as if he'd lost track of where he was. Seeing that Damie had fallen asleep, he rose from the rocking chair stiffly and walked about to stretch his legs. As he came back to the steps where the other men sat, he quietly asked the outcome of the birthing.

"Tis a boy," Rohan replied solemnly without looking up. Ezra shook his head at his father to indicate that this was not the right time for cigars and congratulations.

"Eh... splendid. And the lady, is she well?" Mr. Dennis ventured.

"Aye, they're both sleepin' noo. Thank ye. I expect ye got here just in time. I dinna ken hoo I can e'er repay ye the kindness ye've done," said Rohan clumsily.

"You'd have done the same for us if we were in need, I'm sure." The words rang in Rohan's ears, bringing to mind the day the doctor's rig had overturned. The day when another babe had come into the world. That day he had been thanked and had answered Gus in much the same fashion. That was the day that he'd arrived home too late.

The grief bit suddenly like the strike of a rattler. He knew there was a great deal of work left to be done in his heart before he could love this new child under his roof. There must be a resolution of his anger at the one who had caused such pain to Miryam and Jon and himself, the one whom this child would ever represent in his mind.

Ezra saw him wrestle with his thoughts, "You carry a heavy burden, sir. Sometimes a shared load is easier to carry."

Rohan made no response. His mind was far away.

A very small dark boy in the carriage popped up from among the nest of blankets where he had slept, and peered over the side like a rabbit testing the air for the scent of a fox. Seeing no danger he climbed down, using the spokes of the great wheels as his steps, jumped to the ground and ran to the far side of the yard where he promptly pulled down his tiny trousers and peed in the grass along the picket fence. Having completed this necessity, he sought out Ezra, the one who had found him along the roadside.

Ezra held out his arms to the child, who only came close enough to almost touch his fingertips but did not enter the offered embrace. His eyes searched for answers in Ezra's face, but found none. He saw compassion, and safety, but not what he needed just then. He looked to Rohan. He looked longingly, until Rohan's eyes rose from where he had been absently lost in watching the progress of a heavily burdened ant toward its home.

In Rohan he apparently found what he needed, a grieving heart. The small boy knew instantly upon seeing Rohan's deep sadness that at last he'd found an understanding he could rest in. He went to Rohan without hesitation and put his arms around his neck, and curled his little legs into Rohan's lap.

Rohan could do nothing less than put his arms around the child and draw him in. He sought Ezra's face, and found his own astonishment reflected there. "He has not spoken, nor wept, nor made any physical contact with any of us since I found him alone and sobbing, and lifted him into the carriage three days ago," Ezra said, watching the boy's face as small tears emerged from the dark eyes.

"All we could do was keep him warm and fed. He'd not allow for even a hand to hold from Damie."

"Why me, d' ye suppose? Wha' hav' I tha' he couldna find wi' you all in the carriage?"

Ezra considered the question from the viewpoint of a lost child. His conclusion came at last, completely sensible for the child's heart. "You have grief. You can understand his brokenness. He has lost everything, and you among us here know what that kind of pain is.

"Rohan, you don't have to tell me why you're grieving. It's not my business, but try to let go of it before you become silent and alone like this boy."

Damie stirred from her rest and rose. "I believe I'll look in on the mother and baby," she whispered, taking in the tender scene on the steps.

Inside, Miryam and the baby were awake and Miryam was trying to get him to nurse. Looking up, she asked frantically, "Why doesn't he suckle?"

Damie took one look. She tried to seem unconcerned but her brow furrowed momentarily. The last thing a new mother needed was to get discouraged about breast feeding her baby. It could begin a downward spiral of depression for her and failure to thrive for the child. "Let's see," she offered, "perhaps he's still tired from his ordeal. It was hard work for him, too, don't you think?" She uncovered his feet from their wrappings. "We can make him just a little less cozy and see if we can keep him awake long enough to suck."

This maneuver accomplished a few swallows of nourishment but the baby appeared dazed and succumbed to sleep again far too soon. "We'll give him a bit more time, then we'll try again?" encouraged Damie.

Miryam was too tired herself to put up much of an argument but lay back and closed her eyes, opening them a moment later to say, "Thank you, Damie. I do so appreciate you being here." She reached out to touch the dark, wrinkled hand and held tightly for a long minute before closing her eyes again.

Damie left the baby in her arms and went back to the porch. Rohan had to untangle himself from the clinging boy to stretch his long body. He'd been in the same position way too long. Not knowing what to do with him, he left him on the steps and said, "I'll be back in a little while," and went into the house.

"Ezra?" Damie whispered, taking him aside, "that child isn't sucking, and I think there's just something not right. There's no ambition in him, I'm afraid. You might want to examine him. I know what the old folks say, but I hope you know something more useful, else he won't make it very long."

As he approached the bed Rohan's heart was weighted in turmoil. How could he be a father to this baby? The child was still nestled against his mother, but Miryam was awake again. It seemed that sleep eluded her. She motioned for him to come and sit on the bed. Then she waited for him to speak. He looked closely at the baby as he slept, noting that, along with his dark hair, and a striking squareness of the jaw, his tiny body was stocky and muscular even now. His own build was lanky and angular, as was Jon's. "E'eryone will see he's nae mine."

"Can't you prove them wrong?" Miryam said quietly. "Can't you raise him, and teach him, and love him anyway? He will be as much yours as Jon is. You must show by your way with him that he belongs to you."

Rohan could hear horses rounding the bend at full gallop. He got up to see who it was, "Must be the doctor." As he came out of the house, he saw that Jon was in the seat beside the doctor. He had not realized how much he'd been hoping for his son to make it home for the birthing, how much he needed the boy's steadfast optimism in the face of the ordeal they had come through and the ordeal they now plainly faced. Rohan made an enormous effort, in greeting them, to smile. "Tis a boy an' all's well."

The doctor shook his hand heartily upon hearing the news. "So you have another son?"

"A son? Aye... a son." Rohan's attempt at enthusiasm lacked a certain quality of joy, the doctor thought. His demeanor was stand-offish at best, even with Jon, but the boy came to him and grasped him by the shoulders, while the doctor retrieved his bag from under the seat.

"It's good to be home, Da." Jon grinned. "Did you birth the baby yourself?"

"Ach nae, this fellow, Ezra, did a fine job. He's a doctor, too." Rohan's weariness caught up with him but he rallied enough to make introductions all around and say, "Doc, ye can go on in."

The doctor went to check on his patients, and father and son embraced, Rohan holding his son dear. Then Jon broke away, pulling his father to the doctor's wagon, exclaiming, "Look here at my dog, Da. Remember I wrote you about her? Sass is her name, cause she likes to talk back at me."

The pup showed signs of growing into a fair sized dog. As Jon began to untie her from the back of the wagon seat she licked his hands and whined to be let loose. "I didn't want to take any chances with her since she's never been here before. Thought she might jump out and start cha-sin' a rabbit. So what do you think of her? Da?"

Though he didn't know it, Rohan's jaw was set in a grim line. John pretended not to notice as he took Sass through her repertoire of tricks. "She knows the names of everything in the tack room and she'll bring you just what you ask her for! She won't chew on the leather either, I made sure of that! You should have seen her when she was little. She tried real hard and learned real quick!

"Da? ... Da, are you hearing me at all?"

"Oh," Rohan stammered, returning to the present. "Wha' are ye sayin'?"

"Never mind, I was just telling you about Sass."

"She's a fine dog, son." Rohan said absently, ruffling her ears, then he turned and walked a few steps toward the house, but hesitated to go further. He turned to Jon, motioning for him to walk with him along the line of the picket fence. The boy waited, as he'd learned to do long ago, knowing that to try to pull a conversation from his father was like trying to pull a maple sapling from the ground. It would be of no avail to try. Da spoke only when he chose to and no sooner.

Finally Rohan shared his dilemma. He knew what he should say and do for the new child. He still didn't know if he could actually do it, but he needed to set the boundary lines in the right places for Jon. "This bairn, he looks nae a thin' like us. I expect ye may ha' thought on tha' already... Folks are gang' t' say thin's aboot him tha'll hurt. But I will nae ha' him shamed an' mocked." Rohan was finally coming mentally to grips with this reality, but not yet emotionally. "He's oors t' watch o'er, t' protect. Can ye do tha'?"

"Yessir. I think I understand." Jon wanted to quit the subject. "Can I see Ma now? And the wee bairn?"

"As soon as the doc's through."

"What's his name, Da?"

"Aye, his name... Ye'd best ask your Ma. I'm nae hand at tha'."

Rohan and Jon exchanged the necessary words about the morning chores. Since the baby had arrived in a whirlwind, nothing had as yet been accomplished. Jon set to his work – to milk Miss Wilhelmina, gather eggs and spread some feed in the hen yard, and gather wood to get the stove fired up for a proper hot meal. There were many more mouths to feed today.

After a fair while the doctor emerged, to say that the patients were well, but to Ezra he spoke privately, "You have seen how he doesn't eat and doesn't cry?"

Ezra nodded.

"I can't actually see anything wrong. Do you have any thoughts as to what to do for him?"

"I believe that the first and foremost thing we must do is to pray," Ezra responded, after giving brief thought to medical answers.

Their eyes met. Ezra caught Damie's attention, and the three bowed their heads briefly, then agreed to continue along that line.

The doctor gave Rohan directions as to what he must do to for the next few days. It had been, as they both admitted, a long time since there had been a baby in the house.

"When folks hear that the baby has come, they'll be bringing you food and wanting to sit and visit. If you or Miryam is tired, tell them, very nicely of course, to come back at another time. Yawning conspicuously is helpful. It's all right to do that. If folks are coughing, tell them I said to cover their noses and mouths with a kerchief. It's important. Blame it all on me if they get uppity. Change the nappies every time they're wet or messy, no matter how often. Wash his bottom with a clean cloth every time. If his bottom is red, use bag balm on it. Keep the dirty nappies in a bucket of water outside. Outside! Do you usually help Miryam do the washing ?"

"She does the scrubbin', but I do the carryin'..."

"You will do it all for her, but don't wash the nappies with the rest. The water must be extra hot. Boil them for ten minutes! Hear me? Ten. Then rinse them three times with more boiling water. The soap is very harsh on the baby's skin."

"Aye," Rohan replied, but did not think he could remember it all.

What was stuck in his mind was Ezra's question of him, "Do you hate this child?"

Jon stepped up and said, "I heard it all, Doc. We'll do as you said."

"Miriam will want him circumcised?" Doc asked.

"I didna e'en gi'e it a thought," Rohan answered, "but I expect so."

"I'll be back in a week to do it." With those instructions completed, he climbed into his buggy and rattled away, leaving Rohan, Jon, Ezra, Mr. Dennis, Damie and the boy to ponder the next few hours together.

The small boy had returned to his silent, isolated stone-faced little self when Rohan left him to see to Miryam. Seeing Rohan unoccupied, he was again at his side. When Rohan made to move toward the house he found he was anchored by thirty some pounds of waif holding onto his shirt tail. The big black eyes filled, then overflowed with tears when he got Rohan's attention.

"*A nighean*, did ye think I'd forget your breakfast, laddie? Come in the hoose noo wi' us, eh?" Rohan's big arms lifted the tiny boy up to perch on his back and they all went in to talk about the situation.

"Weel, it seems I ha' an appendage." Rohan began as he took a seat at the table. As unaccustomed to making conversation as he was, he took on the role of host with as much grace as he could gather up. He didn't want the boy to feel rejected, given his obvious state of distress, but even if his kitchen skills were excellent, it would be difficult to make much of a meal while attached at the hip to an approximately three year old child.

Damie and Ezra proposed that they could put together enough of a meal for them all by combining their own food stores and the MacVoy's. This settled, Ezra procured the food he had laid out for their meal outside, which had been untouched in the hubbub, and brought it in. All together they had eggs scrambled with cheese, sausage, and bread with fresh butter and jam, and strong hot tea. Jon left, then, to continue his chores. As they ate, they assessed the situation at hand. Miryam dozed on and off, but offered her comments when she felt it was important.

"First off, wha' shall we do aboot this wee fiend here?" smiled Rohan, stroking the boy's fuzzy, debris strewn head. He had grown fond of the child whose face lay buried in his shirtfront in an emotionally drained sleep known only to those who have been to the very farthest edge of life and survived the journey.

"I think we need t' gi'e him a proper name. He feels alone, an' abandoned t' be certain. We dinna ken his circumstances but surely he canna feel tha' he has any worth wi'oot a name."

Mr. Dennis spoke up, "I agree. Even if his folks might be found later, he should have a name until then, or until he speaks and will tell us what his true name is. Does anyone have a suggestion?"

Silence reigned as each one thought of friends and relatives whose names they admired, of famous men, of inspirational stories or sensational fables. Damie, though, had a heart for the prophetic. "Isaac," she said softly. A sweet, knowing smile played at the corners of her mouth. "Isaac – it's Hebrew, it means *he laughs*."

Miryam spoke drowsily from her nest of bedclothes. "...from the Torah..."

Damie's eye's widened considerably, "Miryam is Jewish?"

Miryam spoke again, "Yes."

Damie went to her bed and sat down, reaching for Miryam's hand. "Miryam," she said, "it is not by chance that we have come today. Not only has your child been safely delivered into this world by Ezra, but I am to believe that I've been brought here to say the words which should be said for him."

"What words do you mean?"

"I was once a slave, owned by a Jewish family. I cared for their children every day of their lives. On the day that each was born, the Prayer for a Newborn Child was always said for them. We can say it together today."

Miryam was overjoyed, but a shadow crossed her face. "I have never heard of that. Jon was not prayed for in that way either. Could we pray for him today, too," she asked eagerly. Mama and Papa would be so pleased.

Damie hesitated for just a moment, but replied, "I can't think why not. God's time is not like ours. Why wouldn't a prayer for a grown son be effective now? And why not for our small Isaac as well?"

"Would you get Jon, Rohan?" asked Miryam.

When Jon came into the house he remembered to ask Miryam what she would name his new brother. She replied, "Joseph Samuel." It was customary to name a Jewish child after someone in his family. Miryam remembered her father saying that he had relatives by those names. Damie asked Miryam, "Do you know what Joseph means?"

Miryam did not.

"It means *he will add*," replied Damie. "This child will add something to your family, something good, to be sure. Do you know what Samuel means?"

"No, I don't know that one either."

"It means *I have asked God for him*," answered Damie.

Miryam's face took on a triumphant glow, "I did that, didn't I Roh?"

Rohan wasn't quite willing to respond verbally, but nodded his assent.

Damie began solemnly when they were all assembled around the bed.

"This prayer, or a variation of it, has been said for generations of children. I'm afraid I can't say it in Hebrew, but I'll say the English. I'll change it a tad bit so that it applies to all three of these young men – this infant Joseph, this handsome Jonathan, and this boy Isaac:

> *Lord Adonai, We are humbled*
> *by the awesome power of this moment.*
> *From life has been brought forth life.*
> *Through Your love have they been fashioned,*
> *these children of love.*
> *May these children be a blessing to all they meet,*
> *and may they count us among their blessings as well."*

Chapter 20

Before an Amen could be said, Isaac gave a resounding wail which startled everyone. He was dutifully checked for an open pin, but when that was not found to be the cause of his eruption, Miryam held out her hands for him. His piercing cries were demanding milk, she said, for her full breasts were suddenly flooding her nightgown.

"Give him to me, hurry!"

The men, except Rohan, turned away to give her time to get discreetly arranged. As quickly as she could, she opened her bodice and directed a frantically rooting baby to her nipple.

"He's hungry! He's really hungry now!" She drew the sheet up over her exposed shoulder and grinned at Damie!

"You were right. It's not just by chance that you came today!"

Everyone gathered around, on the bed or pulling chairs close by and shared stories of births and families, some odd family names, and happy times they'd known. Damie had actually known a a circuit riding preacher who had named his daughter 'Encyclopedia Brittanica'! Miryam realized that they had become almost like a family and yet she did not know Mr. Dennis's given name. It was Edwin, he volunteered, but admitted he was named after his auntie Edwinna. They all laughed in empathy at his reddening face.

Rohan was even more reticent than usual, absorbed in thought concerning the dark haired newborn in his wife's arms, and the dark skinned boy in his own. His life was getting complicated. The one new child was his responsibility, and he wanted none of it. The other one was not really connected to him but, at the moment, seemed as if he was permanently attached. Isaac slept like one who had lived through the trauma of war.

He was to Rohan quite beautiful in his repose. "Wha' strange journeys life does ta'e us upon." he thought to himself.

At last hunger and the necessities to move about and to visit the privy required everyone to disperse. Rohan laid the sleeping Isaac on Jon's bed. Ezra, Jon, Edwin and Rohan would make up beds of straw and blankets in the barn with the smithy fire going through the night for warmth. Damie and Isaac would share Jon's bed, and Miryam and Joseph would have room to sleep and nurse and change nappies in their bed. Damie would be close by to help Miryam with her ablutions and there would be no men in the house to be concerned with for modesty's sake.

Sure enough, there were callers the very next day. The Himmels were the first. Rohan and Jon were in the yard dealing, not too happily, with the laundry. Rohan's face was harrowed by the smell of the bucket where he was sloshing the nappies. Gus thumped Rohan heartily on the back and offered a cigar. He accepted it to be polite, but since he had never gotten the habit, he could not take more than a puff without erupting into agonized coughing. Seeing the spectacle cured Jon of wanting anything to do with a congratulatory smoke. The men were soon into the laundry again, trying to make light of the stink of the baby's many contributions to the day's task.

Ezra, Edwin, Damie and Isaac had gone to town to see Reverend MacClure about placing Isaac with a family, and to put out inquiries for finding information about his own family.

Ava went into the house with her heart in her throat. She alone, of all the folks who knew the MacVoy family, would be their steadfast advocate against the flow of gossip that would soon follow. She came to Miryam's side and looked at the sleeping mother and the swaddled child. "So peaceful," she thought. "O Lord Gott, may You to dem de peace from abuff giff. Dey surely vill it be needink!"

Miryam stirred, saw Ava standing there and smiled. "Ava, it's so good to see you! Look here, he is so beautiful!" She slowly uncovered the baby so as not to wake him from his infant dreams.

Ava's breath came with a sharp intake. "Oh!"

Miryam understood completely. "I know, I know – but look at this sweet face. He is the answer to my prayer for another child." She watched Ava's face as she came close to peek at the wee one.

Her heart, too, was won quickly. "Surely he precious iss! I never de beauty uff a baby's face can enuff see. Unt look at de tiny finkers! Unt de button nose!"

Then Ava grew pensive. Thoughts were flying in her brain. "You to de udder folks in de villich are needink to an explanation giff."

Miryam rose to his defense quickly. "I will just ignore their remarks. I will not pay them any attention."

"But he vill not ignored be. He too different iss. But I haff of something yust tought!"

"Ava, it will be all right!"

"Yust to me you listen please. Diss so easy iss, unt easily unterstoot. It for him, vitt his dark looks, so different from Rohan, vill a coverink be."

She went on to explain her idea.

"My family from Pennsylvania to de vest came." Ava went on to tell that her grandparents had known of the Scots-Irish who lived there who were called the Black Irish. "Dey, of the skin unt hair, very dark vere. Not as dark as de slaves like, but surely not de paleness of you like."

"Black Irish? I never heard of such people." replied Miryam. "Who would believe that? Besides, Rohan is Scottish, not Irish."

"Very true it iss! Dese people Scottish vere, too. But to dose who no better knew, dey Irish vere called. De story alvays told vass dat de Spanish soldiers who to Scotland came, married, and vitt de Scottish ladies de dark haired bebees made. Dat like your little one could be! It could a vay to protect your wee child be, don't you tink so?"

"I could not lie about that, Ava."

"You vill not to lie. You, de same story dat I haff told, to anyvon who qvestions, vill tell! I myself many times have seen it in my own neighbors! Eefen in de same families de dark hair vitt von child iss, unt vitt anudder de red hair iss. It all de time happens."

"It could be a way to stop rumors, I suppose. For Joseph's sake, I'll remember that."

"Yoseph?" Ava spoke the name again, "Yoseph! A very nice sound it giffs. A happy name!"

It was in the warmish mid afternoon of the following day when the Dennis carriage arrived at the MacVoy ranch again. Rohan was harvesting the dried nappies from the picket fence where they had slumbered to dry overnight. He was more than glad to see the entourage, and especially Isaac. Even though he was not feeling paternal toward Joseph, something had awakened in him while holding Isaac in his arms that first day.

He welcomed Ezra and Edwin, shaking hands, and extending his hand to Damie to help her down from the carriage. To Isaac, Rohan opened his arms. Isaac settled very naturally into his embrace, laying his head on Rohan's shoulder as if he had not fully rested since he was last in his arms. Ezra confirmed that this was indeed the case.

There had been a family willing to take the boy, but the young child had dug in his heels and would not be removed from Damie, Ezra and Edwin. Promises were made. Threats were considered. But no one had the heart to forcibly separate Isaac from the only people he actually knew to be his friends. Even though he still had not spoken, he knew that he was safe with them, and thirty-odd pounds of muscle and determination was enough to convince the adults that he had to stay with them.

"We're on our way home, but I wanted to stop to see how Miryam and young Joseph are faring. How are they?" inquired Ezra. "Is the nursing still going well?"

"Weel, I canna say so from direct experryence, p'rhaps you'd best ask Miryam. She's complained o' some soreness." He motioned Damie and Edwin to the rocking chairs on the porch, "Please make yourselves comfortable. I'll put the kettle on."

Ezra went to Miryam's bedside where a chair stood. Jon and Rohan had taken turns helping with the baby while she tried to relieve some of her soreness. "Nothing seems to help," she said. "I've massaged here where there's a lump, but it's hard and hot, and it hurts even to touch it."

"Is the other breast fine?"

"Yes," replied Miyam, "what is it?"

"It's mastitis. A clogged milk duct. Nothing to worry about this early on, it's not infected."

Rohan had been standing nearby, holding Isaac, listening. Miryam's health was his foremost concern.

Ezra turned to him. "When the kettle is hot, make some compresses. Damie can tell you how.

"Miryam, keep a nice warm compress on the lumpy area for ten minutes every hour. It will ease the pain and the clog will break down with the heat. You can keep nursing as usual. You might want to rearrange pillows so Joseph doesn't put pressure on the tender place. Try to stay in bed as much as possible. Rest is important for any new mother. Will you?"

"She will," Rohan answered for her.

In the kitchen, Roh finally convinced Isaac to shift around to his back and ride there with his arms around Rohan's neck. But even so, the boy's cumbersome presence presented difficulties as Rohan tried to get the tea for the company and fill a tray to take to the porch. "Isaac," he said, peering over his own shoulder, "might I put ye doon so's I can get some food ready?"

The large black eyes said no.

"But laddie, I've only *twa* hands an' e'en though you're small, you're becomin' a wee bit heavy t' carry. Hoo aboot if ye stand aside me on this chair an' keep watch o'er all tha' I do? Ye can learn hoo t' make tea? You'll surely be needin' t' ken tha' someday, eh?"

Isaac consented to being close enough to touch Rohan at any given moment.

The kettle was rumbling. The teapot and cups, the sugar bowl, and spoons were laid out on the tray.

"What else are we wantin', Isaac? Aye, some cream! Come an' see where 'tis!" Isaac climbed down from the chair and knelt down to where Rohan was putting his arm through the door in the floor where the wheel brought cold water up from the *burn* into the trough for keeping their milk cold. Rohan retrieved the jug of cream and watched Isaac's amazed face as he pondered the invention. Then Isaac reached down into the frigid water himself, drawing his hand back quickly in surprise at how cold the water was. Rohan gave a loud guffaw.

Ezra continued to visit with Miryam, asking after her well being and Joseph's. Rohan and Isaac served Edwin and Damie hot tea on the porch. Jon finished his chores and joined them. As supper time came near, Rohan realized that it was up to him to put a meal on the table but he didn't quite know where to begin. He took Jon aside and asked him, "Hoo many eggs ha' we got?"

"Four, I think."

"Weel that willna do for a quick supper…" He pondered what Miryam usually had on hand. "Then gang t' the soddy an' look for a large piece o' lamb, an' while you're there, look in the root cellar for tatties. Aboot ten o' 'em, an' bring *twa* jars o' anythin' else t' fill in the chinks wi'. Isaac? Will ye help Jonnie here t' carry the tatties back t' me? Are ye strong enow?" Isaac was about to protest until he understood that he was helping Rohan, then he was eager to comply.

Rohan grabbed up some wood for the stove and went into the house. He was uncertain how to put it all together but would do his best. "Miryam?" he said softly at her bedside. She did not stir. "Miryam? Might ye be awake?" he said a bit louder.

"Yes, but don't wake Joseph please, I just got him to sleep."

"I've got t' feed e'ryone. Hoo do I cook a leg o' lamb?"

With some blackened pots soaking on the stove, having mostly succeeded at cooking his first meal for a crowd, Rohan sat with Isaac on his lap, just listening to the conversation. It was well understood that Miryam was not yet up to cooking or housework. Ezra assessed that she might be anemic, being near forty and having a child. She was ashen and weak, with pale gums and fingernails. She could barely stay awake long enough to feed Joseph. Usually, Roh or Jon gathered him up when he cried, changed his diaper, and handed him to Miryam to feed him. Later someone burped him and laid him to sleep in his cradle. She had not been outside the house in three days. A chamber pot was employed with much muttering behind the curtain around her bed, and the bowl and a pitcher of warm water was all the bath she could manage.

Meanwhile, Rohan would need to be fixing the only foods he knew how to, eggs, *parritch,* pancakes, potatoes, and shaving off bits of the roast for every meal. There would always be a goodly supply of milk. Jon had thus far managed most of the chores but would need some assistance with those that were typically two-man jobs before too long.

Jon caught Edwin's attention as Rohan's head sank to his chest and a faint snore began. Damie tried to lift Isaac from his arms but the boy's resistance was defiantly strong. Ezra broached the subject that had been on his mind since the recently failed attempt to place Isaac. "Isaac has taken quite a shine to your father, Jon."

"I think the feeling is mutual. What will you do with him now?"

"Well, I had a thought. Before your father wakes up, let me see what you think about it."

"I think I'm having the same thought, but it might have some drawbacks. You go ahead though, sir."

Ezra cleared his throat. "Could he stay with you? I know it's an imposition, but is there any advantage?"

Jon interjected, "Da is happier with Isaac around…"

"He could be more work for you though, and that's the last thing you need right now."

Damie got unobtrusively up to clear the dishes. As she did so, she spoke quietly, "If I might offer a suggestion…"

Edwin looked up. "Damie, are you sure?"

Damie nodded. "Ezra, your father and I have talked a little about this. Just thinking… It seems as if I could be of help, at least for a while." She hurried on before much objection could arise. "I can certainly keep everyone fed and clothed and keep house, and care for Miryam until she's on her feet, and of course the baby – well that would just be a joy for me."

Everyone's eyes shifted, each checking the reaction of the others around the table. No one had a word to say against the idea.

Again, Edwin asked, "Are you sure you want to do this?"

"You don't need me on your travels, do you? Of course not! You only brought me along so I wouldn't be sitting alone on my porch waiting to die, didn't you?"

"Well, I wouldn't put it that way. You're a far cry from dying, Damie. We wanted you to come with us for your company."

"I do know that, dear. But wasn't there just a slight thought that you didn't want me to be alone?"

"Yes, there was that."

"Well, if I stayed here, I wouldn't be alone and I would be doing someone some actual good at the same time. It's been a while since I could say I'd been of any real use to another soul! I want to be doing something for a change!"

"Is anyone going to ask me what I think?" asked Miryam from the bed. They all turned in the direction of the curtained off bed. "If so, I'd be much obliged if Damie would stay for a while. Sometimes I'm not sure which end of this baby to feed and which end to put the nappie on."

This produced a round of suppressed snorts and titters, but Rohan's head remained lazily down on his chest with Isaac still snuggled in his arms. They talked quietly for a while voicing the possibilities.

Only Jon raised the final question, "So we're happy, but what if Da doesn't like the idea?"

"Save your breath t' cool your dinner wi'," came Rohan's response. "Let's ha' the wee mannie stay here. Tis all right wi' me."

"You've been playin' possum, Da," hooted Jon. The others shared the laughter.

"So, hoo long do ye think it'll be 'til Miryam is herself again? I dinna mind sleepin' in the barn for a few weeks, but if twill be longer, we can make some changes."

Ezra replied with some hesitation. "You can never tell with anemia. I'd have to guess a few months."

"Weel then, let's get us a plan."

Edwin and Ezra departed the next morning to attend to their business obligations, promising to stop and visit whenever they were in the vicinity. Damie shed a few tears, but was truly happy with the decision she had made to stay, and Isaac was thrilled!

With the addition of Damie and Isaac to the MacVoy's household, friends and neighbors were invited to come on the following weekend to put an addition on the back of the house. Where years of sharing the same large room had been sufficient before, the need for more space required some thought. Miryam and Rohan would occupy the new bedroom addition, which also had an alcove for Joseph, and a store room. Damie would have the privacy of their former curtained area for herself, while Jon would keep his bed but with the addition of a trundle for Isaac.

At first the plan was to build the foundation for the new room right up to the window level with the readily available stones and a lime mortar. Then they would make trips to the sparse woodlands to find trees for the wall frames. This was not highly successful, so they solicited their neighbors to bring as many boards as could be spared with them to the raising. They spent their days pulling more stone from the ground to build the addition as high as possible, thus using the precious wood for only the roofing and window frames. These were built on the ground and added, by means of scaffolding, piece by piece, to the house.

Miryam enjoyed making curtains for their own new windows. She could easily contribute by sewing while still bedridden. It had been her special request to have two of them. The glass was brought out by Ralph and Bettina for the grand finale of the project. Moving day was a hustle and bustle, but achieved a much needed change in the crowded main room. Moving Miryam's trunk and their chest of drawers to the new bedroom made a much larger area for the family to share. A new smaller bed was built for Damie and placed in the corner where theirs had been so that she could pull the drape around herself at night. Ava and Gus donated a chair and footstool from their overstuffed house for Damie to relax in the evenings.

A semblance of order began to fall into place as Damie cooked much more interesting and nourishing meals than Rohan would be able to muster up. Her contribution to the care of young Joseph was almost seamlessly meshed with her care of Miryam. Miryam's strength was not improving rapidly, but she did gain a bit each week as Damie encouraged her to get out of bed for a little while longer each day to sit in a chair and do a few kitchen chores with her. After a month, if the weather was warm enough, Miryam finally was encouraged to go outdoors to sit on the porch and enjoy the sunshine. She was then able to manage by herself for a morning while Damie did the baking or worked in the vegetable garden.

Joseph's cradle had been moved to the porch for the afternoon as well. As they rocked and visited together, Damie asked if she might go to church on the coming Sunday. Since Joseph's birth and Miryam's confinement, the family had ceased their habit of attending weekly services. Damie wondered if perhaps they might be ready to return to church soon. It had always been part of her life and was sorely missed.

"Why yes, I guess I hadn't thought much on it, but Rohan and Jon should certainly be going back now and I will in a few weeks. I'm glad you mentioned it, Damie. You've been such a help to me in so many ways, I want you to be happy here, too."

"I've been thinking on Joseph, and how his name means that he will add something to your family. What do you think that might be?"

Miryam smiled a slow smile and looked at her baby, then up at Damie. "He's given me such joy. I had lost that part of my life. I wake up eager to see what he will do each day, just waiting for his smile. Whether it's just a gas bubble or not, I can't get enough."

"What about Jon and Rohan? Do you think he adds something to their lives?"

"Jon, yes. Rohan, no. Roh is taken up with Isaac. He doesn't notice Joseph at all. But that will change, don't you think?"

Damie nodded, pondering. "Do you know the story of Joseph in the Bible?"

"No, I was only taught prayers in Hebrew and then what they mean in English. I know traditions, but not why we do them. The Torah is our holy book, but I truly don't know anything else that's written in it." She thought about that for a long moment, "That's very sad, isn't it?"

Damie nodded, and resumed her train of thought. "The story of Joseph's life may give you some idea of what he will bring to your family." Damie, ventured further into Miryam's thoughts. "When you go to your church, do you believe what is said about God there?"

Miryam did not want to offend Damie, but felt she could be honest in her answer. "I don't know about the gods they speak of. Are they anything like *Adonai*?"

"Let me tell you the story and you let me know what you think about it. Does that set well with you?"

"I'll listen. I want to know more. I don't know what I believe in… so please, do go on."

Damie settled herself more comfortably into her rocking chair, fluffing the back cushion 'til it was just right, and cleared her throat. The tradition of passing the time with good conversation and wisdom from generation to generation was well honored in her people. She was an accomplished story teller, she had been told, and she wanted to do her best for Miryam.

Her narration began. "Joseph's mother had passed on, you see, so he was the baby of the family, and the favored son of his father. There were other brothers, but the father gave only Joseph a beautiful robe. This brought much jealousy among his siblings, who resented their father's unmerited blessing on the boy. One day the father sent Joseph out with a message of greeting to his brothers as they tended their flocks in the desert.

"The brothers saw the opportunity to get rid of their bothersome little brother but mercy intervened and he was sold instead into slavery in Egypt. The brothers killed one of their sheep and put its blood on Joseph's beautiful robe. They presented it to their father as evidence that their younger brother had been slain by a wild beast and was lost. His father wept in great sorrow.

"Joseph became a slave in a faraway land, but he had faith in God. Sure enough, when the time was right, God's plan was fulfilled that Joseph was made a ruler of the country to which he had been carried off. God revealed to him there would be a famine. So at God's instruction, Joseph arranged for the crops to be stored in years of plenty so that there would be food for the years of famine.

"The famine was so vast that even Joseph's brothers had to come from very far away to buy food. Joseph did not bear them ill but forgave them. The family was reunited. Joseph knew that what was planned as evil, God had turned to good. The very plot on his life was instead the reason that so many lives were saved.

"Just as that family was reunited, the presence of your new son may lead to the uniting of your family."

Chapter 21

As he grew, the infant Joseph captured the hearts of his mother and brother, of Damie and Isaac. Jon heard the story of the Black Irish and understood the need to employ it. He took delight in the tiny baby, offering to hold him as his mother prepared meals or did other chores around the house. He never tired of rocking little Joseph to sleep, and even learned to change the wet nappies, though he never ventured to change the messed ones. He was a good brother to the sweet natured baby and caused many a smile to steal across his mother's face as she watched them together. Jon dandled, and doted upon, and deeply loved young Josey - but Rohan did not.

Damie took up the slack as best she could by diverting Rohan's attention to a hearty meal, a commentary on the books she had read, or by telling one of her many stories as they sat together in the evening by the fire. Her ease with conversation helped him to adjust to Joseph's presence with less awkwardness.

When they tell me that my early years were difficult, I don't remember that at all. Jon was my brother, but also my playmate and as close to being a father as he could be, determined not to ever let me suffer being unwanted. Though he saw what the others all did, he also saw my need to be held, and my innocence in spite of the violence my genetic father had done. Isaac played with me, too, sometimes giggling quietly, but still never spoke.

Da never said "I love you," but apparently said mean, hurtful things instead. I do not remember them. Usually, when we hear angry, toxic words spoken, we end up believing them. In the absence of the vital reassurance of real love, we believe that nothing good can survive the hurt and emptiness we feel. Darkness unabated swallows up light.

But once a light, no matter how small, is kindled, the darkness no longer dominates. The light is the focus of our minds. When we purposefully look at the light we are no longer afraid of the darkness. Mama, Damie, Jon and Isaac all shed the light on me that I needed to grow strong. It was the light of their love that protected me from Da's anger and grief.

Rohan busied himself with many a chore, some real, some trumped up so as to be unavailable to help with the child. He neither held nor spoke to the baby, but ignored him entirely. He devoted much time and effort to the boy, Isaac, instead. The child was at Roh's side every waking moment, and this soothed him. Gustav, Ava and Ana visited often, with Rosie in tow. Jon and Ana had finally spoken. Each had kept the embers of their initial acquaintance smoldering during the time of Jon's visit east. They took short walks together around the house and kailyard just to be away from the adults.

After supper, the family often sat around the cradle watching the sleeping baby, remembering when other children had been that small, and sharing stories of various childish antics they had witnessed. They delighted in touching his tightly curled fingers, examining his tiny toes. His striking appearance was never spoken of, but keenly felt. Rohan did only what was necessary to keep up appearances, since it was his nature to be a responsible person.

At the kirk, when the congregation saw Roh stand up at the Christening with his wife and his son Jon, silent looks of concern passed from one to another through their friends and neighbors. Some had noticed the drawn look about Rohan over the past months, but now they could just attribute it to the sleepless nights experienced by most parents of infants. Many, however, had been able to keep speculation alive with comments about the dubious heritage of the small dark haired baby in the home of a lanky red-headed Scotsman. The folks in town stared as well at the appearance of Damie and Isaac with the family at church. Little was said to their faces, but the word 'heathens' was overheard more than once. Whispers were rampant and some turned away from the family, largely encouraged by Gertrude Lubbock.

But with the help and prompting of Reverend MacClure, each family member pledged to raise the infant in the love of God, and in the fellowship of the church. Rohan felt that in this ceremony he fulfilled his public obligation. But he often stared at the child, asleep in Miryam's arms. Who was his father? Who was that rogue of a man? How was he to care for a child he could not love? Yet how could he look upon that innocent face and not love him? Instead he felt resentment rise up in him like a flood. He could no longer deny the child's part in his life. He knew that he would have to interact with him sooner or later and it made him rage within.

Rohan sought the company of young Isaac as much as Isaac sought him out. Yet he watched with a stony heart as Josey grew into his first months. He took up too much of Miryam's time! Of course it would have been the same with any infant, but this was not his baby. The endless dirty nappies! The crying in the middle of the night, interrupting his sleep! He couldn't make a noise if the child was napping, and there were times when, even though she tried not to upset him, Miryam had to ask Rohan to help her with something concerning young Joseph.

He was an easygoing babe, as they come, but whenever he did cry, Rohan became unhinged. He was harsh and impatient. Rohan complained that the baby was annoying. It was hard for him not to lose his temper completely.

Isaac watched with confusion as Roh changed from a contented companion and friend to a cantankerous grump. He felt secure as part of the family, but did not understand the dynamics of their interactions with the baby, who was often quickly whisked away when his father's mood flared wild. Though still a small child himself, Isaac learned to climb onto Roh's lap when he sensed tension in the room. There he would play at pulling on his beard or making patty-cake motions with Roh's big hands.

Their favorite game was 'creep moosie," when Isaac would pretend to fall asleep on the settle and Rohan would walk his fingers up the boy's leg like a mouse until the suspense and tickling could be tolerated no longer. The child would pretend to wake up, making wide-eyed surprised faces. This always brought gales of laughter from their audience. If Rohan was particularly ill natured, Isaac would in turn play the little mousie game with him, going up his broad chest to his neck and then into his ear. The desired effect was to make the testy father cease from his dark mood and promise to find something for them to do together.

Near midday in the late summer, Mr. Dennis and Ezra drove their carriage into the yard. Accompanying them was another Negro. Sass barked gaily to welcome them, so Isaac left his perch on Roh's side at the workbench to see what was causing the to-do. No sooner had he reached the doorway than he shrieked and ran to the carriage. The stranger leaped from the still moving vehicle to meet the child, pulling him into his arms.

"Papa! Papa! Papa! Papa! Papa!" the boy repeated joyfully as he pounded his flat hands on his father's chest.

"Nathan, is it really you? I thought you were lost forever!" wept his father.

Rohan stood in the open barn doorway, surveying the scene with a heart in turmoil. He could not keep this child. This boy who had kept him from falling into a bottomless well was no longer his own. The joy he saw was overpowering though and he had to shed a tear at the wondrous reunion the father and son were experiencing.

Miryam and Damie had come to stand on the porch and realized the momentous occasion. They wept openly as Isaac's voice was heard for the first time since he came into their lives in the spring.

Isaac suddenly broke away from his father and rushed to Rohan, pulling him out of the barn. "Come! Come!" the child implored. He brought the two men face to face. They looked at each other and then down at Isaac. The boy wondered at their bewildered countenances. They should know what to do! He waited. Because no words were spoken as yet, he took one of his father's hands and one of Rohan's and brought them together in greeting. He waited again.

"I see tha' you *twa* ken one another," ventured the Scotsman quietly. A slow smile played at his mouth.

"Yes," replied the man, "we certainly do. I am Nathan's father, William."

"William?"

"Yes, I have no other proper name. I was a slave, given only something to call me to work by."

"Pleased t' make your acquaintance. I'm Rohan an' my wife, Miryam is there on the porch, wi' our friend, Miss Damie. Would you come in an' sit wi' us? Tell us aboot you an' your son?"

"The entourage poured into the house, where glasses of cold water were served, and some muffins procured from the cupboard.

"Tell them your story, Willie," prompted Edwin. "I'm sure they're wanting to know."

William hesitated. It was not going to be easy to tell with a small boy listening, but he would say what he could without upsetting his son too much.

"I will make it short so as not to frighten the young one," he said while nodding toward Nathan as he perched near the muffin plate.

"We, my wife and I, Nathan, and our baby daughter, Emmaline, were in a small wagon train north of here when a band of ruffians attacked us. I suppose it was because we were all former slaves that they thought we would be easily overcome. But we were prepared for such incidents and managed with a few shots to chase them off. It should have ended there, but they returned after nightfall."

Willie stopped and looked out the window over the sink, without speaking for several minutes.

"Well, the long and short of it is that some of the folks we traveled with were k... they perished." He used the word to spare his son's ears. The bandits were drunken or they'd have done more, but they didn't find those who hid among the supply wagons. My wife was spared, and my children. But since I was among those visible, I was shot. Just a nick, but it scared the daylights out of me. They tied my feet together and dragged me along the ground until they tired of the game and then cut me loose, thinking I was d-e-a-d.

"It was a blessing they were so drunk, because they didn't do a very good job of it all. I was still breathing when some of our party found me the next day, just a short ways from camp. My friends found a doctor at the next water stop, Little Tree Grove, and left me there to mend, if indeed mending was possible.

"But, the thing was, Nathan got out of the wagon and went to look for me without my wife knowing. She had checked on them when the fighting stopped. They were both asleep. It was only a few hour's journey to our final destination, so she thought it would be wise to continue with the train. She reached our claim, set up our new home camp by herself as best she could, and would return for me when she got word from the Little Tree town doctor that I could travel.

"When the wagon train departed from her it was almost dawn. They helped her get a fire going and took their leave. She was exhausted and decided to let the children sleep on 'til morning. But in the morning she saw that Nathan had awakened and was gone."

William's eyes closed as tears rolled down his face. The listeners could only imagine the trauma of a tiny boy alone in the prairie. They kept silent as they waited for the story to continue.

"My wife was distraught, of course but did not know where to begin to look for him. She called out, searching the area as far as she could every day, carrying Emmaline on her back, but there was no Nathan."

His arms went around the boy then, as much to comfort himself as to benefit the boy.

"It took three weeks before I could ride a horse and join my family. We had to come to accept the fact that Nathan was never coming home."

"But we found him along the road!" interjected Ezra. "And because we asked everyone we came across whether they knew this child, we were leaving a trail to his whereabouts."

"I rode for days, hearing folks say they had seen a boy of Nathan's description who had been lost. I went from town to town, asking about him, sometimes for a week at a time away from home. But after four months I, too, had to give up. It was not until Edwin and Ezra came through Little Tree Grove that I heard again of the small boy who might be my son… And now the story is complete with him sitting here on my lap."

Damie rose from the table and set about quiet meal preparations. She gathered ingredients and made up a stew while the others talked. Miryam kept looking at the faces of her loved ones with new appreciation for their presence, knowing now that the little dark skinned boy who had been so much a part of their lives would no longer be with them. She wondered if Damie would leave as well.

Jon's thoughts ran in the same vein. He watched his father's expressions as tales were told of travel and hardships, joys and new life for William's family, now that Isaac, or Nathan... was found. Rohan's face ran the gamut of emotions as he listened and began to absorb the reality that his tiny shadow would no longer follow him through the movements of his days. Jon saw him well up with unshed tears, blink them away, then set his face in an impassionate, stoic countenance. Soon after, the same thing would happen once again.

Rohan could no longer contain his heart's ache and rose. Excusing himself to some task that would take him away for a while, he left the house and walked to the paddock where a mare and her late-spring foal were grazing. He stood thinking about how in the animal kingdom the parents and their young seem perfectly in tune. The mare would nudge her foal if he wandered too far from her. He would, in turn, come to her for a quick tug of milk, then frolic nearby.

He couldn't quite wrap his thoughts around losing Isaac. He had carried the boy on his shoulders, had tickled him, wrestled with him, dressed him, fed him, tucked him into bed at night with a kiss, sang songs to him, taught him to measure out grain for the horses, let him carry a few cups of water in the heavy bucket to their stalls. He had let him milk Wilhelmina amid squeals of delight when he actually got the milk to flow and grunts of frustration when his efforts left the bucket empty. He felt like an empty bucket himself. How was he to get through the days alone?

Damie strode purposefully across the yard to where he stood. She carried a sleepy Isaac on her hip and wordlessly transferred her warm bundle into his aching arms. Then she left him to come to grips with this new development. Roh's eyes overflowed with the river of hurt that he could no longer hold back.

"*Mo anam cara,* my soul mate, my wee friend..." He buried his face in the child's fuzzy hair and wept until he ran out of tears. Isaac stirred in his arms, looked up into his face and caught a droplet from Rohan's cheek on his tiny finger. He examined it briefly, then licked it off with a grin. This brought a chuckle forth from Roh's broken heart and he hoisted the boy over his shoulder, head and arms in the back, legs waving in the front. He opened the paddock gate and shut it behind him.

He went to the mare and placed Isaac upon her back, keeping his hand near to catch him if he should fall. The boy stroked her as he lay across her back, sharing the experience with a conspiratorial grin at Rohan. It was Roh's way of saying, "You can remember me whene'er you see a beautiful horse. They're strong an' will carry you as I ha' carried you. Dinna forget me, wee bairn, as I willna forget you." Isaac seemed to understand completely.

Jon called from the house that dinner was ready. The company talked into the late hours, made sleeping arrangements for the night, and retired. The small town of Little Tree Grove was a very long day's journey away, but promises were made to gather again and renew the friendships they had just begun.

Come morning, there was more peace found in the hearts of those who would part from each other. The tears still flowed, but were intermixed with heartfelt blessings poured out on loved ones who were not lost, but forever found in memories not to be forgotten. As the carriage bore away the dear friends, Edwin and Ezra, it carried also Damie and Isaac, and their new friend, William. Damie would travel with her family. Isaac - Nathan, would grow strong with his family, fully remembering the shelter he had found in this temporary home.

"God be wi' ye, *mo chridhe*," whispered Rohan as the carriage disappeared from sight over the swell of the land. He turned and wrapped his arm about Miryam's shoulder as they went to the house. There was a new life to start and somehow they both knew they must begin it hand in hand.

Chapter 22

Joseph became a square faced little boy. Rohan saw a keen mind in him and inwardly admired the quick learning ability in the child. But love was withheld, not with malice or aforethought, but because Rohan did not know how to feel it for him, or how to give it, or even if it was there at all. He avoided contact with the child as much as possible, giving verbal direction rather than guiding him by taking the small hands in his own and teaching by doing the chores together as he had done with Jon and Isaac.

Still, Josey adored his father, simply because he was his Da. He tried to copy all the mannerisms of this man who raised him. He seemed to study each detail of speech and gait, but where Rohan took long easy strides, the boy always moved with a jaunty, bouncy step. The child seemed to know that Rohan was guarded in his relationship with him, but he did not mind it much. He was so enveloped in the love showered upon him by his mother and by Jon that he was content to just study Rohan as he worked. He watched and listened and secretly mimicked him, and was rewarded with a large round of applause by those who saw his attempts, but not by his father.

The townspeople had duly noted the boy's appearance from infancy and some remarks had been made behind closed doors. The worst of the gossipers was Bettina's sister, Gertrude Lubbock. She had been crippled with rheumatism for many years and had not managed to weather the storm of her pain gracefully. Her passion was passing on rumor and ill tidings. She felt important in doing so, and this gave her a feeling of accomplishment that kept her mind from settling on her own troubles. If anyone was in a mood to murmur, they went to Gertrude, who would give ear and add fuel to any fire where kindling would catch the flame.

Gertrude had a look that she used to employ frequently to quell any dissenters with her opinions. The look was a hard, cold stare, often directed at Miryam. Whenever their paths crossed, the very air between them became icy with unspoken accusation and innuendo on Gertrude's behalf, and shrinking fear on Miryam's behalf. She wanted no confrontation to darken the life of her small Joseph. Miryam began to cross the street when she saw Gertrude's crippled figure approaching.

Bettina loved her sister dearly and tried to still the wagging tongue, but was largely unsuccessful. As time passed, the talk of Joseph's being an "ugly duckling" was stilled, out of respect for Miryam's reputation, which was above reproach. As Miryam had said on the day of his birth, Josey had been accepted by the community because of the way Roh had treated him in their sight. However, at home, a cold, still, quietness of exceeding formality deepened between the boy and his father. The boy grew strong and sturdy, though remained small of stature. He accepted his father for the man he was, knowing no other. And there were rare times when Rohan wanted to love him. But he could not bring himself to step over the imaginary line he had drawn in the sand of his emotions.

I saw Da as a man whose tongue was tied. He would look at me with words on his heart but no way to say them. I knew that I confused him. I knew that there was something deep in him that needed to be said. But I could never bridge the gap between us, so I looked to Jon for the fathering I wanted, and he supplied what Da was lacking.

They say that when gold is first mined, it has impurities in it which make it appear dull or dirty, but when it is heated, the impurities are separated out, leaving a beautiful, shining lump of pure gold. God uses the heat of our trials and hardships to separate out the impurities from the righteous people that He created us to be. Trials are difficult, even painful, but then we are made clean to be used by the Lord for His purposes, which are wonderful.

Da's trials were too much for him to carry at times. He raged and fumed without rest for months on end. Then, by a miracle, he would have a respite. Had he asked for help, it would have been given, but he would not. Mama and Ava prayed for him long and often. Mama did not understand the prayers, but somehow, with Ava's prompting, she knew that God did. And the scripture written by Peter came into their prayer time regularly - "The Lord is not slack concerning his promise, as some men count slackness; but is longsuffering to us-ward, not willing that any should perish, but that all should come to repentance."[13]

Bettina tossed and turned in her sleep. Gertrude had been ill for months and it seemed that she was not improving a bit. "Oh God," she had prayed before getting into bed, "Please do what is best for her. You know she has been a bitter woman for all these years. Please help her to let go of all her hurts and rest in your arms."

Ralph sat up in bed, startled. "Bettina," he shook her shoulder, "Bettina!"

"Uh! Ralph, I haven't slept well for weeks and now you're waking me in the middle of the night?"

"She'll be all right, Bettina," Ralph assured her. "I've just had a dream about Gertrude."

"Gertrude?" Bettina turned to stare at her husband. "What are you talking about?"

"She is going to be all right."

"Do you mean she'll get well again? How do you know?"

"Well, I don't know that, exactly, but she will not suffer anymore. She's content now."

Bettina sank back into her pillow. "Ralph, I can't make heads nor tails of you right now. Speak up, or I'm going to close my eyes again and try to sleep."

"I've had a dream, and it was God's way of telling me that you don't have to worry about Gertrude anymore. She is in his kingdom, safe and sound."

Bettina threw off her covers, "Do you mean to say she has died?" She was out of the bed in a moment and lighting the candle at her bedside. "I need to get dressed, I need to go over there!"

"I don't know if she has passed yet, I just know that you don't have to worry about her..."

"Then why in the world did you wake me?"

"You were tossing and fretting and grumbling and pleading with God for her. I thought you'd want to know!"

"Oh, well I guess you're right. I have spent all night trying to sleep, and then when I do fall asleep, I dream that she's crying and in pain… So what is it that makes you so sure she's 'content' as you say?"

"I dreamed of her. It was so clear and so plain. She was in a beautiful pool of water. Imagine! She's never been in any body of water larger than her bath! But there she was, and she needed help to get out, so I was to lift her out. I didn't know how to do it because she'd be too heavy for anyone to just lift her straight up. But when I got to her I did just that. There was no weight to her at all!

She was naked… Now don't look at me like that! She was in a little body, like a child's body. And I got a big white sheet and I wrapped her up in it and sat her down in a chair, and she was smiling, so relaxed! She's going to be all right, Bettina. I know it in my heart."

"I hope you're right. It would be a mercy for her to be free of her pains."

"I do believe it was a gift from God to reassure us."

"Then I will believe it as well. Let's try to get some sleep now, I am weary down to my bones."

Chapter 23

For the first time in his life Rohan began to take down the bottle of whiskey from the kitchen shelf frequently. He had always kept a bottle for medicinal use and it usually lasted a few years. But this everyday use was becoming a problem. When he had drunk too much, he sang all the drinking songs he knew at full volume, until it was time for Josey to go to bed, at which time Miryam had to send Rohan out to the barn.

"Haven't I asked you nicely to stop your bellowing? You might be surprised that the walls have ears." No doubt he was only trying to drown his sorrows, but there came a time when it backfired on him. Though Miryam had pleaded with him to stop his singing before it was repeated, one Sunday morning they descended from the wagon and were near the portal of the church when Josey began to sing with gusto about the "Little Brown Jug." Rohan vowed to use only appropriate words and songs from then on.

Winter arrived with its usual gusto as fall had lingered just enough to let Miryam gather in her pumpkins and apples and the last of the carrots. There was a light dusting of snow on the ground. The trees were bare, but the sky was a deep blue. A pair of cardinals that were perched in her tree looked in the window. They seemed to be quite interested in watching Miryam lift the freshly baked cookies from the oven. As they peered in at her, Miryam thought, "How strange I must seem to them, hiding behind this glass. But perhaps they know that I need to see them today. Perhaps *Adonai* has sent them to remind me that He is has made us all and sustains us all, whether we have wings or hands."

"Josey," she called. "Do you smell something delicious? Come and see!" Miryam treasured her Joseph. She cupped her small boy's face lovingly, putting her thumbs into his chubby cheek dimples. He munched his cookie and gave her a bright smile. "We could plant potatoes in your dimples, you know." She kissed his nose and said to him, "It's getting on time for supper. Would you please go find your father?" She bundled the boy in his warm duds and unceremoniously whooshed him out of the door. "Tell him to come in and wash up for dinner."

"Dada? Where are you Da?" called Joseph in his little voice. "Da? Da?"

Rohan was at the edge of the woods and heard the boy calling to him but could not bring himself to answer. He was not the boy's Dada, and he never would be. He had put up with all he could from the boy's endless store of love, but he would not let him call him Da. Finally, he bellowed out. "Boy! Come here t' me right noo!"

Josey ran as quickly as he could on his short legs to where his father stood waiting. Only Josey really knew what made him love the tall, gruff man. Perhaps he knew what existed under Rohan's stiff demeanor. He had seen Rohan with his brother, Jon, and he had felt the bond between the two. Even from a distance, Josey seemed to be able to grow strong and healthy on the love which overflowed from that other father-son relationship. He let it warm him as if there were no chasm at all between himself and Rohan.

Rohan stood over the boy and spoke sharply, "Havna I telt ye agin an' agin? Ye call me Fither, nae Dada!"

"Yes D... Fither. Mama says t' come in for supper noo," said Josey softly, not understanding the reason for the reprimand. He stood looking at his father, who stood looking at his shoes.

What had he done wrong and why wouldn't Dada look at him? "Why canna I say Dada?" he asked.

But Rohan couldn't answer. He simply could not summon decent words for the boy. It was beyond him even to interact in a civil tone.

He retreated into his own private battleground as he gathered his tools and headed for the house. He would not even look back to see if the boy followed, but he knew it was so. It seemed that Rohan looked each day for opportunities to find fault with Joseph, but rarely could he do so. He ignored the innocent, youthful questions, and did everything short of actually provoking an argument. If he could get the boy to disobey, he'd have grounds for his anger, an outlet for these feelings he could not live with. But Josey rarely acted out of disobedience. Rohan's anger had nowhere to go. He felt like a pot of stew boiling over a hot fire, and he wondered when he'd burn dry.

Josey followed Rohan toward the barn, taking the longest strides he could so as to place his small feet into the footprints left by Rohan' large ones. He felt a bit sad at having made Da angry, but Mama said that Da was hurt inside and that sometimes the pain made him say things that he really didn't mean to say. Josey ran ahead to open the barn door for Rohan and to help him put his tools away. Rohan did not say thank you or even make eye contact, but Josey was too busy helping to notice.

When they got to the house Josey hung his little coat and hat on the peg beside the door, and washed his hands in the basin before going to the table. He sat at his place and waited patiently for the rest of the family to join him. Jon lifted the heavy pot of chicken and dumplings to the table while Miryam poured milk for herself and each of her sons, and strong tea for Rohan. The lantern had been lit and an amber glow filled the room. At last they were all seated and Rohan bowed his head.

Though it was customary for him as the head of the household to say the blessing at their meals, tonight Rohan remained silent. They waited, knowing better than to interrupt his thoughts. When the silence was almost unbearable, especially for Josey, Rohan spoke.

"He's callin' me Da agin... I won't have it! He's t' call me Fither!"

Miryam did not know how to respond to this outburst and so kept still. The silence was too much for Rohan and he erupted from his seat, knocked over his chair, grabbed his coat, and left the house.

Jon looked at Miryam, and then at Josey, and then went to find his father. "Da!" he called as he ran to the barn, looking into each stall, and finally around the far side of the building. He saw his father, bent double, leaning against the barn, agony on his face. "What's wrong Da?" Jon said rushing to his side.

Rohan stiffened, straightening to his full height. "I willna ha' tha' boy callin' me Da!" he grimaced, his jaw clenched shut with anger.

Jon, still thinking that Rohan was in pain, asked him, "Are you hurt? What's ailin' you? Da, tell me!"

"Nae! I'm nae hurt! I'm angry! Tha' boy in there has nae right t' call me his Da. Tha' polecat tha' raped your mither is his Da! He's nae kin o' mine! I willna stand for it! I just willna have it! Look wha' tha' thief has done t' this family, he's stolen my whole life oot from under me. He's ruined it!"

"No Dada," said Jon in a penetrating, but quiet voice. He usually took the trouble to speak just his mother's proper English, but he let himself fall into his father's way of speaking.

"You ruined it. You've thrown awa' wha's been gi'en you. You've ta'en it an' trampled it under foot. Tisn't tha' little boy tha's eatin' at you. It's you, cuttin' Josey oot o' your life. You're treatin' tha' wean in there like he's a criminal an' he's done nothin' to you!" Jon stared long at his father. Finally, he took a step backward. He had made a decision, and in the manner of a stubborn Scot, he spoke, "If he canna call you Dada, then I willna either."

Jon walked away, ashamed of his father and ashamed of himself. This was not the way to handle a bad situation, by making it worse. It was said now, though, and he wouldn't take it back.

He remained aloof from Rohan, calling him Father, and using only stiff formalities that were not at all necessary, and which rubbed salt into the open wounds between them. Josey was protected from Rohan's attitude because Miryam and Jon sheltered him, and because Rohan made himself scarce. He seldom presented himself at meals, retreating to the barn with his dinner plate in his hand whenever possible.

Josey knew only that his Dada was not feeling well and couldn't be friendly because of it. He excused the ill mannered behavior and poured out more love to fill the gap between them. This frustrated Rohan even more, since there was nowhere to lay the blame but upon himself.

Rohan took to visiting the Himmel's. Theirs had become a home away from home for him during his black moods. The family accepted him as a man who desperately needed help, and they gave him their loving companionship.

On the Himmel's farm, Dan was ever mindful of Rohan's presence.

He always remained away from the house until he checked to see if there was a visitor. Ava, Gustav, Ana and Rosie were used to Rohan's unexpected visits and just let him sit with them and think. He came often, remained silent, and always left as broken as he had come.

Gus did not know what Rohan thought about, only that he was deeply troubled. Only Ava knew the secret of his pain. They both had a high regard for this man who had given them a new start, with food and with friendship, at the time of Rose's birth. They prayed for him every night as they turned back the bedclothes. On occasion Gustav would drive Ava and their daughters to see Miryam and her sons. The women would talk about recipes and dressmaking while the younger ones played or in Jon and Ana's case, sat and talked for hours. In season, the women made preserves from the fruits they could gather. Miryam did not feel so alone now that she had Ava to talk to. Holding in the hurt of Rohan's isolation from the family made real closeness difficult, though, because Miryam did not feel that it was her place to share Rohan's ill behavior with children under foot.

Gus silently helped Roh with whatever he was doing on the days they visited. He felt that if he could just be there, Rohan would only bring him into his confidence. His enduring friendship was rewarded one day. Rohan broke down in the middle of mucking out a stall. He sat down in the clean straw and wept openly. Gus sat down with him and just waited, his hand on the big man's back. Rohan told Gustav the whole story of Joseph's conception. Gus let Rohan fume and cry while he prayed under his breath for release from this bitterness. He, also, had known its sour taste in his mouth. His father-in-law had disowned Ava for marrying him. Leaving their home with its sad memories had almost been more than he could stand, but still he waited on the Lord to do whatever He planned for their lives.

Gustav shared his story and his sureness of God's provision with Rohan, urging him to trust the Lord for resolution of this painful situation. After many long moments of consideration, Rohan rose, speaking with a clenched jaw, "Gus, I dinna mean t' be disrespectful, but I dinna ken God, an' I dinna think I choose t' ken Him."

He went out of the stable without uttering another word.

Chapter 24

Rosie was having a birthday party. Rohan brought his family to the Himmel's to celebrate. Josey was delighted to see her. They dashed off to find something to play with until it was time to have the cake. Dan planned to keep out of sight and was back behind the barn greasing the axels for the wagon wheels when the children ran by.

"Who's that?" asked Josey, slowing to a walk.

"Daniel hiss name iss. He my Papa's friend iss. He tinks can fix guut," Rose replied.

"Let's watch him."

"Oh, very vell, but den de swink I vill to you show dat Papa put for my birthday in de barn up. It from the loft hankink down iss."

"How old are you now?" asked Josey.

"I fife years old am," she said proudly, holding up all five fingers of one hand. "Oh, vait!" She examined her hand and then tucked her thumb away out of sight. "Four! Unt do you know vat else for my birthday I am getting?"

"What?"

"Accolades! Papa says dey for a girl are de best ting!"

"What's acc.. acc.. lades?"

"I am not yet knowing, but I'm sure I vill like dem!"

Rose became sullen for a moment and then confided in Josey that she had recently been naughty. "Papa to me said dat if naughty I again am be-ink, he my next birthday vill away take unt I vould always four years old be! I fife years old vant to become, so I a guut girl from now on vill be!"

Dan chuckled to himself upon hearing the exchange. Rosie was certainly a chatterbox! As he turned to see who her visitor was, he saw the spitting image of himself standing next to her. The boy was shorter by far than Rosie and had the biggest, darkest eyes. His straight, jet black hair stood up at his crown in a cowlick. The boy's face was as square as could be. And there was the same gap between his front teeth that Dan had always been known for. Dan stared unblinking for a long minute before standing up to look surreptitiously around the corner of the barn toward Gustav and the tall thin man with the curly red hair way across the yard. Yes, he knew who this boy was.

Upon the advice of his close friend, the reverend Jamie, Dan had come separately to the kirk for the wine and the cup that had become so dear to him. He stayed outside in clement weather when the church windows were open, singing the hymns, and listening to the readings and the sermon. In bad weather he snuck into the foyer where he remained unseen to participate in the worship.

From the moment that Gus had taken him on to work for his room and board, Dan had trod a cautious path to avoid contact with the MacVoy family. They visited every few weeks or so in fair weather, but he was able to discern the day of their expected visit by casual conversations with Gus. Ava, knowing the situation, would let him know of the MacVoy family's movements if she knew they would possibly collide with his own. Dan never suspected that she was helping him to remain anonymous. He arranged to be gone at those times, making up any reason that would get him safely away. Once he had to leave Ava's kitchen quite abruptly as Rohan rode unannounced into the yard. Dan gave a chore left unfinished as an excuse.

He had almost been discovered a few times when spontaneous visits happened, but during the winter months there was little chance of an unplanned visit. When in town, Dan was vigilant while about his errands, always wearing his hat, keeping the brim down low, and drawing no attention to himself whatsoever. Dan had known that he was the boy's father, even from the day of Josey's baptism. Until recently, the tall Scotsman with the pretty Jewish wife had brought his family to church every week. Dan had watched them from his seat in the rear of the sanctuary. The tall teenager with the mop of fine red hair was called Jonathan. The infant was christened Joseph Samuel MacVoy. He looked as out of place in his family as a goat among sheep. No one had ever said a thing to him about it, but he knew this was his son. Josey's hair was black as coal, as was his father's, so Dan resolved to keep his own hat on whenever possible. He even resolved never to smile and reveal the tell-tale gap between his front teeth.

On the day of Rose's party, as he worked on the axel, he realized that it was the first time he might have to cross paths with the family directly. He did not attend the town's social gatherings, and spoke to no one unless spoken to. The townsfolk who hired him as a handyman didn't usually stand around and talk, nor really take as much notice of him as of his workmanship. Their interest was only in whether the job he was paid to do was done well.

But Dan was lonely. He knew he should have moved on long ago, but the child and his own longing for a family held him. He would never, ever interfere - but he watched closely whenever he could without being seen. Dan had seen Rohan scold the boy, never hurting him physically, but calling him names, like "wee scoundrel," that would wound his little heart. He had heard gruff exchanges. He had seen the man act a certain way in public and another way when he thought no one was around. Dan, however, made it a point to be where he could see how his son was treated.

After the birthday celebration, Rohan MacVoy gave Josey a stone cold refusal to communicate when they were ready to leave. Gustav and Ava and the girls had said their goodbyes and stood on the porch. Josey was full of chatter and wanted to tell his father about Rose's swing, but though he tried to get Rohan's attention, Rohan ignored him. The child climbed up into the wagon filled with resignation to follow in the footsteps of a man who did not want to be followed.

Dan could feel the disappointment in Josey from far across the yard. He could sense the child's sadness to return to the silence of his relation-ship with his "father." It hurt him to watch, and to know that he had cre-ated more pain than he could ever repair. If Miryam had not conceived, she might possibly have been able to put the day of the rape behind her. Her husband and son might have been able to set it aside as well. But he was afraid that young Joseph would never know the love that a father should have for his son and it was all because of him. Dan turned and went into his room in the barn and closed the door. He buried his face in his hands and wept. He knew that God had forgiven him, but there was so much more pain that he did not know how to deal with.

When I later learned that Dan was my father I understood my "Da." Though my family and the Himmels say that they sometimes saw great sadness in me, I truly do not remember it. As Mama says, it's by God's grace that I do not. It is true, the mercies of God are "new every morning."[14]

When Dan felt normal again, he returned to the yard. He saw that Ava was struggling with something heavy, so he rushed over to see if he could help. She was laden down with a sodden quilt she had just finished washing. "Och, Daniel? So guut that here you are! Could you ofer de fence to dry diss qvilt put?" she puffed. As they labored to lay it gently over the split rails he saw a large brown stain in the center. "Did you know dat diss qvilt Miryam's mudder made? I am sure it lovely vass, until it vass rrruined."

He paled and stepped back.

"Daniel," Ava took his hand in her two hands. "I know."

"What?" he stammered.

"I about all uff it am knowink. I a smart voman am. But you are not to be vorryink. Remember dat a vonderful plan Gott alvays hass. Do not effer forget, do you hear?"

He stared at her a moment, then averted his eyes. He rallied to help Ava arrange the folds over the fence rail so the whole quilt would dry. In his mind he went back to the MacVoy home, where he himself had brutally caused the blood of this stain to be spilled.

"Oh God," he thought. "Will this ever be gone from my memory? Will it always torture me? What can I do ta take the hurt away from this family?"

Ava was explaining that she was going to repair the quilt, taking out the ruined cloth and replacing it with four new pieces. "Dey vill each der names on it see, vitt der birthdays. De qvilt den vill a special meaning for all of dem haff. Ve must alvays remember dat ve vere each by Gott planned. Not vun birth a mistake iss, Daniel."

Dan felt ill. "Would the pain always be there?"

Ava took him by the shirtsleeve, "Gott vill all tinks make new, Daniel. He can, unt He vill."

"How, Ava? It is impossible an' you know it as well as I do."

"Daniel, you to me listen! De Guut Book us tells, 'Faith iss beink sure uff vat for ve are hopink, unt beink certain uff vat ve cannot vitt our own eyes see.'[15] Dat means dat ve out uff our smartness must step. Ve all search for sometink for to hold fast vitt, unt ven ve very much search, eefen vitt tremblink, dat place iss vere our faith beginnink iss. Dere no giffink up vill be! Do you unterstant?"

Chapter 25

Reverend MacClure had noted the MacVoy family's situation early on as well. Dan had shared over the years, filling in the details, when necessary, so that he might to receive godly counsel. MacClure held the secret close. Dan's heart was breaking over Rohan's lack of love for the boy, but his silence was absolutely essential. He had nowhere else to turn. Having to always keep to himself, he had made few close friends in the area.

In light of the MacVoy's situation, the good reverend thought that it might be a beneficial time to teach about raising children in his Sunday sermon. He had been a widower for many years and childless as well. But he was the eldest of nine children, so all the little ones were dear to his heart. As his congregation settled into their seats, the wise preacher closed his eyes in prayer.

"Let me speak only wha' ye want said today, Lord. An' let those who specially need t' hear be listenin' wi' their hearts." Then he began, with great conviction.

" Jesus telt his disciples, "Suffer the little children t' come t; Me, an' forbid 'em not, for o' such is the kingdom o' God." [16] Noo Jesus understood, bein' God Himself, tha' the hearts o' the wee ones are often a far sight closer t' Him than the hearts o' most adults. Those o' us who're grown up tend t' see things oor own wa', but the weans are more open t' the wa's o God. The Fither God says tha', t' us adults, children are a reward from Him, an inheritance from the guidness He has promised us. Saint Paul telt us tha' we mun teach oor children the truth tha' God loves 'em, tha' the Bible is inspired by God, an' tha' tis profitable for learnin' doctrine, for correctin' us when we're wrong, an' for instruction in right livin'. [17]

"King Solomon wrote in his proverbs tha' we mun 'train up a child in *the way he should go, an' when he is old he willna depart from it.'*[18] *We mun teach oor children tha' the Word o' God is truth for each day. Ye ha' t' impress the words o' God upon your children. Make an imprint o' those words in your child's heart. T' do tha', ye mun ken those words for yourself. Ye canna be firm enow t' make an impression if ye dinna ken wha' you're sayin'. An' it mun be done all o' the time. In the book o' Deuteronomy, tha's one o' those first five books, it comes right oot an' says tha' we mun make sure God's words are in our hearts. And we mun teach 'em diligently to our children, an' talk of 'em when we sit doon in our hooses, an' talk of 'em when we walk aboot, an' when we lie doon an' when we rise up. We mun aboot God when we lay those children doon t' sleep at night an' keep talkin' when we get 'em up e'ery mornin'.*

"*It e'en says, noo understand this, folks, I have ne'er seen it myself, but I hear the Jewish folks ha' the scriptures written oot real tiny like, on bitty pieces o' paper*" He held up his thumb and forefinger pinched close together.

"*An' they put those wee papers in wee little wooden boxes an' tie 'em on their hands an' on their foreheads. This here passage in Deuteronomy says t' do just that! Noo I'm nae sayin tha' we should do tha', but we need t' ta'e this here Word o' God,*" he held up the Bible for emphasis, "*verra seriously. If God thought somethin' was important enow tha' He telt folks t' write it doon, then we plum ought t' be payin' attention!*

"*Why I hear tha' those Jewish folks ha' those same wee pieces o' paper in other wooden boxes, an' they nail 'em up on the doorposts o' their hooses. They touch 'em like this,*" MacClure touched his fingers to his lips, then to an unseen object in the air beside him, "*e'ery time they gang in an' oot tha' door, t' remind 'em hoo important God's words should be in e'erythin' they do. So be thinkin' aboot tha'. Be mindful o' wha' your children see ye doin' an' wha' they hear ye sayin'.*

"*Noo I can hear ye all thinkin' tha' your nae gang t' read this whole book for memory an' then try t' teach it all t' your babies, an' your older children. You're sayin' t' yourselves, 'So, hoo much do I really need t' read? Hoo much do I need t' teach?' But ye see, God looks at the heart. He looks at the person ye are inside. He looks at your attitude. Ye dinna need t' be memorizin' an' gettin' all the words in perfect order for the recitin' o' it. The words o' God are not just wha's written in this book an' on these pages. The words o' God are wha' tells us who He is.*

"An' for tha' we ha' a real human bein' t' see Him by. He sent Jesus. He put human skin on His own Son. Jesus is e'en called the Word o' God. The Bible says tha' God's Word, Jesus, "is a lamp t' oor feet, an' a light t' oor path."[19] *Tis His Word tha' shows us the wa' t' go each day. Jesus is the signature o' God. Ye know when ye put your name on a piece o' paper tha' it really an' truly means somethin'. Tis a way o' identifyin' all tha' ye stand for. Jesus is the identity o' God wearin' a human cloak. The disciple John tells us hoo it all happened."*

MacClure picked up his Bible and began to read,

"'In the beginnin' was the Word, an' the Word was wi' God, an' the Word was God. He was wi' God in the beginnin'. Through Him, all thin's were made. Withoot Him, nothin' was made tha' has been made. In Him was life, an' tha' life was the light o' men.'[20]

"There's your lamp for your path agin. D' ye see it?

"This Jesus, who was God from the beginnin' o' all time, came t' us as a child. Bein' a child, an' learnin' thin's as a child learns, was important enow for God t' do Himself. So ye best know for sure tha' He wants ye t' regard your children as bein' precious an' important in your life, too. The Bible says tha' twould be better tha' a man should ha' a millstone tied aroond his neck an' be thrown in t' the sea than t' harm a little child."

He paused a long minute, and then closed with, *"Amen."*

Miryam's heart stirred. She had seen, and touched those "tiny wooden boxes" from the time she was a little girl. She remembered staring when her own grandfather had worn them, one on his right hand and one on his forehead, but no one ever told her what they were for.

And she had been given a *mezuzah* when she married Rohan. "To remind you," Mama had said. She had dutifully asked Rohan to nail it on the doorpost. She had mechanically kissed it for years but then gotten out of the habit. How strange, she thought, that the reverend would speak of it. She silently vowed she would try now to teach Jon and Joseph about the words written there. Still she felt an emptiness in that she did not know the true significance of the all-important words on those "wee bits o' paper" that Reverend MacClure spoke of.

That book of Deuteronomy that he mentioned was in the Torah. She remembered it because it was so hard to pronounce as a child. But by the time she had grown up no one even mentioned the Torah anymore. Her parents kept traditions, not scriptures, at the forefront of their faith. It was their firm belief that keeping the law and holding fast to those traditions was what brought one to God's attention. But to Miryam, the law was a vague memory of endless "Thou Shalt Nots." Nothing she wished to dwell on. So what was in the words of the Bible that she should learn for herself and teach her children?

Later when they'd been home from church a while and the noon meal had been cooked and enjoyed and cleared away, Miryam thought again of the Bible. She did not own one, but Rohan did. He had been given it when he left Scotland, but had never read it. His only use for it was in keeping family records of births and deaths. Their marriage had been recorded by Miryam's steady hand as he showed her where to write. Jon's birth was also in Miryam's hand.

"My own scrawl wouldna be guid enow," Rohan had said.

During the sermon, Miryam had realized that Joseph's birth had never been recorded.

"Rohan," she asked, "Where is your family Bible?"

"Wha' will ye be needin' tha' for?" he replied.

"I need to write in it when Joseph was born," Miryam answered.

Rohan considered a moment. Something did not seem right about that to him. "But tha's for recordin' my own blood relatives, an' tha' is nae Joseph."

"Am I not your wife? Have you not pledged yourself to me in marriage to be one flesh with me as we said in the marriage vows?" Rohan did not answer her, but she persisted.

"I see! Then my child is your child! Bring me the book, please."

Rohan slammed around until he found the Bible, slammed it down on the table, and slammed the door behind him as he left the house. It had been a long time since Miryam had seen him so angry. Well, she was a bit angry, too. Didn't Rohan hear anything that was said in the sermon about children?

She laid the book on the table and opened it, noting its weight and its fragile pages. What an important looking volume. She found the page near the front where their marriage and Jonathan's birth were recorded, along with Rohan's family's momentous events. As she wrote in the name, Joseph Samuel MacVoy, and his birth date, she realized that she had not mentally relived the day she was raped in quite some time. To her, and to Jon, there was no presence, nor daily remembrance of Joseph's biological father in their home. She did not know when the nightmares had ended, but they had not awakened her in panic for a long time.

Miryam began to turn the pages carefully. Her parents owned many books, but few as impressive as this. Jon's letter from the east came to mind then. He had said something concerning her parents arguing about a passage in the Bible. He said that it was not from the Torah, but from the prophets. She went to her writing box and took out his letter. "Isaiah," she read aloud, "chapter 53." Her own father now believed that Jesus was a Jew, and that He was the Messiah. She would have to find it somehow.

To the best of her recollection, the Messiah was always someone that Jews were waiting for, but she did not know who he was supposed to be or why he was important to them. She decided to find the place. As she turned the pages, she came upon a paper, folded in half. The words were handwritten in the old style, and very faded with time. It was poetry, written in a rough hand, not Rohan's, but perhaps his father's?

"Whene'er I look unto the heavens
to ponder the mighty God,
I wonder how He came to love me,
Who walked this guilty sod.
He suffered here to set me free,
to bear my sin and shame.
He has looked upon me with His favor,
and called me by His name.

Tis God Who set the sun to shining,
and all the stars in space.
And I wonder how He came to love me,
Who died to take my place.
A debtor, I, who could not pay,
so He gave, Who did not owe.
By His blood I stand, I am forgi'en,
redeemed in that precious flow.

I shant forget the love of Jesus,
Who took away my pain.
And I wonder how He came to love me,
Who o'er the earth does reign.
He left His throne, a servant to be,
to show God's power and grace
He bids me now to come before Him,
to see His lovely face."

Miryam wondered, "Have I ever looked for *Adonai*? Have I ever pondered Him? Is it true that He cares about me, and all my life's good and bad times? Could this Jesus have really been the Messiah? Did He set all the stars in space? If He truly loves me and gave His life for me…?"

The questions came faster than she could even begin to answer them. "What response should I give Him? Does He ask something of me?"

Rohan came in, sheepishly standing at the door and looking only at the floor. "I'm sorry," he said.

"I know," she said. "Rohan, would you sit with me for a bit?"

"Well, I ha' thin's needin' t' be done…"

"Just for a little bit…" She patted the table across from where she sat. "I was wondering what you might remember about your Da. You've not talked to me about him much in all these years."

Rohan took the chair. "I dinna remember much at all. He wasna home often in the day tha' we hardly took notice. He worked all the time. We were nae well off, I can tell ye tha'. Why d' ye ask?"

"I was reading the Bible records in the front here. There are many generations. Did anyone ever talk about these folks? Do you recognize any of the names?"

Rohan looked over the pages. "I really dinna remember. Nae much was e'er told. But there were stories aboot a few. There was an uncle who died fightin' off the English. There are lots here who were marrit an' burrit but ne'er spoke much of. The only thin' I can remember aboot my Da is tha' he was e'er so tall. O' course I was still wee small when he met his reward.

"Wait noo a minute. I do recall tha' he an' my mum would boo their heads an' hold their hands before we had oor supper, an' tha' he ha' a cushion on the floor beside their bed in the corner o' the big room. We children slept on one side, an' they on t'other. Da knelt there e'ry night after we were abed, while Mum cleaned up the dishes. Then after, sometimes he would play his fiddle."

"Your fiddle?"

"Aye, an' we loved t' hear it. We would watch him play an' listen until oor eyes were too heavy t' stay open anymore... Tha's all I can say aboot 'im."

"How did ye come by the Bible for your own? Didn't any of the rest of the family want to keep it?"

"Ye see, I were the only boy. Twas my responsibility t' keep it... I suppose for the records written in it."

"How was it given to you?"

"When I was t' leave home, I had nae but one other shirt an' a pair o' breeks t' put in my packet. But my mither got it oot o' the cupboard, an' set it before me, sayin', 'This has been in oor family a long time noo, an' noo it be yours t' keep. Ye may lose many other possessions ye might gather o'er a lifetime, but ye mun ne'er lose this.'"

Rohan stopped a moment and stared at Miryam, then he went on, "An' she said somethin' strange tha' I didna recall 'til just noo. She telt me tha' my Da ha' kept it safe all o' his life because he was telt by his own Da tha' there were precious words in there tha' mun be passed on t' each generation t' come.

"'It has 'the secret for life inside,' she told me. But I mun 'look for it wi' all my heart, all my soul, all my mind, an' all my strength...' I ha' nae thought o' tha' since I left the old country."

As Miryam closed the Bible carefully, she saw the folded paper again and pulled it out to show Rohan. "Does this look familiar to you?"

He read the words slowly. "Aye, I ken it from my childhood. Da sang it while we were fallin' t' sleep verra often." He folded it and handed it back. "Keep it safe there, will ye? I'm gang t' the barn. Then I'll get the wood in for the night." It was time to get the evening meal ready, so Miryam put the Bible away, her earlier pursuit forgotten.

Rohan went to the loft as soon as he got into the barn. He brought his fiddle down and brushed the dust from the case with a cloth in the tack room. "Hoo many years," he wondered aloud, "has it been?" He opened the stiff clasps and lifted the lid, letting a deep sigh escape as he did so. It surely was a beautiful instrument. His Dada had given it when Rohan was only a small boy.

"In the old days," his Da had once said to little Rohan, "we played e'ery night after supper. My Da, an' my uncles played the old songs, tellin' hoo folks lived, an' loved, an' died. There were sad songs, an' lively tunes. Tha's hoo I learnit t' play, an' hoo ye'll learn, too."

He had learned his fiddling from the uncles, for Da had died soon after. Da had a wonderful gift of playing and such a voice as Rohan had not heard since. He remembered the song from the paper tucked into the Bible. It had a lilt that had always lifted his spirit.

"Hoo did it go agin? *"Whene'er I look unto the heavens t' ponder the mighty God..."*

He would have to get that paper for the words, but he surely did remember the notes. He hummed it as he lifted the fiddle from its bed. "Sure, an' the rosin is in here, too. Are ye still in tune?"

Plucking the strings one by one Rohan made some adjustments to the pegs and then tucked the fiddle under his chin.

Miryam had stepped out to get a breath of fresh air while her meal was cooking when she heard it. She looked up, startled, then she realized what she was hearing. The music seemed to fill the very air she breathed. The vibrato was like an angelic serenade. She closed her eyes and let it wash over her. Oh, she had missed it so. Now that she heard that sweet,

sweet sound, she knew what had been lacking the past several years. Rohan had put his music away, and with it a part of himself. A part of him that she had fallen in love with had been hidden away by the daily ordering of their lives. It was as if the paths of their days had been worn smooth, and then become rutted, leaving the joy of running through life's meadows behind.

Rohan felt it, too. As he played, the tunes in his memory took over, playfully at first, and then purposefully, leading him beyond himself. This was the same urgency he'd felt at the fall church social so many years ago. There was, indeed, something more to living than he could grasp. An energy, a will, an entity apart from himself was finding expression through him, and he knew it. Somewhere in him he found a connection with it. It was both a longing and a fulfillment. He let it continue for some time, and then sat down, exhausted – and wondering what had just happened. Was this feeling from God? When he asked the question, he heard an answer.

It resonated in his mind and heart, "Yes!" He had to acknowledge it, but at the same time it gave him a fearful awe. "If God be this real, an' this close, I mun be quite a burden t' Him."

Rohan watched a moth flutter around the lantern. He knew what longing it must feel as it was helplessly pulled so close to something so dangerous and beautiful. He realized that the very same yearning was also in himself. His heart spoke to him from its depths, uttering words of worship and truth he had never felt before.

"O Lord, like a moth t' a flame,
I'm drawn t' Your heart.
Let me lose myself in Ye.
May Your light burn on in the night.
Ye say the mornin' will come
an' I know tha' Ye speak the truth.
May Your lantern shine brightly
in my eyes tha' were once blind with fear.
Kindle Your lamp in me 'til nae darkness hides."

Rohan did not know that his heart was being prepared for the incoming of the presence he hoped for, but at last he knew that he could no longer turn away from it, any more than the moth could leave the beautiful flame. He gently put the fiddle away and returned to the house.

Chapter 26

The leaves, colored pink and green like rhubarb, had long fallen from the maple that shaded the house. The Indian summer of a few weeks ago had bidden farewell to warm days. Josey was three and a half years old. This might be the last clear day for a good while. Winter storms were brewing and she knew that there were many things to get done today before the bad weather hit. She knew she had to hurry. If she could just get the house swept out, scrubbed from the summer grit, and set to rights again, she'd feel ready to settle in for winter. Josey came up and tugged on her apron.

"Mama?"

"Yes, Josey."

"Can I ask you somethin'?"

"Yes."

"Why is Dada so angry at me? Was I naughty?"

As she knelt next to Josey he put his head against her shoulder and snuggled against the softness of her dress.

"Did I do somethin' wrong?"

"No, honey, you didn't. Dada is just not himself anymore."

This required deep thought on Joseph's part. After long moments he asked, "Then who is he, Mum?"

"No, I meant he just isn't the same as he used to be. I can't reckon it all out for you, Josey, but he's got a hole inside his heart that he doesn't know how to fill. He needs to let go of his hurting, but he keeps holding on because that's all he's got. Maybe some day he'll find something worth letting go for. Maybe he'll find something that's far better than his hurting to hold onto."

"I'll find somethin' Mama, somethin' lots better!" said Josey, and he scampered off to find a special gift that would fix the hole in his Da's heart. He thought he knew just what to do. It would be a special surprise.

I remember looking in the woodpile for just the right piece of wood to inscribe with the word that would make Da happy. I was sure that he would see that he was important to me and that knowledge would please him at last.

Jon had overheard the conversation and he came to Miryam. "Ma? When do you suppose Da'll come 'round? He's been out of touch with us for close to four years now. He doesn't talk hardly at all anymore and he barely listens, either."

"Jon, I wish I knew. He just needs to stop looking behind him at what could have been, and start looking ahead at what can become of the future. He's still angry." Miryam felt the need to add one more note of explanation, "He's never forgiven himself for not being here either."

"I suppose that's the hardest part, feelin' like it's all his fault," Jon said under his breath. "He can't really think that. Can he?"

"I'm afraid he does, and I'd appreciate you being a little more understanding," said Miryam quietly, as she grasped Jon's hand in hers. "He needs support and not criticism. Give him all you can, and hope for a change of heart."

"But Ma, he's hurting Josey, too. Not just you and me and himself."

"I know... I just hope for the day to come when he'll be well again." Miryam touched Jon's cheek lovingly. "You'd best get back to work now, it's almost time for milking."

As the day drew to a close, an early snow began to fall in huge lacy flakes which covered the ground in no time at all. "How silent it is," thought Miryam, as she watched the fluttering whiteness fill all the uneven places in the yard until everything was equally blanketed. It changed everything she could see, all the world was made new in so short a time, and all without a sound. She longed for a fresh start for her family as well.

She turned from the window to admire her family. Rohan sat in his favorite chair, his head resting back on the cushion, staring at the ceiling in far away thought. The children sat before the fire, playing checkers,

Jon teaching Josey ever so patiently. She could tell that Jon was letting him win. Soon he jumped up shouting with excitement,

"I won, Mama!" He ran to Miryam and flung himself into her arms. Then he remembered his gift for Rohan. He'd found a piece of flat firewood and with an old nail had painstakingly scratched the letters 'DADA' on it. He went to the hiding place he'd made behind the rocking chair and fetched his prize. "I made this for you today," he said shyly, as he handed it to Rohan. "It's for you to hold on to."

Rohan took one look at it, rose up from his chair and thundered, "Don't call me tha'! I'm nae your Dada!" He saw the boy only through his rage, and had brought his hand back to strike when abruptly he came to his senses and left the room without a word. Miryam followed him into the bedroom and closed the door behind her.

She worked hard to collect her emotions, then carefully spoke just loud enough for Rohan to hear, but her words were not lost. "When are you going to leave the past behind you? Who else but you can he call his Da? He has no one else. He doesn't know about anyone else. He's never known anyone but you! It's not his fault. You know that! Don't break his heart!"

"He's nae my flesh an' blood! I canna change tha'!"

Miryam spoke evenly and quietly, testing her will to the utmost. "Am I your flesh and blood? But you took me as your wife and we pledged our love to each other. You can do the same with Josey. You can't carry on like this any longer or you'll lose us all."

"What d' ye mean? Lose ye?"

"You're hardly a part of this family any more, Rohan. You treat us as if we have no feelings at all. You'll lose touch altogether if you don't change your ways." Miryam stood fast, letting her words hit their mark. But, at last, seeing no response, she turned and left the room to try to repair the breech in the security she had tried so long to build around her family.

Rohan's eyes were fixed on the door. He wanted to call to her, wanted her to come back in and hold him while he let the agony flow out of him. His heart was cut to the quick and he stood there emotionally bleeding, still unable to make a move toward his family to bind up the wound. He had almost struck a small boy in a rage that might have been fatal. He slowly turned and lay down on the bed. When Miryam came in after tending to the children, banking the fire and latching the shutters for the night, she found him still there, on top of the covers. His eyes were shut, but his face was contorted, wet with tears that glistened when she lit the lamp.

She changed into her nightclothes and crept under the blankets, then put her small white hand on his large brown one. Rohan reached over with his other hand and touched her cheek, then turned to seek sleep. It was a long time in coming, though, for both of them.

I do remember that one time, feeling briefly that I had done something terrible but not knowing what. When Da raised his hand against me, apparently Jon had seen it coming, though I did not. He reached out and pulled me into a big hug. The heat of the moment was dissipated by the affection he showed when I needed it most. The traumatic rebuke which might otherwise have scarred me was reduced to an unidentifiable restlessness and a sadness I could not grasp or acknowledge. I did not choose to be around the rest of the family as much after that night, but took refuge in playing in the meadows by myself. It was a solitary time, but also a time when I believe God was shielding me from harm.

As winter passed them by, each family member bore their burdens alone, not speaking of them, to spare the others from knowing the full weight of their private pain. Rohan bore his agony in silence, as usual. Miryam bore hers in sudden outbursts of emotion, coming from nowhere. Jon got angrier and angrier, seeing his father act out so childishly. He followed suit as he stomped around while at his chores, slammed doors, and frowned continually. Young Josey stayed in the recesses of the ranch until he was called in for meals or chores.

Miryam grieved for her family. As she did her chores she wept for them. Washday had become a particularly hard day of the week for her. The smell of the wet clothing reminded her of the day she had never finished her laundry chores, so long ago. It had taken years for her to stop looking over her shoulder as she went about her work, looking for danger on the horizon. The prickling of that fear had eventually subsided, only to be replaced by this grief for what had been lost.

Miryam often lay awake long into the night. Why were the heavens silent as she called out for help? Surely, if there was indeed some great 'god' out there, he had heard her! Perhaps he was letting her know that she should be a better wife. Or perhaps he was quixotic and just played with her pain. Her grief had blinded her to the ways she could show Rohan that she loved him, in spite of his attitude. For, deep inside her heart, she knew that she did still love him. It was a commitment she had made when she had married him, and it would not change now. The winter had been long and lonely for all of them.

One early spring night, a dream she had gave her new hope. She dreamed of the two horses that had come to her as a young girl while she was picking flowers. But in this dream they spoke to her, saying, "We don't know your language, but the gentleness of your voice we can understand."

How very odd, she thought when she awoke. But how like her relationship with the god she heard of in the kirk and like the hope she had that *Adonai* was indeed real. There was a language barrier that was seemingly insurmountable. If only she had been able to speak to the horses… If only God could speak plainly to her… If only she could speak to Roh…

As dawn filled the room with pale yellow light, Miryam thought about how she might be more supportive of Roh's heart. She could no longer stand by and let Rohan recede into himself. The time for that was well in the past and she knew that to allow it to go on would be to lose sight of the man she had loved for these many years. She feared that he would go around the bend and over the horizon, and would ever after be a stranger to her and to her sons. So she resolved to speak to him often during the day to ask his opinion on various and sundry unimportant matters. She had to keep him talking! She had to remind him that he had a life, a home, a family that loved him. Rohan's anger had hedged him in. But Miryam persisted, asking herself, "What can I do that will break down the wall he has built?"

"Rohan," she would call across the fence, "do you think it's warm enough to plant the beans yet?" She knew full well that it was not, but she could bolster him by letting him have a say in the right time for gardening.

Rohan," she would say, "can you give me a hand with these rugs, please?" She had carried them outdoors many times before, but perhaps, if she could keep him nearby, she could reach him in some way.

Some days she wanted to scream at him, "Don't you think this has hurt me, too? Have you forgotten that I'm the one he raped? I could remember that day like it was yesterday if I chose to, but I've chosen to put it out of my mind! You can't imagine the awful way he looked at me and the way he touched me, and his whiskey breath in my face!" But she could never say those things to Rohan, because to do so would be to bury him beneath more guilt than he already carried.

Though she could see no outward improvement, Rohan was responding to her attentions. He did not speak when spoken to, but often, a reply would come into his mind in answer one of her comments. When Miryam spoke of the weather, of an impending thundershower, he'd look into the distance to gauge how long it would be before it would reach their property. There were words that could have been said, had he only been able let go of them.

Mama told me the verse that God had placed in her heart at that time. She'd heard it in the kirk and had clung to those words each day to remind her that she was not alone in her struggle to bring peace to her household. She let me help her memorize the words, but now I know it was for my benefit as well. It was Psalm 18:29 – "By my God I can leap over a wall!"

She said to me, "Da has built up walls to shield his heart from troubles. He doesn't realize that his walls are what keep the troubles in!"

Spring arrived with a series of thunderstorms which threatened to shake the house from its foundations and set it adrift into the accumulation of water in the yard. But Miryam had always loved thunderstorms.

One day while Ava was visiting, their conversation was interrupted by such a loud clap that she screamed, then collapsed into laughter at her foolishness.

"Och, I a guut soaking storm do surely enchoy!" shouted Ava over the noise.

Josey was not so sure that it was a good thing. He and Rosie cowered by their mothers as the rumbling seemed to come from the depths of the earth.

Ava sympathized, but knew just what to say. "Do you know dat de man called Job in de Guut Book a bit afrait uff de tunder wass, too? Miryam, let me to your Bible go unt fetch it."

Miryam told her where to find it and she brought it to the porch where they sat watching the lightning.

Och, here it is, chapter 37. "Poor man, at first he afright wass, but later, he wass not so much." She read the words in her halting accent, slowly and soothingly for Joseph, but with emphasis on the mighty power of God and His creation.

"Hear attentiffly de noisse uff Hiss voice,
unt de sound dat goett out uff Hiss moutt.
He directett it unter de whole heaven,
unt Hiss lightnink unto to de ends uff de eartt!
After it a voice rrrrrroarrett!

Ava paused and looked at the children with her eyes wide open in wonderment. The children responded in kind and God's thunder and lightning added to their expectant excitement. Ava continued.

"He tunderett vitt de voice uff Hiss excellency
He tunderett marvelously vitt His voice.
Great tinks doett He vich ve cannott comprehend."[21]

"Listen to Hiss voice, Yoseph! See His beautiful lightnink! He makes us stop vat we do, to His vonder see!"

But Josey clapped his hands over his ears, still unconvinced that all this terrible noise was somehow a wondrous thing.

"Vait, I anudder vill to you show." She turned the pages until she found the passage. "You read it dis time, Miryam. You can better do it dan can I."

Miryam was amazed that the fancy Bible held words about so common a thing as a thunderstorm. She read with awe in her voice as the skies broke open in resounding crashes and bright streaks of light.

"When He uttereth His voice, there is a multitude of waters in the heavens; and He causeth the vapours to ascend from the ends of the earth: He maketh lightnings with rain, and bringeth forth the wind out of His treasures."[22]

Ava quickly reached and turned the pages to another reading, pointing her finger at the place for Miryam to read from. Miryam cleared her throat and began.

"The heavens declare the glory of God,
And the firmament sheweth His handiwork."[23]

Miryam looked to the horizon where lightning flashed, and listened to the roar of the thunder with a new appreciation for the presence of God in her daily life. "Don't be afraid of it, Josey," she whispered into his ear. "Just climb up here on my lap and we'll enjoy it."

Chapter 27

Rohan was in town to do the month's errands. There were new boots to buy for Jon. He'd thought his son was fully grown at last, but then he'd shot up again, and his feet were now bigger than Rohan's. The child, Joseph, was also growing in leaps and bounds. Though very slight in stature, he was quite strong. At four years old, he was doing his share of the choring. He was now very quiet, almost to a fault, completely different from the outgoing child of a few months ago. The outburst which had followed the child's gift to Rohan was not forgotten by any of the family members.

At the mercantile, Gertrude Lubbock was at the counter sorting out coins from her recticule. "Ahh," she spoke with a side glance at Rohan, seemingly to herself yet loud enough for all to hear, "the man who raises stray pups for his own. A noble endeavor, to give a home to the whelps of others."

Ralph interrupted her with a loud cough, and a great deal of noise as he rustled around behind the counter. "A good day to you Rohan, a lovely day for planting your spring vegetables. Can I interest you in some seeds for your garden?"

Rohan caught the ill intent of Gertrude's remarks and would not answer, but managed to restrain himself long enough to walk out the door with a deliberately even pace. Rohan still thought of that awful day when Miryam had told him that she was with child, and the day of Josey's birth. Ezra came to mind then. Ezra had spoken of the meaning of love: "to give and forgive, unconditionally." These words, from a perfect stranger, returned to prompt him to find some answers. He carried deep doubts about why God did not prevent the crime against his wife, and why he had been prevented from being there to have helped her. He recalled that

Ezra and Edwin had been on their way to see the reverend. Maybe that might help him, too. He went to the church to see if his friend, Jamie, was there. Could he answer these questions? Would God answer his heart's profound ache?

Reverend MacClure was at the church sweeping the floors in the small sanctuary and singing his favorite quiet verse as he worked.

> *"O come now, Beloved, His kingdom draws nigh.*
> *Come pray t' the Fither, the Lord, the Most High.*
> *He is the Guid Shepherd, o' all life the Giver,*
> *Almighty, Victorious, His reign is forever!*
> *He bids you from heaven t' answer His call.*
> *So come now, Beloved. O come one an' all."*

He looked up as he saw a long shadow fall across his path. Rohan hesitated in the doorway. He had never spoken to his Scottish friend about anything of consequence. Their friendship was based on far more casual things, like their mutual heritage and the workings and going on in the town and surrounding countryside. How could he approach the problem, now that he had been foolish enough to have come here. His disturbed countenance told of his inner pain.

The Reverend MacClure knew the problem, and he was well aware of the condition of Rohan's heart. For, though Rohan did not know it, he wore his doubt and his shame as often as his favorite shirt. His features did not hide his feelings, and though the town may have thought Rohan gruff for other reasons, MacClure was used to looking deeper for the source of people's pain than whatever surface excuses were made. He knew that a broken heart and a doubtful spirit were often the cause of an angry man. He could see that it would be hard for Rohan to speak until spoken to.

"Mornin' Rohan," he said. "I ha' wantit t' talk t' ye for a long time noo." He knew that would open the way for Rohan to hear him out. "Ye feelin' puirly? Ye looked mighty peaked last Sunday in services."

"I only feel puirly on the inside, my ootside is tolerable well," replied Rohan.

"What seems t' be the matter, on the inside tha' is?"

"...I dinna ha' liberty t' say wha' it tis. I just ken I should act better than I do aboot it. There's a gnawin', like a wild animal caught in a trap... Ye ken hoo they do? They thrash an' pull 'til they just die."

"Aye, I've heard tis tha' way."

"For me, I feel as if my heart is aboot ready t' break, an' I'm afraid I'll hurt somebody, or run so far from the pain tha' nary a one will e'er find me. Sometimes I want t' run out in t' the meadow an' just keep runnin'. Leavin' all the problems behind me."

"Rohan, wha' is it tha' hurts ye so badly?"

"Like I said, I canna tell ye, but tis a wrong tha's been done t' me an' t' my family, an' I canna shake it. Why did it ha' t' happen? Why did God let it happen? Isna He supposed t' be guid, an' lookin' oot for us all the time an' steppin' in t' help when somethin' has gang wrong? I canna believe in a god who doesna help the people he's supposed t' love so much!"

Rohan turned away from the minister and stuffed his hands into his pockets. He shook with silent sobs, and began to walk toward the door.

"Rohan," Jamie said softly, "Wait. Ye an' me are much alike. Nae just tha' we both come from the auld country. We both ha' carried heavy burdens. My own burden is the reason tha' I became a minister. What God permits in oor lives can be used for oor own guid. It doesna always seem guid t' us. Bad things surely do happen. But in the long run, they can make us stronger an' more able t' help others, because o' wha' we ha' been through..."

MacClure saw that he hadn't lost his audience yet, so he continued. "Noo we can go through life kickin' an' thrashin' agin His plans, sayin' He's nae been fair in wha' He's doin', but tha' doesna change thin's any. It just makes life hard on us, an' on e'erybody aroond us. Think o' those horses ye raise oot there. They're pretty wild 'til they get broke, right? We're kind o' like tha'. Sometimes, when we kick too hard, God might pen us up for a while so we dinna get hurt. We can try an' go through life thinkin' tha' we dinna need Him, tryin' t' run awa' from His love, but it doesna get any easier. We're just pullin' tha' lead rope tighter aroond oor own necks. God isna gang t' lift His hand t' ta'e the rope off us cause we're just choosin' t' be ornery."

"I ken tha' I'm *crabbit,* all right," admitted Rohan. "I just dinna ken what t' do aboot it."

"Well, when we keep on bein' tha' wa' we're choosin' t' walk ootside God's ways. We're deliberately closin' oor eyes an' ears t' His direction an' t' His safety. Stayin' angry is a sin. Tis like walkin' right in t' the divil's territ'ry an'makin' oorselves right t' home there. Only one thin' can come oot o' that kind o' behavior – sufferin'!

"Ye see, God made us, an' He knows what we're like. The only thin' we can do is t' walk clean awa' from that anger. Really... t' turn tail an' run from it is wha' we should be doin'. Anger's like poison."

Rohan thought about his friend's words.

"But what aboot the one tha' wronged us?" he countered. "Am I supposed t' just forget wha' he did? Just carry on as if nothin' e'er happened?!"

"Well ye canna do anythin' aboot it anyways, nothin' that'll change wha' happened. Look here, if ye ruminate on it long enough, it'll addle your mind 'til ye canna think straight." He paused to let this sink in. "Or... ye can learn t' trust God t' do wha's best for us, or wha's maybe best for somebody else."

The reverend, seeing no forthcoming response, continued. "Sometimes wha's so painful for us can actually help someone else get through a bad spell. Tis for their benefit, not oors, but we can be happy knowin' another person has been helped because o' us.

"Like a mother when she's in labor," MacClure went on. "From wha' I hear, she's nae really enjoyin' the pangs o' birthin'. But she knows, in spite o' the pain, tha' she'll be bringin' a wean t' life."

Rohan thought back to the day when he'd given all those supplies to Gus and Ava when little Rose was born. It had been a great feeling that swept over him, to give from his heart to one who needed the gift and who would appreciate it. "I ga'e half o' my provisions t' a puir family once. We ate sparely for a while, but it surely made me right canty t' do it. Miryam was happy aboot it, too"

Thoughts of Miryam engulfed him. "But why did Miryam ha' t' get... A hurt was done to Miryam... Why did she ha' t' suffer tha' bad?"

MacClure searched for the right words. "Well ye see, Rohan, God's like a parent t' us. We see oor own young'uns sufferin' but we know it'll help 'em learn t' git through life better if we let 'em bear a hardship once in a while. When ye ha' got children, ye mun let 'em learn thin's by experryence. They mun do thin's their own way, so they can learn deep down inside. They dinna want t' ta'e their parent's word tha' up is really up, an' when ye climb up ye got t' get doon somehoo.

"I ha' heard ye tell the story tha' Jonathan was just a mite when he climbed up in the hay moo an' was too scairt t' get doon. Ye said tha' ye ha' telt him a hundred times nae t' go up tha' ladder, did ye nae? But he had t' learn the hard way tha' ye kent wha' ye were talkin' aboot. He dinna trust ye t' tell him the truth, but then he had t' trust ye nae t' let him fall when ye was helpin' him climb backwards doon tha' ladder, did he nae?"

Rohan could see that Jamie was beginning to make some sense.

"Aye, we got pretty close after tha'. We were close for a guid long time, until this thin' happened. I ha' nae been close t' anyone lately."

"Ye ha' t' let Jon make his own mistakes. T' learn the wa' o' this world. An' when he got all befuddled, he'd come runnin' t' ye for help. If ye'd ha' held his hand an' done everythin' for him, he'd ha' ne'er learnit anythin'. Noo look at him, he's a grown man. Does a man's share aroond the farm. He learnit all tha' from ye bein' his fither. If ye would ha' pamperit him, he'd be a weak man today in the thin's tha' coont. We canna shield oor children from life's hurts or they willna grow strong enow t' survive."

"But wha' aboot Miryam? She's nae a child."

"We are all God's bairns. God doesna always shield adults from harm neither. When we come t' realize tha' we're fully dependent on Him, God gives us shelter on the inside, instead o' the ootside. The inside is right where it hurts ye so bad noo. Am I right? Tha's where we need His protection the most. That's why God doesna stop the hurtin'. Pain is a great teacher. When a child touches a hot stove he learns nae t' touch it agin. When tha' divil hurts us, we can learn nae t' dawdle aroond him any more. The only wa' t' keep oot o' his path is t' follow God's wa' instead. God warns us t' keep us awa' from the divil in the first place, but we dinna listen."

"Miryam listens... she dinna follow the divil. Why did she get hurt?"

"I'm nae sayin' tha' bad thin's willna happen t' guid folks, but the folks who follow the Lord, an' who cry oot t' Him will surely be answered by Him. When He answers, they know! E'en though they may be in the midst o' a terrible storm, He has nae forgotten 'em. E'en though they hurt in awful ways on the ootside, they ha' a secure place on the inside where nae harm can come t' 'em.

"God permits pain in oor lives t' build character an' strength in us, an' He understands wha'e'er we have t' endure. Look at His pain when He tried t' explain who He was t' those Jews, an' they turnit awa' agin an' agin an' agin. Then He sent His Son! He let His only Son be brought up before the law – an' then murdered! An' He was nae guilty of anythin'! Think aboot His hurt when He sent Jesus t' carry the sin o' the whole world, all the sin o' the past, an' the present, an' the future, too!

"For e'ry time someone is neglected, for e'ry time someone is looked doon on, for e'ry time someone is rejected or scorned, for e'ry shameful word e'er thought or spoken, for e'ry lie e'er told, for e'ry rape, for e'ry shootin', for e'ry robbery, for e'ry adultery, for e'ry murder...

"For e'ry sin known t' man, an' those only alone God knows, Jesus was the only one tha' could bear the hurtin', an' the punishment."

Rohan was squinting with his confusion. "Why would He want t' do that? I'm nae guid enow for anyone t' die for me! Why would He care aboot me? I'm nobody! Nobody!"

"But t' God ye surely are somebody. He knows ye inside an' oot. Your sin separates ye from God, just like your anger separates ye from your family. Ye came in here today wi' your heart broken in two because o' this wrong tha's been done ye. How do ye think God feels? The world was so full o' sin tha' He just had t' do somethin' t' take the sin awa'. He doesna want ye t' be separated from Him anymore. When was the last time ye felt Him close t' ye? When ye knew tha' He truly exists?"

Rohan was silent. He remembered the times he played his fiddle. God was close by then.

"But," Rohan questioned, "couldna He just make thin's right t' begin with?"

"He kent tha' folks need t' choose t' love Him. He had t' give us the ability t' choose Him instead of just gang oor own way. Jesus kent tha'

His death would look like a wasted thin' in oor eyes, but when He obeyed His Fither an' died in oor place He bought us all back from slavery t' the divil. He paid a huge price for us t' be freed. He was the only one who could pay the price for oor sin - because He was innocent. Only His own blood was pure enow. He was the only One who dinna need t' be freed, so He was the only One who could help.

"Think once aboot it… When a body's locked up in prison, the only one who can let 'em oot is somebody who is already free, right?"

"But why, why did He do it?" Rohan just could not comprehend this Jesus.

"Because, He is the only one that holds the key."

"What is this key you're talking aboot? I dinna understand ye."

"The whole key t' the kingdom o' God is love. He did it for love. He loves us, nae matter who we are, nae matter wha' we've done t' push Him away. He did it because He wanted to. He decided t' do it. All we mun do is let Him love us, let Him come in t' oor lives an' make us better people, fit t' be walkin' an' talkin' with Him e'ry day, like Adam an' Eve did in the beginnin'. He did it so there'd be somebody t' share His love wi', like a family."

"Could He want t' share His love wi'… e'en me? I'm nae a guid man, I used t' think I was. But I'm nae e'en much o' a family man any more. Could He really want me? I wish I knew for sure."

Rohan's eyes met the Reverend's for a long moment, then before any more words could be spoken, he blinked hard and fast and rushed from the church.

"Rohan! Ye can be sure, ye can!" called the minister.

But Rohan was running. He didn't know where to go, but he had to cry! Where can a man go to cry where no one will disturb him or think overmuch about it? He headed for the graveyard. There wasn't any of his own kin buried there, but an old friend had passed last year, and he found the grave through his mask of anguish and knelt there. "Oh God, hoo do I ken for sure tha' ye want me for your family? I ha' made a bad mess oot o' my own!"

Rohan rested his forehead on the coolness of the grass as he watered the ground with his tears. His sobs of grief were barely audible but served to loosen the sorrow long pent up in his soul.

He spoke to the earth beneath him as if to God. "Hoo can I trust ye when you've shaken everythin'?"

Then he heard in a firm strong voice that seemed to rumble up from the ground,

"HOW CAN I SHOW YOU THAT THE ROCK
UPON WHICH YOU STAND IS SOLID
UNLESS I SOMETIMES MAKE THE WHOLE
WORLD AROUND YOU TREMBLE?"

Suddenly he felt calm enough to able to carry on. He rose with a determination to try to see his world from a new perspective, to look for meaning where he had only seen tragedy before. Let the nay-sayers do their worst. He would have to try to do his best.

Chapter 28

Mama said that Da wouldn't take us to church anymore because he was wait-
ing for God to talk to him alone. He'd said he needed some answers from God
but He needed peace and quiet to be able to hear. So we didn't go to church
for a few months. And though Mama was sure God was talking, it seemed
that Da didn't hear what He was saying.

But Mama read from Da's Bible when he was doing his chores on Sunday
mornings. She liked Psalm 130, especially because it spoke of forgiveness.

"Out of the depths have I cried unto Thee, O LORD. Lord, hear my
voice: let Thine ears be attentive to the voice of my supplications. If
Thou, LORD, shouldest mark iniquities, O Lord, who shall stand?
But there is forgiveness with Thee, that Thou mayest be feared.

I wait for the LORD, my soul doth wait, and in His word do I hope. My
soul waiteth for the Lord more than they that watch for the morning:
I say, more than they that watch for the morning. Let Israel hope in
the LORD: for with the LORD there is mercy, and with Him is plente-
ous redemption. And He shall redeem Israel from all His iniquities."

Ralph and Bettina liked to sit near the front of the kirk where they
could see and hear best. The Sunday choir was the worst it had ever
sounded. Mr. Fellows tucked his ample chins to his chest and boomed out
notes that were quite powerful, however out of tune. Jeanette Wilkey war-
bled unsteadily toward the high notes which continually eluded her, while
Helen Bastable made a futile attempt at a contralto harmony. Warren
Manning stretched his skinny neck and was nearly as red as his vest as
he rounded up his tenor crescendo. It was more than poor Ralph could

bear. And when at the last measure, the organist struck a wrong note, which sent Miss Wilkey into a frantic tizzy, he could stand it no longer and did not restrain his laughter. Bettina jammed her elbow into his ribs, but was unsuccessful in stopping his hearty guffaws.

When they emerged from the church, Ralph tried to make amends. "Would you like me to take you out with me to deliver the letter to the MacVoy's?"

"Ralph, I don't feel like it! I shouldn't wonder if this whole town thinks you're a crazy person after the way you behaved today while the choir was singing!"

"Horse feathers! They all know me and they've probably wondered how I managed to hold it in so long."

"Well all right, we can go to the MacVoy's, but you must restrain yourself from comments about the choir. Do you promise?"

"I pledge to you that I'll be on my very best behavior, dearest."

When they arrived at the MacVoy's the letter was ceremoniously opened. Miryam's mother was not famous for writing nice letters. Both Rohan and Miryam wondered what the subject of her frustration was this time. Miryam began to read while the listeners sipped their tea.

"Dear Miryam,

I see now that this new faith your father has accepted is much closer to the truth than I had thought could ever be. I couldn't stand for him to talk about it all the time with me left in the dark about what the Torah may have to say. So I began to read it for myself, from the 'Old Testament' and the 'New' one, too. What stories, what tsoriss, what misery!

This Jesus your Papa talks about? I always thought of Him as a goy gonif, someone who pulled the wool over the eyes, but now I am going to call Him Yeshua. And I'm still going to use the word Adonai for the name of 'the Lord'. I still believe, like other Jews, that His name is too holy to speak aloud. I know now that I used that as an excuse to not talk about Him at all while you were growing up.

But that has changed now. I have taken great pains to write this all down because I have been so wrong for all this time and didn't know it. I want you, now, to know what I have denied my whole life, that Adonai's plan was that His spoken Word, Yeshua, would spring up in the fields of men's souls and bring the Bread of Life to all who hungered for it.

Yeshua blessed and broke loaves of bread to feed thousands. At His last Passover, He took bread, gave thanks and broke it, and gave it to His disciples, saying, "Take and eat; this is My body."[24] What a meshugge thing to say, I was thinking!

But it was because He is the Lamb of God, the Passover Lamb! Yeshua poured the wine into the cup of salvation at that last Passover feast with His disciples, saying, "This is My blood of the new testament, which is shed for many for the remission of sins."[25]

The name of Yeshua means salvation! When you read that passage from Isaiah, which Papa talks about all the time now, it all makes sense! He is Elohim!

I hope you understand why I write so much here. It is very exciting to me! I now understand that the Jesus of the goyim is also the Yeshua of Isaiah! He is our Messiah!

My Miryam, I love you,
Your Mama"

Miryam was stunned. Her eyes stared straight ahead. Rohan waved a hand in front of her, which brought her back to the table they all sat around.

"Never would I have believed it. I don't believe it still. Mama said she loves me. If this Yeshua is real, I want to know Him," she murmured under her breath.

Ralph whuffed a small tickle in his throat and pushed his chair away from the table. Bettina looked at him, questioning. But he persisted in getting their things together to leave. Bettina managed to say the polite thank you's and gave a brisk hug to her friend as Ralph opened the door for her. They climbed into their buggy and waved as Rohan stood in the yard. When out of hearing Bettina pulled at Ralph's shirt, "Why the bum's rush back there? Miryam was ready to talk about God!"

"It's not time yet," Ralph answered. "There was a holy moment. I'll grant you that. And the time will come. But I believe the Lord said to me that He has some work to do first. It's His timing, not ours." They grasped hands silently for a moment, each knowing that the other was praying the same thing – that a change was about to come that would bring peace to the MacVoy's home.

Chapter 29

Rohan left to attend his chores, while Miryam's thoughts remained on her mother's letter. She sat down in her rocking chair and laid Rohan's Bible across her lap. She slowly turned the pages of the book seeking the answers it might hold for her. She passed through the pages, reading a paragraph here, a line there. It seemed to be true that her people had not been faithful to *Adonai,* the Lord. He had called them to be His own, but they had turned away from Him time after time. Yet it seemed that He would not give up!

She knew the word her mother always had used, *goyim.* It meant people who were not Jews. To her parents, Rohan was *goy.* She knew that only too well. *Goy* meant gentile, and *im* meant people. "Gentile people." The *im* meant the word was plural. She knew that in the Jewish Scriptures God was called. *"Elohim."*

"But, wait" Miryam spoke with alarm, "that would mean Elohim is a plural word!" A plural God? That could not be! She sought affirmation in her childhood prayer, and quickly began to say the *Sh'ma,* a tradition as old as Moses.

"Sh'ma Yisrael, Adonai Elohenu, Adonai Echad…" There it is! The answer!

"Hear, Israel, the Lord is our God, the Lord is One."

She spoke aloud again, "Echad means one, ONE God. One person. There is only one of me, one Miryam." But wait, that would be where she should say *achat,* another word for one. There is only *achat* Miryam, she knew that meant "a singular Miryam." But she also knew that *echad* meant one, as in one family. Her people, the Jews, were one nationality, *echad!* One People!

"It's true!" Miryam almost shouted it.

Her thoughts ran to and fro as she grasped the enormity of this. Jesus was the God of Abraham, Isaac, and Jacob! He was the one plural God of a plural people, her people! Yes, He was the living God of this book. He was the God who knew her. The Torah spoke of the Lord, the Salvation of Israel, of the Lord's Messiah, and of the Spirit of the Lord – not more than one God, but more than one facet of Him.

She came to the Psalms. They told of deep yearnings in the hearts of her people – of cries in the darkest of nights, and songs of thanksgiving for answered prayers. She, too, had felt that longing. She saw that these people wrote genuine stories, of life's fullest measure of sorrows and joys.

There were places in the MacVoy family Bible where someone had marked certain verses. She could hardly imagine the audacity of writing in a book! These Psalms were of great importance to someone. The marked passages were like a map, showing the way to a sojourner. One after another, she read aloud the marked passages,

"Thou art my hiding place. Thou shalt preserve me from trouble. Thou shalt compass me about with songs of deliverance…"[26]

There was a slip of paper tucked into the crease. The person who had marked these passages explained the reason for doing so. It was what Rohan's own father had said to him. His Da said that there were "precious words" that must be passed on from generation to generation. His Mother had said that the Bible had "the secret for life inside." It read,

"O God, Thou hast taught me from my youth:
and hitherto have I declared Thy wondrous works.
Now also when I am old and gray headed,
O God, forsake me not; until I have shewed Thy strength unto this gen-
eration, and Thy power to every one that is to come." Psalm 71:17-18

Miryam turned the pages rapidly, searching for more underlined passages. One place read,

"Come my children, hearken to me. I will teach you the fear of the Lord."[27]

Another passage spoke of the same wondering she felt in her own heart concerning the Lord.

> *"I remember Thee upon my bed, and medi-*
> *tate on Thee in the night watches."*[28]

Miryam felt that she was hearing wisdom directly from those who had diligently read this book, almost as if she was walking in their footsteps. Her heart felt a kinship to those who knew far more than she did about the God of her people. What more did this Bible have to say to her? She looked for the book of the prophet Isaiah, and the words that her father had written about. When she found it, she was taken aback by the harsh words the prophet wrote, saying,

> *"And when ye spread forth your hand, I will hide mine eyes from you. Yea,*
> *when ye make many prayers, I will not hear. Your hands are full of blood."*[29]

He spoke of the desolation of a people who had turned away from God.

"Have I turned away from God?" she wondered. "Not purposefully, but I have never turned toward him purposefully either. All I know is what I could memorize as a child. I've been like a child, knowing only how to recite the letters in the *alef bet*"

She went to the next marked passage,

> *"The LORD Himself will give you a sign,*
> *a virgin will be with child and will give birth to a son*
> *and will call Him Immanuel."*[30]

Here, someone had written in the Bible's margin, "Immanuel means God with Us."

And then she read the next,

> *"For unto us a child is born, to us a son is given,*
> *and the government will be upon His shoulders.*

And His name will be called Wonderful Counselor,
Mighty God, Everlasting Father, Prince of Peace."[31]

These were the very words which her father had sent to her. Words which had meant so much to her grandfather! Miryam knew then that a world had been opened to her that she had never imagined existed. It was a kingdom where the God of wonder and might ruled. It was a place where a King and a Prince and a Spirit ruled forever, and she could feel a place inside her heart, that had been asleep for so long, come to life. It was as if she could breathe fragrant, clean air after being confined for a lifetime to staleness. She was so eager that she nearly tore the pages as she looked for the 53rd chapter her father had written about. When she found it the words leapt from the page. The passage was titled, "The Suffering Servant." It read,

"Who hath believed our report? And to whom is the arm
of the LORD revealed? For He shall grow up before Him
as a tender plant, and as a root out of a dry ground:
He hath no form nor comeliness; and when we shall see
Him, there is no beauty that we should desire Him.
He is despised and rejected of men; a man of sorrows, and ac-
quainted with grief: and we hid, as it were, our faces from
Him; He was despised, and we esteemed Him not."[32]

Miryam could only imagine what Yeshua must have felt when His own people rejected Him. She had heard many times from Reverend MacClure that Jesus, at His death, had been beaten so terribly that it would have been hard to look at Him. And the next words she read rang true to life.

"Surely He hath borne our griefs, and carried our sorrows: yet
we did esteem Him stricken, smitten of God, and afflicted.
But He was wounded for our transgressions, He was
bruised for our iniquities: the chastisement of our peace
was upon Him; and with His stripes we are healed.

All we like sheep have gone astray; we have turned every one to his own way; and the LORD *hath laid on Him the iniquity of us all."*[33]

This was what the Passover was about, the next verses confirmed it. Miryam felt her burden lifted as she read on,

"He was oppressed, and He was afflicted, yet He opened not his mouth:
He is brought as a lamb to the slaughter, and as
a sheep before her shearers is dumb,
so He openeth not His mouth."[34]

This book, this Bible, stirred in her a hunger for more and more of the God she had never known. He was more than a relic from the past, more than a distant, unreachable being. She remembered Reverend MacClure saying that even though Jesus had been crucified, He was alive, right now. She prayed, for the first time in her life, with a heart that was waiting to hear an answer. "Tell me who you are – I want to know you."

Miryam went right out into the yard and looked up at the sky. Overwhelming yet inexpressible love flooded over her, as she saw that all of her life was a gift from her heavenly father. She thought of all the things which had a way of pleasing her, a way of making her smile without really knowing why - like whenever she saw a lady bug, or a nuthatch with his blue back and his striped head, or the fat woodchuck who lived under the bushes at the edge of the barn, or the deer that made their leisurely way across the yard twice each day going to and from their daily grazing places.

The popping and rustling of the fire in the hearth at night, the warmth of her nightdress when she draped it over the settle to toast up before bedtime, the laughter of her loved ones, the song of the chickadees, the bright pink breast of the bluebird, the early morning yellow melting the night away, the tiny shoots of new spring plants emerging, her delighted surprise whenever she came upon a salamander or a toad hiding under a leaf in the kailyard

Each of these simple pleasures was a gift from God, designed especially for her since she was often the only one to see the sleek rabbit as he wandered around in his lavish fur coat finding a fallen apple or a stash of nuts left by the squirrels.

She had tried in vain to find truth in the things around her, in her daily life, but truth was instead something greater than she. She pondered the matter from a different point of view. It was a Who and not a what!

Truth is the knowledge that You love me even though I don't deserve it.

Truth is knowing You'll never leave me.

Truth is when Your love takes the pain and aching in my heart and works the tenderness out, carefully and masterfully, until I am whole again.

Truth is the light You have kindled within me that shines out through all the wounds I have suffered, showing the way to a better place.

Truth is knowing that I don't have to hide anymore.

Truth is safety and trust amid life's fiercest storms.

Truth is a skillful mingling of my grief and my giddy joy that produces a wine that will age to perfection.

Truth is giving just because it feels so good to offer what I have to someone who needs it.

Truth is the exchange of a life of ragged edges for a life of completeness.

Truth is the giving of a pure life to pay for an impure one, a debt paid by the One who does not owe anything to anyone.

Truth is the release of my white knuckled grip on all that I hold too close, into the competent hands of the only ONE who can measure it back to me as needed.

She knelt down and leaned forward to place her head to the ground in worship. This carpenter she had heard of from the *goyim* was truly the Lord. His words were truth. There was a way to start over. Mercy has a way of sweeping away all the stains, all the pain, all the resentments and all the blame from the past and creating a fresh start for each moment.

Mama told me that she felt herself washed and able to begin afresh with the promises of God. She said that it was as if she was clothed with a new understanding and love for Da that she had been unable to grasp before. She was looking at him with a different, loving heart.

As the next days passed Miryam wondered to herself, "Could God work within Rohan's heart, to call him away from the destructiveness of his anger?" She felt the sting of tears well up in her eyes.

Yes, she had read it!

"Come now, and let us reason together, saith the Lord. Though your sins be as scarlet, they shall be as white as snow..."[35]

She prayed for Rohan to hear the call of his Heavenly Father, and turn toward Him. She knew that God would not forsake him. But would Rohan answer?

It was washday again. Miryam made a decision. She would pray over each garment as she washed it, rinsed it and hung it. That way each member of her household would be sure to be well prayed for.

That was good for wash day, but what about the rest of the week? She then decided to pray as she washed the dishes as well. Each plate and cup and utensil was lovingly cared for. This inspired her to pray as she cooked, that the food would somehow nourish and bless her family's souls as well as their bodies. The prayers flew home to God on the wonderful smells of freshly baked breads and biscuits, the hearty aroma of stews and soups, the sweet fragrance of jams and pies, and cakes, and the enticing scent of cinnamon in Josey's favorite dessert, applesauce, which he called "applefuss."

Miryam began to recover from the grief she had borne. She began to hum the tunes to her favorite hymns. She had not realized that, in the years of attending the Christian kirk, she had learned so many.

One day as she swept the front room she found herself singing! On the porch she laughed at the antics of the chipmunks as they chased each other among the stacks of firewood. She listened to the birds' songs early in the morning as she made breakfast. She stopped to admire a bird as it landed on her rose bush. She felt the stony heart of pain within her soften and become flesh again.

As often was her habit, Miryam took her prayers to the outhouse. At least there she could pray uninterrupted. She spoke aloud, fervently, while seated on the "throne of grace." She poured out her heart, had a full head of steam going, and was fully assured of the Lord's ear when she heard a timid knocking at the door to the outhouse.

"Mum?" came the little voice, "Who's in there with you?"

Miryam had to laugh. "No one, Josey. It's just me."

"Then who are you talkin' to?"

"I'm praying to *Adonai*. I'm just praying."

"Oh… is He staying for dinner?"

Miryam grinned but replied in an even tone. "Just run along, go see what Jonny is doing."

That night Miryam was chuckling in her sleep. Rohan lay next to her wondering what on earth she was dreaming about. Her chuckling became louder and then she burst into a delighted laughter that made Rohan himself begin to grin. Whatever she was thinking, he wanted to know the same joy. It had been a long time since he had had a good laugh.

She was stirring, waking, still laughing. When she became fully awake, she realized that Rohan was looking at her curiously. "What?" she asked.

"You surely were havin' a guid time! Wha' was it all aboot?"

"Oh, what did I do?"

"You were laughin' an' carryin' on!" answered Rohan. "Wha' was so funny?"

"Oh! It wasn't so much funny as joyful," Miryam said. "We were in a banquet hall, you and I, and Gus and Ava. And Bettina and Ralph … and you'll never guess who else."

"Who?"

"It was Gertrude! We were all just tickled about something. We laughed until our sides ached."

"I dinna believe I e'er saw ol' Gertie laugh, or e'en smile for tha' matter. Why were ye laughin'?"

"We were so happy, like at a surprise party when the person walks into the room and everyone shouts and laughs." Miryam went on to describe her dream. "Gertrude was laughing the most of any of us. She was near to falling off her chair, so I hurried to her just as she was just falling over and I caught her up in my arms."

"Tha' must ha' been hard on ye, she's a big woman!"

"But she was no weight at all to me. She was like a feather in my hands. She looked at me and she just laughed! She knew me, but she wasn't rude or angry. She looked at me with love and we laughed together. Then I woke up!"

The clock chimed twice. "Well," Rohan smiled, "I'm glad you ha' such a jolly time, but I ha' t' get up early, so if ye'll keep your party quiet, I'll get me some more sleepin' done."

"I'll try to keep it down, Rohan," Miryam joked. "Good night again."

Chapter 30

Rohan had decided that perhaps he wasn't a good enough listener to hear God speak to him out of the blue, so he had begun to take the family to the church again. As the family made the trip to town each week, young Josey asked question after question about how the Bible stories came to be written down and whether they were true or made up.

Rohan had wondered the same things but would have felt foolish asking. But lately he had felt God speaking to him, just as he had asked for. He had listened with a new heart during the last few Sunday sermons as intently as young Josey and thought deeply about this God who seemed to have such love for His people.

Josey knew that his name, and his brother's and his parents' names were all from the Bible, and so it was that he asked to hear the stories often where each of their names were mentioned. The woman named Miryam in the scriptures was the sister of the priest in the tabernacle. Mama had told him that it was like a kirk for the Jews.

Da's second name was Peadar. Rohan Peadar MacVoy. This was the Gaelic way of saying Peter. The man named Peter had promised to stick by Jesus no matter what. Then when he became afraid, Peter lied and said he didn't know Him. But then Jesus loved him so much that He forgave him and led Peter be a teacher for others to know Him better.

The young prince named Jonathan was King David's good friend, who protected him from his enemies. And the man called Joseph was a man who believed God and helped people by following God's ways.

Today as they bumped along in the wagon, bundled against the blowing snow, they listened to Miryam read the story of the prodigal son who had left his home and lived recklessly and shamefully, and who had finally returned and found his father rejoicing at his homecoming. "This fither," thought Rohan, "loved his son in spite o' the way he acted. Why canna I love this boy, Joseph, who always behaves? Hoo mun God think o' me an' the way I behave?"

The family reached town and Rohan watched the boys together as they hitched up the horse and as they walked, hand in hand, toward the church. Jon had always loved his little brother dearly and reached out to him to make up for Rohan's negligence. Rohan knew this well. Then, as if by chance, Rohan and Josey ended up sitting side by side in the tiny sanctuary. Miryam knew that it was no coincidence, for she and Jon had often ended their bedtime prayers with a petition aimed at Rohan's relationship with the boy.

The pew was hard as they sat together, the winter air nipping at their feet in the cold room. The small potbellied stove was not nearly enough to warm the church as the singing began. They rose and lifted their voices in the cold air. The effect was thin, but strong.

> *"How can it be tho' I live in this flesh*
> *that I may grow by Your spirit in knowledge of You?*
> *That tho' dead in my sin, I shall have life anew?*
>
> *How can it be that one so small as I*
> *Should be loved by One so great?*
> *To see with Your love, not ruled by hate*
>
> *How can it be that You, Who made the sun and stars*
> *should grant me the privilege of prayer?*
> *That by loving Your ways I should learn to care?*
>
> *How can it be that Your hands*
> *which bore crude nails, would also bear my name?*
> *That in Your death and rising You have taken away my shame?"*

The congregation settled back into their seats for the lessons.

"The first reading is from Psalm 63, verses 1-8," Esther Mitchell began in her quivery voice.

"O God, Thou art my God; early will I seek Thee: my soul thirsteth for Thee, my flesh longeth for Thee in a dry and thirsty land, where no water is…"

Rohan's mind wandered as the reading went on without him. "My flesh longs for understandin.' I'm in a thirsty place."

The reading must have ended as he was lost in his thoughts.

"Let us rise and sing," announced the choirmaster.

> *"Though lies have made, by dread and fear,*
> *a prisoner of my heart,*
> *may truth's bright coals rekindle now*
> *and strength to me impart.*
> *O let that spark within me grow*
> *until it's burning strong.*
> *I'll bear His light of righteousness*
> *tho' wrong has ruled so long.*
>
> *His fire still burns within my soul*
> *and I'll not give up now,*
> *I'll fan to flames the gift of God*
> *as I before Him bow.*
> *His mighty blaze shall set apart*
> *the dross from what is pure.*
> *And I my King shall celebrate*
> *and for His Name endure."*

Reverend MacClure took his place at the podium and introduced a guest to give the sermon. The MacVoy's were both quite surprised to see that it was Jon who rose from his seat to speak. He had indeed spent a longer time than usual to dress this morning, but they had thought that was because he and Ana had taken such a liking to each other. With raised eyebrows they exchanged glances.

Reverend MacClure continued, "Young Jonathan here has been studyin' wi' me aboot God's plan for man. He's doin' this t' prepare for bein' baptized, o' his own choosin', when the weather gets warmer. He's put a great lot o' hard work in t' this report he's goin' t' read, so I ask for your full attention."

Jon could not look at his audience, but stared instead at his papers. At the sound of a slight rustle from the congregation he stuck a finger inside his collar to loosen it and began. His voice was high at first but evened out after a few sentences to its usual tenor.

"Our God visited earth to pay the ransom for us with His own sinless life. Jesus taught that love and justice must walk hand in hand. He lived what He taught, a pure life. His mercy shields us from the punishment we deserve, and His grace showers us with blessings that we could not earn on our own merit. All who seek Him are cleansed from their sins, past, present and future.

"When Jesus had paid the price for our sin, God raised Him from death to new life. This new life is open to all who believe, to all who accept the gift. Until God's gift of new life in Jesus has been received, we cannot own it. But when we acknowledge Him in our daily lives we are in the relationship that God planned from the beginning.

"God defines sin as missing the mark, falling short of who He intends us to be. Every man, woman and child has missed the mark every day since the fall of man. As man has known from the beginning, the price for sin is dear. It is separation from God.

"Rituals and covenants have been made and laid down throughout history, and in primitive cultures today are still practiced. The plan given by God was the sacrifice of an unblemished lamb, or other innocent living thing, as payment for sin. God knew that man could not offer anything that would fully absolve himself, so sacrificial offerings had to be made continually to cover sin with blood. Even then it would never be enough for man to stand blameless before God.

"God's only solution was to interject Himself. As the Torah shows, the Spirit of God has rested on His people while they obeyed Him. But disobedience brought discord again and again. As God's redemptive plan unfolded, the Holy Spirit of God overshadowed a young virgin, Mary, implanting Jesus within her. The life in her womb was fully God and fully man. Jesus would be the only divine man, born of a virgin. As a human being, Jesus could pay

the debt incurred by mankind. As His holiness took on flesh, He could pay the price for our sin by offering Himself as a blood sacrifice. He would die on our behalf.

"The New Covenant teaches that the fulfillment of the Old Covenant has been accomplished as the prophecies of the coming Jewish Messiah were fulfilled. There is not one word of the Law which has not been fulfilled in Jesus. He is the anointed Lamb of God, the Savior. He could offer the only pure, holy and perfect sacrifice to redeem imperfect man. As we come to the Lord's table, to the banquet He has provided, and as we partake of the body and blood of Christ, we are given the only antidote to the poison of evil. It's in Luke 22:19 - 'And He took bread, and gave thanks, and brake it, and gave unto them, saying, This is My body which is given for you: this do in remembrance of Me.'"

When Jon had finished, he looked up and spoke from his heart. "My heart got hurt really bad a few years ago and I struggled with how I was going to behave and react to all the hurts in my life. It has taken a long time of thought, and some prayer times with some good people..." He looked at his mother, at Ralph and at the reverend, "but I know now that I was not forgotten by God. So I choose to accept His plan for me by being baptized as a Christian. I was raised both Jewish and Christian and it was confusing at times, but I can see now that being a follower of Jesus is really a continuation of all that my mother's Jewish roots have taught me."

He stopped and glanced for approval from his pastor and found a beaming response.

"Well, I guess that's all I need to say," he finished, and left the podium a bit taller than when he had arrived.

"Thank ye, Jon," grinned MacClure. We'll be lookin' forward t' your baptism in t' the family o' the Lord. Now let us sing!"

The service was long and Josey was tired from his early morning chores.

"Cows dinna ken tis Sunday," Rohan had said to him. "Wilhelmina mun be milked just like any other day."

Miryam had brought the blanket in from the wagon, anticipating the chill in the small building. She had wrapped Josey up in the blanket's warmth as he sat trying to stay awake. The organ sounded the first line as an introduction and Miryam turned to share her book with Rohan and found that he was still seated. Young Josey had fallen asleep, his head cradled in Rohan's lap. Tears sprang to her eyes as she sang her thanks to God. Her husband was too gentle a man to move a muscle and disturb the sleeping boy. God was doing His work to wear away Rohan's defenses. The congregation's hearty voices rang out.

> *"I travel a road trodden by the King,*
> *His royal highway through a desperate land.*
> *I search for the signs that He's gone on before me*
> *and my only strength comes from His almighty hand.*
>
> *The road is quite narrow, the travelers few,*
> *but we carry the banner of His most holy Name.*
> *The journey is long yet we march onward singing,*
> *as the weary band cries out His glorious fame.*
>
> *The Word of the Lord is most faithful and sure.*
> *He shows the true pathway to all who would go.*
> *His hope is within us and His love is our charter,*
> *for we're strangers and aliens and we're on our way home.*
>
> *Our vision our Voyage, all lead to His house,*
> *through valleys and highlands, by faith, not by sight –*
> *For faith isn't faith when you see where you're going.*
> *Yet I'll sing of His mercies and I'll walk in His light.*
>
> *I'll walk out his promise for I know whom I trust,*
> *traveling mile after mile, by night and by day.*
> *I've never seen heaven, but my home's where my heart is,*
> *for my King is my refuge and He's leading my way."*

Rohan sat there staring at the wrinkled jacket of the man in front of him. He did not want to feel fatherly toward this boy. He did not feel comfortable with the yearning inside him to touch the black silky strands of hair that fell across Josey's face and trace his finger along the outline of that square little jaw. He fought with himself as he felt the warmth of the small face and hand on his legs. "This boy has ne'er asked a single thin' o' me," he thought. "He follows me aroond like Jon's pup... an' he gets nae more attention from me than I'd give t' a sparrow on the barn roof. Wha's wrong wi' me? I canna go on livin' like this, nae bein' a proper fither t' him."

The swell of voices seemed to make the sun shine brighter through the dusty windows. The words of the hymn rang true as Rohan listened. It spoke of letting God be the one to order the lives of men, the uselessness of trying to live without His guidance, and the simple beauty of being in God's will. Rohan knew the need to be free from the striving he could no longer bear. Yet he did not know how to lay it down, and the strain of carrying it was too much for him. This child had so utterly altered his existence that he could not find anywhere on the whole homestead that was unaffected by Joseph's laughter and chatter when he was small. More recently, the silent solitude of this boy shouted in a resounding silence.

Rohan did not realize that he liked hearing the laughter of the child, until it had stopped.

The order and peace that had once been his had been shattered with the arrival of an innocent child. "Is tha' so bad, tha' my life has changed? Is my life so ordered tha' I canna accept him?" he wondered. "Is this child here t' show me where there is beauty in this world? T' show me where I might be able t' find God's peace?"

When love is the issue, he realized, he would have to learn to speak it for himself and not make Miryam say it for him. He was well aware that she had always filled the gap. A great sense of longing for this child suddenly overcame Rohan. This boy was part of his heart and could be denied no longer. This boy did not know of his conception, and could not be held at arm's length because of his biological heritage. He belonged to Rohan, who had witnessed his every breath since birth and who had seen him through his daily journeys from being nursed at his mother's breast to learning the fine art of polishing a saddle. True, Rohan had led him angrily and resentfully, but led him all the same. No one else could lay claim to the title of father to the boy. Love had come in when there was a chink in the walls Rohan had built around himself. He must tell the laddie face to face, heart to heart. He had let Miryam speak the words to this child his whole life, saying, "Dada loves you," on his behalf. He must not delay. It was time to say it himself.

Suddenly gunshots echoed from the street and a bullet struck the bell in the steeple. The women screamed and the children cried. Josey woke wondering what was going on.

Dan jumped from his seat in the last pew and ran out the door.

He had usually made it a habit to linger in the vestibule where he could hear the service of worship without being seen. He sang quietly, then left as soon as the benediction was said. It meant a lot to him to hear the words from the book of Jude each week.

> *"Now unto Him that is able to keep you from falling,*
> *and to present you faultless*
> *before the presence of His glory with exceeding joy,*
> *to the only wise God our Saviour,*
> *be glory and majesty, dominion and power,*
> *both now and ever. Amen"*[36]

In the extreme cold of the winter day he had come inside to sit at the rear of the church, arriving last, after waiting until all the others had entered the building. Few people noticed his presence, most of all, no one in the MacVoy family, who always sat on the opposite side of the center aisle, and toward the front. He had been able to watch the child grow into a sturdy little boy. His fine, straight black hair matched Dan's own, so unlike the other family members. Rohan and Jon were known for their red hair and their height, while this boy was the smallest of all the playmates of his age. This boy was tough, though, like a wrestler in miniature. Josey did not reflect anything of his parents.

Dan had always wanted children. Now he had a son whom he could not even speak to, let alone acknowledge as his own. His suffering was multiplied by the suffering he could see in the man, Rohan. Rohan did not love the boy. Perhaps no one else could see it, but as one who had lived long under the same roof with a woman who did not love him, Dan knew the signs. Rohan did not watch the boy as he played, as a proud father would. Nor did Rohan reach out a hand for the child to hold as they walked to and from the church.

As a nurturing person, when he was sober, Dan forever wanted to hold out his hand to the boy, but he could not. He knew he was forgiven in the eyes of God, but the MacVoy family was another story. His pain would remain his own. His anonymous fatherhood would be lived out from afar. It was sometimes all he could do not to walk into the saloon for a drink to ease his sorrow.

The sheriff was the only one wearing a gun in the church service, so he left his pew and went out to stop whatever celebration had gotten out of hand. It was the law that the saloon was not to open on Sundays, but this had apparently been overlooked. In the street, a drunken man reeled in the saddle, causing the horse to turn this way and that as the reins were jerked whenever the man lost his balance. He waved his pistol over his head in circles. The sheriff walked toward the carouser, one hand on his gun.

"Alright now mister, you can go on home now. This is no rodeo show here."

The fool in the saddle took one look at the sheriff and shot him in the leg. The men had all been watching from the doorway of the church, but at the shot Rohan ran to his wagon, which was closest, to get his rifle from under the seat.

The sheriff groaned, holding his kerchief to his wound to stop the bleeding. Rohan had not yet been seen. The drunk swung wildly down from the horse, staggered toward the sheriff. He was weaving as he walked, flailing about with his gun in the air, but fully determined to finish him off. Rohan shouted at the man to stop, but was not heard above the whiskey inspired ranting.

He yelled again when the rebel stopped for breath. "Ye stop noo, right where ye stand!"

The man turned and took aim at Rohan who was crouched beside the wagon. "Don't ya go tellin me what ta do! I'll shoot the next one that moves!"

Josey had been watching from the window next to the church doorway. Seeing his father threatened, he pushed through the crowd in the vestibule before anyone knew what was happening and rushed into the street. The stranger was startled and turned again, aimed at Josey, and fired.

Rohan stood and shouted, "No!!! That's my son!!!" He took aim to kill. But the drunk turned and shot before Rohan could pull the trigger. Yet Rohan and the drunken man fell at the same moment.

The town lay in silent shock for what seemed like an eternity as they took in the sight of the child, the sheriff, the stranger, and Rohan all lying in the street. The doctor ran to get his bag. A lone man stood at the end of the street, holding a rifle.

"Someone shot the drunk, was it you?" yelled the sheriff. Dan just turned to leave. But one of the congregation caught up with him.

"Mister, that was quite a shot. You saved their lives! What's your name?"

"It don't matter," Dan answered, and walked away.

The man went back to the church and asked the first person he saw, "Who was that? Who killed him?"

Bettina was thoroughly beside herself. She had seen him raise his gun and make a clean shot at the gunfighter. "It was Dan," she said.

Josey began to whimper and at the sound people sprang to life again. He was barely grazed above the right ear, but no worse. Miryam could hardly breathe.

Jon saw his mother run to Josey so he ran to his father. "Da! Da! Can you hear me?"

Rohan lay still but was breathing. He blinked his eyes rapidly to keep from crying out. It hurt to think, let alone talk. "Josey - is Josey alive?" he whispered hoarsely. And then he lost consciousness.

"I don't know Da. What about you? Da? Da!"

Then Rohan heard Miryam kneeling at his side but was unable to answer. The doctor got his bag and rushed to where he lay.

"Dada! I want to see Dada!" The women were holding Josey back as the doctor worked. "Da!"

"Give me some room if you want to me to save him!" the doctor shouted as the crowd gathered around. "Miryam, Jonathan, you stay." He ripped at the shirt she'd just made for Rohan's birthday. "Open the bandages there inside that package and get me that pair of scissors. Best to get this over with before he wakes up."

Miryam caught his eye. "Will he?"

"I think he'll pull out of it." As the doctor cut away the torn flesh Jon could no longer remain at his father's side. He rose and ran behind the church and retched. Still shaking violently he turned to go back out front. He had to know what was happening!

"It's all right!" Doc breathed a long sigh as if he'd been holding his breath. "The bullet went clean through and didn't even hit a bone! The wound's more in the shoulder than the chest, he'll live to tell about it."

Jon saw his mother embrace Josey. People gathered around his mother and brother as they cried together, but he needed to do his crying alone. He walked down the middle of the deserted street, away from all the people. He wiped the wetness from his face, blinking fast to keep his eyes clear enough to see. He too had seen Dan walk toward the church and take aim.

Jon had at once recognized the gait of this man, the tilt of his hat, the angular jaw line, and the deep dark eyes. And at first, he thought that the stranger who had haunted him had returned to kill his father. It was with full relief that he realized that the stranger had saved his Da's life instead.

Jon ran into the stable and climbed up to the hay loft. He threw himself headlong into the pungent bed and wept tears long bottled up. The fear and the heartache the stranger had brought were washed away. Later, when the weeping was over, Jon realized that he no longer feared or hated the stranger.

Rohan roused as the doctor finished his bandaging and the men were moving him to the hotel. He startled violently and yelled, "That's my son!" Once settled into a room at the hotel, he wept bitterly in his half conscious state and called out, "Josey! Josey!!" He prayed in his dreams and those around his bed heard it as well, "Oh God, dinna let my boy die, ta'e me instead!"

The next few days passed without much change as Rohan tossed in a battle against an infection in the wound. Miryam and the doctor took turns cleansing the shoulder and packing it with fresh poultices of drawing herbs. Jon and Josey went to Gustav and Ava's house to stay. Jon meekly approached Dan. Their eyes met in full recognition.

Dan began, "I know that I will never be able ta say I'm sorry enough ta make up fer what I did ta ya and ta yer ma. All I can ask fer is that ya might someday be able ta see yer way ta forgive me."

Jon extended his right hand. "I already did that on Sunday. Thank you for saving Da's life." He thought for a moment, then added, "We need to go to the farm every day to take care of the stock. Would you be able to come along, and help us?"

"I thank ya fer askin' me," Dan answered. 'Sure, I'll take us over in the wagon."

There was no change even on the fourth day after the shooting, so Dan did the chores and the boys spent the night in town to be with their mother and to be near Rohan.

It was on the morning of the fifth day, when the light of day broke, that Rohan opened his eyes. For several long minutes he gazed at the dark haired boy who slept at the end of the bed. Josey's hand rested on his father's bare foot which stuck out of the covers. Except for a bloody scratch on the side of his head the boy was otherwise well as far as Rohan could see. He wriggled his foot back and forth gently to waken the child.

Overwhelmed with emotion, tears ran down his face. "Oh Josey," he choked out tenderly as the boy fluttered sleepy brown eyes and looked up at him. "Come on up here wi' me." Josey eased off the bed and stood near Rohan's head timidly. Still shaken, he carefully touched his father's hand. He'd never seen anyone so badly injured before.

Rohan touched the soft face and pulled him into his good arm. He kissed the forehead of the boy he thought he'd lost just as he was finally beginning to find himself.

Miryam, Jon, and the doctor all occupied various awkward positions around the room, sleeping where exhaustion had ultimately found them. He had to chuckle. "A body wouldna want t' be caught dead lookin' like ye do right noo."

"Rohan!"

"Da!"

In simultaneous confusion and excitement they all spoke at once and then collapsed into relieved laughter as they all realized that Rohan's fever had broken and he was out of danger.

"Rohan MacVoy, I won't have any more shenanigans going on in this town," warned Doc good naturedly. "I've seen enough innocent blood to last me a long time. The sheriff's hobbling around seeing to the burial. That fella was a wanted man." It seemed to the doctor that there was much to be said among the family, so he excused himself to let the townspeople know that Rohan was recovering.

"I'll just go see what's cooking downstairs. Oh, by the way, the man who killed that gunman was a fella by the name of Dan. He's the Himmel's hired man." As he shut the door they could hear him say, "Mmm Mmm! Does that smell good!"

Rohan cleared his throat a few times, not used to making speeches. "I know tha' I ha' missed oot on a great deal o'er the past years... I think I understand noo wha' love really is. Twas a hard thin' t' figure... But it seems I just ha' t' let go o' all the thin's I was holdin' too tight. My pride... my plans... an' my stubborn ideas. I was blind t' all the clues God ha' gi'en me all along the wa..." He turned his head to Joseph.

"A man by the name o' Ezra... he helped ye in t' the world Josey," said Rohan as he drew the boy closer. "Ezra told me wha' love is. He said twas givin' an' forgi'in' withoot any conditions on it... An' tha' fella in the Guid Book, the fither tha' your Ma read aboot on the wa' t' the kirk, he took back his wayward boy withoot needin' any promises made. An' God gave up His Son for my own sake e'en though I don't deserve it either. I'm gang t' be a new man from this day on... Tha' is I'm gang t' try anywa', wi' God's help."

Rohan MacVoy reached out to Josey and spoke softly, "Come, gi'e your Dada a kiss."

Ralph and Bettina came to the partly open door to Rohan's room. Just as they were about to knock, Ralph heard Rohan's voice. They peeked in to see him awake and holding Josey with his good arm.

"I see that all is well here!" Ralph spoke up. He tried to hold back the emotion as he took in the sight of a man who had been bitter toward the child, now embracing him.

Bettina went to Miryam's side to give her a hug. Miryam saw that, even though Bettina was happy about Rohan's recovery, she was obviously very upset about something. She searched the older woman's eyes, "What is it, Bettina."

The woman just closed her eyes, and tears ran down her face. She did not want to spoil the joy of seeing Rohan awake and whole again with her grief. But Miryam persisted, "What is wrong, Bettina?"

"It's Gertude, she passed away last week and I just seem to well up with thinking about her sometimes."

"Oh, I'm so sorry! When did it happen? I didn't know…"

"I know, Miryam. It's been a while since we talked last. You have been so tied up here. It was last Saturday night, in the wee hours."

"I dreamed of her Saturday night, didn't I, Rohan?"

"Oh ye certainly did, keeping me awake wi' your laughin'."

"Laughing? What were you dreaming? I'm surprised that you would think of her at all, the way she treated you," wondered Bettina.

"Well, we were all at a big party, and she was laughing so hard she was about to fall off from her chair!"

"To the best of my knowledge, Gertrude hasn't broken a smile in years." Ralph broke in.

"I saw her falling and I rushed over to help, but when I got to her, she was weightless. She looked at me with joy on her face and we just kept on laughing. Then I woke up."

Bettina asked Miryam, "You say that was Saturday night?"

"Yes, we were a bit groggy getting up on Sunday morning because of me laughing and waking Rohan up in the wee hours. I had to tell him all about the dream and it was about two o'clock before we settled back down to sleep."

"I do believe that your prayers have been answered, Bettina," Ralph put his hand on her shoulder.

"How do you mean?"

"Well, do you remember my dream a while ago? I didn't think more of it since then, but now it all makes some sense. I said when I woke up that I knew that she was content, not angry anymore. Remember?"

"Yes, I had forgotten it, too. Tell Miryam and Rohan about it."

"She was in a pool. I had to lift her out, but she was light as a feather. She had the chubby little body of a small child, and she was naked as the day she was born. I lifted her up and wrapped her in a big white sheet and she looked at me with an expression that was contentment itself. I knew somehow that she was healed, at least in her spirit. It was as plain as day."

"You say she was in a pool?" asked Miryam.

"And a beautiful one, crystal clear, so deep ... and blue as the sky."

"Well, that makes me think of the pool in the scriptures where the crippled man was waiting each day. Remember the story? He wanted to be the first one to get into the pool when the waters were stirred by the angel. If he was the first one in, he would be healed."

Ralph pondered, "It seems that she had gotten into a pool of healing water, Bettina."

"What about the rest of the dream, Ralph?" asked Miryam. Let's sort it out. It must have more significance if it's a message from God. What were the other details?"

"She was naked and in a child's body. You know, I think there's a great deal of meaning here. The Bible says that a person must be like a child to come into the kingdom of heaven.[37] Not physically, but in the spirit. They must be trusting and humble before God. And she was naked and weightless because she was ready to leave all the burdens of this world behind."

"What about the sheet?"

"The saints of God are said to be clothed in pure white garments,[38] the righteousness of the Lord. Why, Bettina, I believe she must have been ready to meet Him at long last."

"And just think," Bettina pondered, "in Miryam's dream, she died joyfully. What a relief that is to my heart! You said it yourself, she never laughed on this earth, but in her last moments, I believe she was changed! She stepped from this world into the next with a happy heart!"

Martha Fuller

Chapter 31

Rohan mended quickly, returning to the farm after another week. The boys and Dan had managed to keep up with most everything.

"I'll ha' t' find tha' fellow o'er at the Himmel's, Dan, an' thank him," Rohan said. "'Tis odd after all the years he's been there tha' we ha' ne'er met him before."

He was surprised that he enjoyed the time off. He was not to do any lifting for weeks, and because of his shoulder he could not play the fiddle to keep busy, so he sat near the fireplace and thought hard about the ways God was speaking to him. Miryam found herself engrossed in the pages of their Bible whenever she had no chores to do. She discovered the New Testament book of Philippians, the second chapter, and read it with Rohan.

> *"Let this mind be in you, which was also in Christ Jesus: Who, being in the form of God, thought it not robbery to be equal with God: But made Himself of no reputation, and took upon Him the form of a servant, and was made in the likeness of men: And being found in fashion as a man, He humbled Himself, and became obedient unto death, even the death of the cross. Wherefore God also hath highly exalted Him, and given Him a name which is above every name: That at the name of Jesus every knee should bow, of things in heaven, and things in earth, and things under the earth; And that every tongue should confess that Jesus Christ is Lord, to the glory of God the Father."*[39]

Rohan knew that there was work left to be done in his heart, and in his attitude. But for the first time in his life he felt he could trust God to lead him through it.

Though he could not yet play his fiddle, Rohan began to compose a tune by humming little snatches of a melody. It wandered about in his head, and followed him into his dreams. Then words came to fit the tune as well. They reflected his struggle while he had fiddled at the church social, and while he had played his fiddle in the barn. The song expressed his desire to be a godly man. He wrote it down painstakingly, changing a phrase here and a word there. When it was finally complete, he brought it to his wife.

"Miryam," he said, after taking a deep breath, "I'm tryin' t' own a humble heart... an' a listenin' heart. But there's still a knot in my gut tha' I need t' deal with. Ye understand? I dinna want t' make excuses. I just want to be honest aboot it. Ye know I havna got a wa' with words, but this is my best attempt t' tell God hoo I feel lately It has ta'en me a full week t' write it. I tried to spell it oot proper, like in my school days.

"I wrote it all doon for ye. Read it oot an' see if it's right."

Miryam's eyes swept over the page. She could see at once that this was written by the man she had fallen in love with long ago.

> *"O, sweet Master,*
> *I am a mute instrument awaiting Your touch.*
> *Pluck the strings of my heart*
> *and bring forth the song of the living God.*
> *Draw life from me to magnify Your name.*
> *Breathe into my hollow form,*
> *and coax Your music to flow through me*
> *for Your glory.*
>
> *Pick me up and play me,*
> *in supreme mastery of my being.*
> *It was You Who created me to be played.*
> *It is You Who springs forth in each note of joyous praise.*
> *O let my voice rise up in worship worthy of You.*
> *Let me give You all that I am,*
> *and all that You wish me to be."*

She rose from her seat and kissed his hands. "I can hardly wait to hear you sing it for me."

Spring found its way to Miryam's garden and her flowers fairly sang with their colors. Josey had celebrated his fifth birthday with delight at being hugged by his Da. Though Rohan had thought of paying the Himmel's hired man a visit, he didn't make the time to do it. It was a long, lazy stretch of hot days. It had been many months since Rohan and Miryam had shared a secret time in bed. There were, of course, two children who always seemed to be around. Privacy was hard to find.

The busyness of their lives caused them to rise early and retire early. They had finally resumed lovemaking after a long period of mourning the loss of the intimacy that they had shared, but those times were brief and under cover of darkness. There still lurked a shadow of shame for them both to overcome, though neither was guilty of any wrongdoing. They heard Jon and Josey get up early. The two went off to the barn for chores, returned and then left again on foot past their parents' window. Jon called through the curtain, "Da? We're going to the fishin' hole!"

"Chores done?" asked Rohan, though he knew they would be.

"All finished!"

"Gang on then!" said Rohan, turning to Miryam with a smile. It wasn't often in twenty-odd years of marriage that they had this luxury. "We're alone," he grinned, "an' this nightgoonie o' yours has wa' too many buttons on it."

Miryam had so looked for the day when Rohan could hold her and show her the love they had known in their younger days. His mood lately was gentle and easy going, especially with the string of fine weather. The sky had held on to its perfect blue for weeks and the rains that they needed came only at night, softly falling as they fell asleep to the sound of it. This morning they were relaxed and ready for long kisses and warm embraces.

Rohan's fingers played with the buttons on her bodice. One by one they fell open, until he could reach inside her nightgown to touch her. He came to the long stroke of an unexpected scar, and then another which intersected it.

"What's this?" he demanded, raising himself on one elbow to open the neck of Miryam's bedclothes.

She had forgotten it. The "x" had healed years ago but a scar remained. She had put balm on it repeatedly, but it was still visible if she looked for it. Only a tender touch would have revealed its presence. Now the tender touch that she needed so much pulled away from her.

"Ye never telt me aboot this?" Rohan bellowed.

"Things were bad enough without me adding to it," she explained.

"He put his mark on ye? He ..."

"Rohan..." Miryam got no response.

"Rohan? You can't hold on to this forever. I had even forgotten the mark was there! I'm the same person you married, and I want you to love me for who I am! Your getting angry is not helping us to grow old together, and love each other, and make love together. Now you're acting as if this man made love to me! He didn't! Only you can do that! I love you! Only you! That's what making love is, it's building love, helping it grow!"

Rohan was getting dressed while Miryam spoke, and was ready to walk out the door. "Don't you leave, Rohan MacVoy! I'm as angry as I've ever been in my whole life, so don't you walk out on me!"

"Ye're angry?" he asked incredulously. "Ye're angry? I thought I could forget tha' day fore'er. I was almost free o' it!"

"Well I am free of it and yes, you make me furious with all your storming and stomping and bullheadedness. Let it go or you'll be sleeping in the barn tonight!"

"The barn? Then I guess tha's where I'll be gang noo!" Rohan buckled his belt and left, slamming the door so that the house fairly shook.

Apparently the barn was too small to hold Rohan's anger. Miryam soon heard him gallop away.

Chapter 32

Bettina and Ralph sat on the porch, "watching the world go by," as he so often put it. Watching people as they moved about their work, or their errands, was nearly an occupation for them. It certainly kept them informed of the goings-on. The cat lay in Ralph's lap with her motor running and her downy belly exposed. She let her head droop over his knee, on the verge of imbalance, but Ralph was her favorite chair, and she knew he wouldn't let her fall.

They both watched as Mrs. Shawnessy emerged from the mercantile with what looked like seventy parcels. She prided herself with always having the nicest hats in town, and she trimmed them all with new ribbons and notions as often as most women changed their dresses. It was unfortunate that the day was windy, and that Mrs. Shawnessy was fully burdened with her frilly purchases. She over stepped the end of the plank walk, and her ribbons caught in the wind like falling leaves. She was able to remain upright, but this did not deter her from a blustery boo-hooing over the incident.

"Thar she blows!" Ralph laughed heartily, though he was only loud enough so his dear wife could hear and chastise him. He enjoyed hearing her scold him as much as she enjoyed doing the scolding.

A gaggle of the town children trailed onto the porch to visit them. It happened often when they sat out in front of the store. The youngsters were happy when they could wrangle a penny from their mothers to buy a sackful of candy, but when Ralph was out front they knew it was a dream come true. Ralph's eyes twinkled as he asked each of them in turn if any had felt poorly that day. They knew what was coming next so each one brought up a different complaint.

"I got the pneumonia!" said one.

"I near broke my arm trying to get the pump going!" said another.

"I lost my two front teeth!"

"I got my bum blistered 'cause I sassed Pa!"

Ralph's eyes were merry. "Oh, then I guess you need a pill." He produced for each child a sweetie from his vest pocket. "This will help you feel right pert again."

"Do tell us a story!" they would beg. Ralph made a production of swelling up his chest and taking a deep breath or two. His words flowed briskly, full of fervor and elegance, which enthralled the children.

> *"And then the noble duke*
> *clasped the blushing beauty to his manly bosom,*
> *and said in a deep musical voice:*
> *'O fairest and loveliest of thy sex,*
> *thou whom I adore,*
> *I lay my hand, my fortune.*
> *My ducal rank I lay at thy feet.*
> *Deign to accept them, my sweet one,*
> *and still my throbbing heart..."*[40]

This type of performance was never completed due to the fits of laughter which overtook the children. Urged on by their giggling, he also sang to them a sailor's ditty in his deepest basso profondo.

> *"Loudly the bell in the old tower rings,*
> *Bidding us list to the warning it brings*
> *sailor, take care - sailor, take care*
> *Danger is near thee, beware, beware, beware, beware*
> *Many brave hearts are asleep in the deep, so beware*
> *- BE - E - E - E- WARE!"*[41]

The children responded with awe, and then with giggles as Ralph made funny faces for them.

Rohan had ridden hard and fast. Letting the wind blow away his frustration. His anger had cooled with his ride. Finally in a better mood, he stopped by and sat down with Ralph and Bettina to bide the time. He had no desire to go home too soon after he had made such a fool of himself. He knew it. He did not mean to blow the roof off but he couldn't seem to stop himself. Bettina went in to help a customer with a purchase. The mercantile's porch was in full deep shade and was a great refuge from the heat of the day. The sun was almost blinding for those who were out in it.

Dan stepped down from Gus's wagon wearily. He needed more nails for his latest job so he walked toward the mercantile. Taking off his hat, he mopped his brow. He had let down his guard at just the wrong moment. Rohan had caught sight of the short, athletic build of a man he had never really noticed before. His hair was a shiny blue-black in the intense sunlight. His face was as square as a new salt lick. Rohan's stomach turned inside him. This stranger had a bouncy walk like Josey did. He did not put his hat back on as he approached the steps to the store, so when he waved in response to Ralph's greeting, Rohan could see that his eyes were jet black. His smile, deeply dimpled, showed a wide gap between his front teeth. He was unmistakably Joseph's father. Though Rohan had seldom been violent, he felt a fury begin to rise.

As soon as Dan stepped into the shade he knew that he had at last revealed his hand. In this dangerous game he had played, he had risked discovery every day to be near the child who would never be acknowledged as his. His heart longed for a chance to just touch Joseph and hold him for even a moment. He had finally come to the point of no return. He could see immediately that Rohan had seen guessed his identity.

"Who are ye?" Rohan demanded.

Ralph could see what was transpiring, but sat quite still, prayerfully interceding.

"I'm no one," replied Dan, keeping eye contact with Rohan. "I'm nobody at all."

"I can well see tha'! You're nothin'! Do ye hear me? Nothin'! Wha' I want t' know is this – do ye know who I am?"

"Yessir, I do."

"Well wha' kind o' man would do wha' you did?" Rohan asked what was not really a question but an accusation. He wanted to strike this man with all the strength that was in him.

But Dan answered very quietly and evenly. This day had been rehearsed in his mind ever since his acceptance of the love of God. He'd had to deal with his past and learn to walk on into the present reality. Restitution was not an option open to him. He had to own up to what he had done and he knew it.

"I was not a man at all then... I was a wild thing, a wolf with my foot caught in a trap, tryin' ta chew off my own leg... I was drunk – on liquor, and on my own anger - and outta my head with grief... There will never be an excuse fer what I did. I can only ask fer yer forgiveness."

"My forgi'ness? Forgi'ness? Wha' aboot my family? Wha' aboot the pain ye've caused us?"

"If there was anything I could do, I'd do it. But there is nothing I can say or do ta change what happened. I've not had a drink since then, an' I never will again. I've knelt before the Lord and confessed my sin, an' He has forgiven me. Reverend MacClure has talked me through the way ta peace with God an' I've found rest from my demons. I'm free of 'em now."

Dan paused and lowered his gaze to the ground. All the courage he had possessed was now spent, but he chose to continue.

"I can only tell ya that with every breath in my body I am as sorry as a man could ever be... I know that's not the answer ya want. But it's all I have to give ya. I'm not the wounded animal I was then. I'm not that man anymore, not a danger ta you or ta anyone else. I hope that can give ya some peace."

Rohan was taken aback. He had not expected to hear a calm voice. He wanted to hear a defense, or an excuse, anything he could lay blame to. Yet this man was a rational man. He was a man who had faced life head on and could still stand up straight. Rohan was speechless. His armor and his angry weapons were useless.

Dan looked at Rohan again. "I ask ya from the bottom of my heart, please... please forgive me."

As he looked into Dan's eyes Rohan saw a deep, deep hurt. A hurt much like his own.

Then Dan stepped forward with a strength not his own, saying, "My name is Dan. I live at the Himmel's place." And then he humbly backed up a step, turned and walked into the store.

Rohan was cut to the quick. "I...I..."

"Rohan, sit down here a minute," Ralph got up and led him by the shoulder to the far corner of the porch.

It was good that the porch was dark, and that they were seated a ways from the busy threshold. Rohan sat doubled over and shook with silent sobs, his face washed with tears. Ralph sat next to him and prayed silently for his friend. It was many, many long minutes before Rohan leaned back and took a breath without the heaving struggling breaths that come with great sorrow.

"I dinna ken wha' t' say, or wha' t' do noo. I ha' carried tha' burden for so long tha' I was thinkin' I would ne'er be able t' come oot from under it. An' then he comes, an' he speaks of peace an' forgi'ness t' me.

"An' I feel it in my heart! I feel it!" Rohan put his hand on his chest, as if reassuring himself that his heart did still beat.

"Wait noo a minute!" Rohan's mind struggled with the revelation. "Dinna he say tha' his name was Dan? Tha's the man who saved my life! Bettina said twas Gus's hired man!"

"Yes, she saw him fire the shot that killed that gunslinger. That's him." Ralph laid his own hand on Rohan's and said, "Now you know, don't you, what God's peace is? It's freedom."

Rohan closed his eyes and prayed as Ralph listened, "Aye, freedom. Dear God in heaven, forgi'e me. Tis my turn t' ask forgi'ness noo."

When Rohan came home, Miryam was sitting at the table shelling peas into a colander. She looked up when it seemed he was just going to stand in the doorway. He was hesitant about something.

"*Vos iz?* What? What is the matter?" she asked.

"I saw him."

"Who?"

"Him. The one."

She could hardly breathe. She never thought she would hear of him again.

"Where? Where did you see him?"

"In town, he's been here for years... He's the Himmel's hired man. The one we ne'er met because he was alwa's gone somewhere or t'other when we visit."

"Did he see you?"

"Aye... He spoke t' me."

"What did he say? What happened? Did you fight?' she asked, looking for bruises or scrapes on Rohan's hands and face.

"Nae, it ne'er came t' tha'."

Miryam searched Rohan's eyes. What had changed in him? There was a quality in her husband that she had not seen since... There was a tenderness, like a man has when he first kisses the woman he loves.

He sat down next to her.

"It was so strange." He tried to remember all the words that were said and relayed them to Miryam.

He told her of his brokenness before God, and the release he had found in his own weakness. Miryam cried. She brought his rough hand to her soft face and held it there. Here was the man she had hoped was still alive. He had returned to her well and whole.

"Do you think he'll still stay around here now?" she asked, anxiety written on her face. "Am I likely to run into him somewhere?" Her only memory was that of pure panic. She wondered how she could manage coming face to face with the monster who had occupied so many nightmares and daytime fears as well. It was true these had subsided over time, but now?

"I think that depends on us."

"Us? You would be able to... What are you saying, Rohan?"

He knelt in front of her, taking both her hands in his own and spoke as he looked into her eyes, "Miryam, I think I've forgi'en 'im. He's nae wha' I expected. I lookit in his eyes an' I saw a great measure o' peace there. I saw a man who is alive an' healthy, where I thought all these years tha' he was... tha' he must be a divil. But he's nae!"

"Then, what is he like?" Miryam hardly believed she could be asking such a thing.

"He's strong, I could see that. But humble, a very meek and gentle man. He's Joseph's father. Josey's the image o' this man. His name is Dan. Miryam, he's the one who shot the gunman in town last winter. He saved my life, an' ne'er e'en came forward for a thank ye. He's a man at peace with God.

"He carries a heavy burden though. I could see it in his face. An' only you an' I ha' the power t' ease it for him... an' I think we should."

Miryam could hardly bear to hear it. She sank back into the furthest reaches of her heart, where she wanted to lash out, to scream at the man who had hurt her so. She had convinced herself that, since she would never see him again, she was totally free of all the horrible memories. He had nearly collapsed their home around them, crushing their family. What could she say now? How could she put aside all the bottled up emotions that had suddenly returned to her consciousness? Didn't they need to be resolved with vengeance somehow?

Rohan placed his hand under her chin, bringing her face up to look at his. "My Miryam, *a chuisle,* my heart's blood. I ha' been drownin' for so long tha' I hardly recalled wha' bein' alive was. I ha' hated him for so long tha' I dinna understand tha' it was killin' me. I canna live like tha' any more. Dinna ye see it? I need t' stay free, noo tha' I understand what love is. I'm choosin' t' forget the pain. I want t' look at Joseph an' not feel the violence o' his comin' t' us. But tis gang t' be hard! Do ye hear wha' my heart is tryin' t' say? I want the hurtin' t' be o'er."

"I do know, I do see," Miryam said softly. "You know, I've been praying for ever so long for you, for us, for the boys. But I never thought that this day would come. I hoped and dreamed for many ways of resolving this, of healing this. But now I'm afraid!

"How can I even look at him? I'm all *fershimmeled*. Will I be able to meet him again without fear? He was so filthy, and raw! He was rough as a cob, and he stunk of drinking!"

Roh reassured her, "Tha' is nae how ye'll see him noo. I think ye can do it. He's a gentle man. He said he hasna had liquor since then, an' he's clean lookin'. An' remember, he's been livin' at the Himmel's for years, an' ye know Ava wouldna hold wi' anyone who was nae right bein' aroond young Ana an' Rosie… Gus has alwa's said he considers him a guid friend, an' he's guid at judgin' character, ye know. An' Ralph says this Dan ha' been counselin' wi' MacClure, an' tha' he's right wi' God."

Miryam gave Rohan a long look. Then she took a deep breath, and let it out slowly. It was like when she was giving birth to Josey. Only now she was pushing the fear out of her heart, and making room for a new life.

"Then we must do it. If your burden is lifted, I want mine lifted as well. And if we can be free of this, we need to tell him that he's free too, and that he's forgiven. Tell the boys to watch out for each other then. Let's go right now."

Rohan went to talk to the boys. Joseph was playing and Jon was relaxing by the creek.

"Jon, can ye watch o'er your brother for a while? Your Mama an' me are gang t' see a man o'er at the Himmel's place"

"Dan?" asked Jon.

"Wha' do ye ken aboot Dan?" Rohan said, eyebrows raised in wonder.

Jon looked at the ground and scuffed his boot around.

"I know he's Josey's father… And that he shot that fella in town at the gunfight."

Rohan was dumbstruck.

"He saved your life… I shook his hand when we stayed with Ava and Gus the week after the shooting. He said he was sorry and I forgave him. Then he was the one who brought us here every day when you were healing so we could do the chores together."

Rohan pulled Jon to his breast and held him there. Then he took him by the shoulders, looked him in the eyes and said, "Ye're a guid man Jonathan MacVoy… An' I'm proud t' be your Da."

Chapter 33

Dan pulled into the yard from finishing his latest job to find a wagon waiting there. The MacVoys were visiting. Gus came quickly out from the house to call him in. Miryam and Rohan had told the Himmel's why they had come. Gustav and Ava had seen the resemblance between Dan and Joseph as the child grew, but they had not felt any warning in their hearts about his presence in their home, or with their children. They kept waiting for the inevitable meeting to occur, but it had taken until now, years later, to come to pass.

"Dey haff come." Gus said, laying his arm across Dan's shoulder.

Dan didn't know if he could raise even a small scrap of courage again. "What can I say ta 'em? It took all the gumption I had ta stand still in front of Rohan. And how can I face the woman?"

"Daniel, mine friend, Gott hass for all tings, times unt seasons. Right now your time iss to stand up for vat ever He planned for you hass, unt for diss family. It all right vill be. Come now in."

Da told me when I grew to be a man that only the faith that is actually put to the test can become our own possession. If we don't go out on a limb, we'll never know the delight of being a forgiven child, the beloved ones of the Almighty God. When we come to Him humbly, He comes to us with unsurpassed love.

Ava and Miryam were seated at the table while Rohan paced a furrow in the floor. Miryam could not look up when Dan entered, but kept her eyes on her lap, her hands wringing her dress unconsciously. Ava jumped up and offered him coffee. As soon as she could pour it, she handed him the cup. Gus pulled out a chair for him. He and Rohan pulled up chairs as well, one on each side of Dan.

Dan thanked Ava for the coffee. He didn't know if he should look at the others or keep his head down. But somehow he turned to meet Rohan's eyes. He was surprised by what he saw there. Rohan did not bear him any ill. Instead his face was compassionate. He nodded to Dan silently, then nodded his head toward Miryam.

Miryam's heart skipped a beat when she heard the man thank Ava for his coffee. His voice was totally unlike the frightening voice she had heard in her mind for years. It was not the voice that had lived in her nightmares. She could not look up yet, though.

When Ava had settled into her chair next to Miryam, Dan cleared his throat several times. He was choked with emotion and found it difficult to speak. Finally the words came.

"Mrs. MacVoy... I spoke... ta yer husband in town... He was kind enough not ta knock me down an' beat the life outta me.

"I surely don't deserve any more than that... But now yer here..."

There were several long moments of silence.

Ava's lips moved in silent prayer.

"I don't deserve that either, that ya would come ta hear me out." Dan's jaw trembled.

"I can only offer my apologies fer all that I done ta hurt ya an' yer family... I..." Gus put his right hand on Dan's shoulder. Rohan put his left hand on Dan's shoulder. He began again with more strength.

"I deeply regret my actions against ya. Please..."

After an interminable pause, his voice broke to an almost inaudible whisper as tears streamed down his face, "In the name of Jesus Christ, please fergive me."

Everyone could feel the presence of a mighty power among them.

Miryam raised her eyes slowly to see the face she had dreaded to ever see again, but saw instead a deeply humble and sincere heart. Quite unlike what she had anxiously feared, Miryam saw the face of her little boy - on a grown man. His face was wet with tears. His eyes held the same sorrow she had seen in her mirror and on her husband's face for many a year. It was like seeing her Josey cry, and she knew she could relieve his suffering.

Her heart thumped a strong, happy beat that nearly burst out of her. It was unmistakable joy that fluttered around her. Without hesitation, Miryam broke into a smile. It seemed that no trace of fear remained.

"Daniel," she asked, "Would it seem right for Josey to call you Uncle?"

Everyone let out the breath they had been holding.

They talked far into the evening. When at last Rohan and Miryam pulled into their yard, they saw that Jon had lit the lantern in the window for them. Rohan looked at Miryam and said, "God always leaves a light burnin' in the window for us, doesna He? Nae matter hoo far from Him we've wandered, as soon as we turn aroond toward Him agin, we can see Him faithfully welcomin' us home."

Chapter 34

The leaves were piled up under the MacVoy's solitary tree. There were plenty to make a soft landing for a small boy to jump in. Josey heard a horse galloping toward them down the road. "Mama!" he called. "Company's comin'!"

He ran to hide behind the tree and surprise the unwary visitor. He peeked out in time to see Jamie MacClure dismount and carry a basket and a big burlap sack to the door where Miryam greeted him. "Oh my! Does that smell good! Just put it on the table there. What kind is it? And what's in the bag?"

"Apples! Ava says tis raisin an' walnut bread in the basket. There's some currant jelly, too. They'll all be along as soon as Rosie finds her shoes. They say she's fore'er takin' 'em off t' play barefoot an' forgettin' where she left 'em."

"I know what you mean. Josey does it all the time, too. Speaking of him, I wonder where he's gone off to." Miryam nodded toward the tree and raised her voice a bit. "I just can't imagine where he might be!"

They heard a small stifled laugh.

"Twould be a shame if he misses the party! All the children will be here, an' lots o' guid food!"

A bundle of energy rushed out from behind the shade tree and ran to the reverend. "Tag! You're it!" he shouted and ran as fast as he could to the barn.

"Oh ye think ye can run faster than me? I'll catch ye, an' squeeze the puddin' right out o' ye!"

The pursuit went all the way around the barn, but then more company arrived, one wagon right after another.

"Josey," called Bettina from their buggy. "Come here and help with these cookies!"

"Can I have one?" he asked, out of breath.

"Only if you don't tell your mother," replied Ralph.

"Ralph!" scolded his wife.

"Don't mind her, boy. She's got a heart of gold."

Meanwhile the crowd gathered and set up the tables and benches they had brought with them.

Rohan came out of the barn with Dan, each carrying one end of the plank board trestle table they had built earlier in the week. They set it up in the shade of the house and dusted off their hands.

Dan was introduced to the folks as Rohan's long lost relative.

One of the ladies said, "I didn't know you had family living so close by!"

Rohan replied happily, "Neither did I! Tis a long story, but it turns oot we're related an' ne'er knew aboot it 'til noo! An' I mun tell ye, tis powerful guid t' ha' him here wi' us. Noo tha' we ha' got acquainted, tis like he's my own brother."

Everyone greeted Dan with their "How do you do's."

Josey snuck up behind Uncle Dan. But Dan could see him from the corner of his eye. He acted as if he was unaware, but was fully ready to catch his little opponent.

"So it's your birthday, Dan?" Ralph asked. "How many of those have you had now?"

"Oh, I'd say about half as many as you!" Dan laughed as he quickly spun around and grabbed Josey up into his arms. "Give yer uncle a hug now would ya?"

"Only if you get me one of Auntie Bettina's cookies," Josey answered.

"A cookie! I'll give ya a tickle!"

Josey erupted into a bundle of giggles as Uncle Dan held him close.

Rohan was showing a neighbor a lively lick on his fiddle, when Josey struggled free of Uncle Dan's arms. He ran a ways off, but quickly returned with a mischievous grin to hang on to Dan's shirt tail as they listened to the music.

Mama and Da always said that after that I became a "scamp!" I made silly faces and wiggled and cavorted to make folks laugh. The sorrow which could have easily followed me from the early years was washed away by days filled with laughter and the joys of being alive and being a family. I was a boy who was cherished, especially by my "Uncle Dan."

Josey called Rosie to watch his Da make magic as music flowed from his fiddle. When the song ended, Josey tugged on Rohan's shirt to get his attention.

What is it, *m' annsachd.*

"Dada?" he asked, using Rohan's Scottish accent flawlessly. "Wilna ye be learnin' me t' play soon?"

Miryam overheard the question, and interrupted, "Josey, don't you mean to say, 'When will you be teaching me to play?' Da is from the old country, but you are not. You will learn this country's ways, right?" she said with coaxing smile.

"Yes, Mama," he answered with a grin, "but when I learn to play his fiddle..." he took a deep breath and picked up the Scottish burr again, "I shall be playin' it just like my Da!"

Catching the playful spirit of his boy, Rohan began to fiddle and sing a lively tune. He fiddled, then sang a few lines in the manner of a bard, then repeated the process, as it's hard to sing with a fiddle under your chin. Those who knew him well were aware that he had written the words to the old drinking song that they all knew.

"Well the man in the moon is laughin' at me tonight.
I thought tha' I had it all set, everythin' was all right.
I'd learned all my lessons an' yes, I was ready for flight
With dreams in my heart tha' I'd locked up all cozy an' tight.

See, the world was a place tha' was dancin' at my command.
I'd wave at the stars an' they'd come an' perch on my hand.
They'd sparkle for me an' ne'er alone I'd stand.
I laughed at the night, I thought tha' I had it all planned.

But You, in your wisdom, knew I was playin' the fool.
I'd ne'er considered tha' Yours was a needful rule.
I wanted t' be the one holdin' all o' the jewels,
But they're not mine for holdin' an' now
—here we are in a duel."

Here, Rohan took his fiddle from his chin and began to dance a jig. The watchers clapped as he lifted his feet and clicked his heels together. Then with a flourish he danced over to Miryam, took her in his arms and planted a very passionate kiss upon her warm lips. Then he returned to his song as a deep blush came over Miryam's face.

"I pull out my sword an' I challenge Your right as a King.
You speak out Your word an' show me You've made e'rythin'.
My skill at fencin' fills the air wi' a hollow ring,
While Your weapon in battle is as mighty as David's sling.

That ol' man in the moon is lookin' down, laughin' at me.
But I'm grinnin' back, cause now I can finally see
Tha' Your justice is right an' my bail has been paid
(quite a fee!)
You sent Your only Son t' be all that I couldn't be."

Joseph MacVoy had been dancing around with a silliness that overflowed to the crowd. When the music was nearly ended, he ran to Dan and said to him in a serious voice, "Look at me, I have something new to show you."

Dan knelt down to see, "An' what is that?"

Still with a straight face, Josey moved his eyebrows to the music, then he broke into laughter and declared, "Uncle Dan, my eyebrows are dancing!"

Rohan finished his song with gusto.

"I can't learn these lessons an' sew 'em all up in my mind.
For my thoughts are finite an' my heart is searchin' an' blind.
But my spirit takes wing by a Spirit so mercifully kind.
An' one day I'll fly home, an' I know I'll like what I find."

Chapter 35

I did not know for many years how I was conceived. When I did learn, I was devastated at first, but Mama has reassured me many times over that I am not a mistake, or a burden to be borne in shame or sorrow, but that I was in the mind of God well before that Monday when Mama was doing her laundry.

She recites for me, whenever I ask her, the words from Psalm 139 in our family Bible. They are words that she found marked out as a beacon to generations to come, in fact, to me.

> "O Lord, Thou hast searched me, and known me.
> Thou knowest my downsitting and mine uprising,
> Thou understandest my thought afar off.
> Thou compassest my path and my lying down,
> and art acquainted with all my ways.
> For there is not a word in my tongue, but, lo,
> O Lord, Thou knowest it altogether.
> Thou hast beset me behind and before,
> and laid Thine hand upon me.
> Such knowledge is too wonderful for me;
> it is high, I cannot attain unto it.
> Whither shall I go from Thy spirit?
> or whither shall I flee from Thy presence?
> If I ascend up into heaven, Thou art there:
> if I make my bed in hell, behold, Thou art there.
> If I take the wings of the morning,
> and dwell in the uttermost parts of the sea;
> Even there shall Thy hand lead me,
> and Thy right hand shall hold me.

If I say, Surely the darkness shall cover me;
even the night shall be light about me.
Yea, the darkness hideth not from Thee;
but the night shineth as the day:
the darkness and the light are both alike to Thee.
For Thou hast possessed my reins:
Thou hast covered me in my mother's womb.
I will praise Thee;
for I am fearfully and wonderfully made:
marvelous are Thy works;
and that my soul knoweth right well.
My substance was not hid from Thee,
when I was made in secret,
and curiously wrought in the lowest parts of the earth.
Thine eyes did see my substance,
yet being unperfect;
and in Thy book all my members were written,
which in continuance were fashioned,
when as yet there was none of them.
How precious also are Thy thoughts unto me,
O God! How great is the sum of them!
If I should count them,
they are more in number than the sand:
when I awake, I am still with Thee..."

I am an old man now. I know I was not an accident or a victim of life's chaos. I know I was conceived in the heart of God before I was conceived on this earth and that my life has been used by Him to prompt those around me to "grow in grace, and in the knowledge of our Lord and Savior Jesus Christ. To Him be glory both now and evermore. Amen." 2 Peter 3:18

Joseph Samuel MacVoy
1945

Endnotes

All Bible references are from the King James Version

1. Deuteronomy 6:4-9 (all Biblical references are from the KJV)
2. Hebrews 9:22
3. 1 Timothy 2:5
4. Isaiah 61:1-3
5. John 14:6
6. Thomas Edison
7. 2 Chronicles 6:18
8. Isaiah 4:2
9. Isa 9:6
10. Isa 11:1, 10
11. Isa 55:11
12. St Augustine of Hippo
13. 2 Peter 3:9
14. Lamentation 3:23
15. Hebrews 11:1
16. Luke 18:16
17. 2 Timothy 3:16
18. Proverbs 22:6
19. Psalm 119:105
20. John 1:1-4
21. Job 37:2-5
22. Jeremiah 10:13
23. Psalm 19:1
24. Matthew 26:26
25. Matthew 26:28
26. Psalm 32:7
27. Psalm 34:11
28. Psalm 63:6
29. Isaiah 1:15
30. Isaiah 7:14
31. Isaiah 9:6
32. Isaiah 53:1-3
33. Isaiah 53:4-6
34. Isaiah 53:7
35. Isaiah 1:18
36. Jude 24-25
37. Mark 10:15
38. Revelation 3:5
39. Philippians 2:5-11
40. "Tony, the Convict: A Comedy in Five Acts" 1893 by Charles Townsend
41. "Asleep in the Deep" 1897 by Arthur J. Lamb

CPSIA information can be obtained at www.ICGtesting.com
Printed in the USA
BVOW05s0127210714

359771BV00001B/2/P